MEDIA AND PERFORMANCE IN THE MUSICAL

Media and Performance in the Musical

An Oxford Handbook of the American Musical, Volume 2

EDITED BY RAYMOND KNAPP

MITCHELL MORRIS

AND STACY WOLF

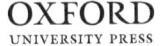

OXFORD
UNIVERSITY PRESS

Oxford University Press is a department of the University of Oxford. It furthers the University's objective of excellence in research, scholarship, and education by publishing worldwide. Oxford is a registered trade mark of Oxford University Press in the UK and certain other countries.

Published in the United States of America by Oxford University Press
198 Madison Avenue, New York, NY 10016, United States of America.

© Oxford University Press 2018

All rights reserved. No part of this publication may be reproduced, stored in a retrieval system, or transmitted, in any form or by any means, without the prior permission in writing of Oxford University Press, or as expressly permitted by law, by license, or under terms agreed with the appropriate reproduction rights organization. Inquiries concerning reproduction outside the scope of the above should be sent to the Rights Department, Oxford University Press, at the address above.

You must not circulate this work in any other form and you must impose this same condition on any acquirer.

Library of Congress Cataloging-in-Publication Data
Names: Knapp, Raymond. | Morris, Mitchell, 1961– | Wolf, Stacy Ellen.
Title: Media and performance in the musical : an Oxford handbook of the American musical, Volume 2 / edited by Raymond Knapp, Mitchell Morris, and Stacy Wolf.
Description: New York, NY : Oxford University Press, 2018. |
Series: Oxford handbooks | Includes bibliographical references and index.
Identifiers: LCCN 2018022230 | ISBN 9780190877828 (pbk. : alk. paper) |
ISBN 9780190877842 (epub)
Subjects: LCSH: Musicals—United States—History and criticism. |
Musicals—Production and direction—United States—History.
Classification: LCC ML1711.M44 2018 | DDC 782.1/40973—dc23
LC record available at https://lccn.loc.gov/2018022230

CONTENTS

Contributors		*vii*
About the Companion Website		*ix*

Introduction   1
By Stacy Wolf

PART ONE MEDIA

1. Theater   11
   Tamsen Wolff

2. The Filmed Musical   27
   Raymond Knapp and Mitchell Morris

3. The Television Musical   55
   Robynn J. Stilwell

4. The Animated Film Musical   79
   Susan Smith

5. The Evolution of the Original Cast Album   101
George Reddick

PART TWO PERFORMANCE

6. The Institutional Structure of the American Musical Theater   127
David Sanjek

7. Orchestration and Arrangement: Creating the Broadway Sound   149
Dominic Symonds

8. Musical Theater Directors   173
Barbara Wallace Grossman

9. Sets, Costumes, Lights, and Spectacle   197
Virginia Anderson

10. Acting   221
John M. Clum

11. Singing   241
Mitchell Morris and Raymond Knapp

12. Dance and Choreography   265
Zachary A. Dorsey

References   *289*
Index   *299*

CONTRIBUTORS

Virginia Anderson, Assistant Professor of Theater, Connecticut College

John M. Clum, Professor Emeritus of Theater Studies and English, Duke University

Zachary A. Dorsey, Assistant Professor of Theatre, James Madison University

Barbara Wallace Grossman, Professor of Drama, Tufts University

Raymond Knapp, Distinguished Professor of Musicology and Humanities, Academic Associate Dean of the Herb Alpert School of Music, and Director of the Center for Musical Humanities, University of California, Los Angeles

Mitchell Morris, Professor of Musicology and Humanities, University of California, Los Angeles

George Reddick, freelance writer, New York City

David Sanjek, deceased. Professor of Music and Director of the Salford Music Research Centre, University of Salford, UK

Susan Smith, Reader in Film Studies, University of Sunderland, UK

Robynn J. Stilwell, Associate Professor of Music in the Department of Performing Arts, Georgetown University

Dominic Symonds, Professor of Musical Theatre, University of Lincoln, UK

Stacy Wolf, Professor of Theater and Director of the Program in Music Theater, Princeton University

Tamsen Wolff, Associate Professor of Drama, Princeton University

ABOUT THE COMPANION WEBSITE

www.oup.com/us/mapitm

Oxford has created a website to accompany *Media and Performance in the Musical*, which includes nearly two hundred audio, video, image, or text examples to illustrate or augment the discussions advanced in the text. To make this valuable resource easy to use, each example is keyed to its appropriate place in the text, and numbered sequentially within each of the essays that use this resource. For clarity, we've used the following notation (these particular indications would refer to examples 5-8 in the first essay):

🔊 Example 1.5 (Audio Example 1.5)

▶ Example 1.6 (Video Example 1.6)

◉ Example 1.7 (Image Example 1.7)

▯ Example 1.8 (Text Example 1.8)

To access an example, simply click on the appropriate icon on the website.

MEDIA AND PERFORMANCE IN THE MUSICAL

Introduction

THE AMERICAN MUSICAL IS A paradox. On stage or screen, musicals at once hold a dominant and a contested place in the worlds of entertainment, art, and scholarship. Born from a mélange of performance forms that included opera and operetta, vaudeville and burlesque, minstrelsy and jazz, musicals have always sought to amuse more than instruct, and to make money more than make political change. In spite of their unapologetic commercialism, though, musicals have achieved supreme artistry and have influenced culture as much as if not more than any other art form in America, including avantgarde and high art on the one hand, and the full range of popular and commercial art on the other. Reflecting, refracting, and shaping U.S. culture since the early twentieth century, musicals converse with shifting dynamics of gender and sexuality, ethnicity and race, and the very question of what it means to be American and to be human. The musical explores identity, self-determination, and the American dream.

The form of the musical—the combination of music, dance, speech, and design—is paradoxical, too. By the middle of the twentieth century, spoken scenes in musicals were expected to conform to the style of nonmusical plays, with characters psychologized and realistically portrayed. When characters burst into song or dance, a different expressive mode took over, one that scholars like Richard Dyer have seen as utopian.[1] Even as artists aimed for "integration" among the musical's disparate parts, in emulation of Wagner's "total artwork," the pieces required different skills of creation, presentation, and interpretation. As Scott McMillin argues in *The Musical as Drama*, "When a musical is working well, I feel the crackle of difference . . . between the book and the numbers, between songs and dances, between dance and spoken dialogue."[2] In part because of its hybrid form and its commercial aspirations, the musical failed to register as a legitimate topic for scholarly study in either music or theater programs in universities until near the end of the twentieth century. Although audiences flocked to see *The Phantom of the Opera* on Broadway to the tune of 140 million people (as of 2017) worldwide since its opening year on Broadway (1987), and the film of *The Sound of Music* (1965) held its place as the most popular movie musical of all time well into the twenty-first century, few college courses taught the history or criticism of musicals. And while young composers, lyricists, librettists, designers, and performers honed their craft and enrolled in professional training programs, they gained knowledge of the musical's history and theory through practice rather than through college classes that emphasized a scholarly approach to musicals.

Beginning in the 1990s, and gaining considerable momentum across the first decade(s) of the new millennium, the study of American musicals on stage and on film has grown rapidly into a legitimate field. Many universities now offer surveys of musical theater or film history; or build a course focused on a composer, a subgenre, or a period in U.S. history; or include musicals in other courses, from American drama to popular culture to African American studies.[3] In departments of music and musicology, theater, film, media studies, and literature, more courses are taught each year about musicals or include the study of a musical play or film as an example of cultural or performance history. Increasingly, musical theater, musical films, and musicals in other media, such as television or online, are seen as viable objects of scholarly inquiry.

Scholarship to support the study of musicals is gradually catching up to the enthusiastic reception of students, as more dissertations are written and books published on musicals each year. Where there were formerly only encyclopedic lists of musicals and their creators, coffee-table tomes, or hagiographies, there is now a growing field of academic studies of musicals. Some explicate and analyze a range of musicals; others trace a chronological history. Some authors stress context over analysis, locating musicals historically, and some books consider musicals from specific identity positions. Increasingly, studies focus on a single musical, often relying on archival research to unearth details about the production process. Finally, books take a biographical approach and center on a director, composer, choreographer, producer, performer, or another member of the creative team.

Even as scholarship has grown in diverse and wide-ranging ways, the teaching of musicals continues to be extremely challenging. This book, in its original one-volume edition, grew out of our mutual passion for teaching musicals and our mutual frustration with available pedagogically oriented materials. When the three of us first met to talk about musicals, we complained—as most professors do—about the lack of a textbook for teaching musicals that adequately covered the wide range of possible approaches to the subject. Each of us had solved the problem in our own way, using a combination of texts and articles and our own expertise. From that start, we found common goals as instructors: first, to situate the musical historically; second, to locate the ideological work of the musical as "American"; and third, to practice a variety of methods and techniques to analyze musicals. Moreover, each of us was well aware of the strengths and weaknesses in our training, of the stubborn disciplinarity of each of our fields, and of the tendency to privilege one element of the musical over another based on our comfort level. We knew that a useful textbook for the study of the American musical needed more than our three voices to write it.

Although we designed our book as a teaching tool, we mean "teaching" in the broadest possible way for students, instructors, and the general reader. We intended our book not (necessarily) to be read cover to cover, nor (necessarily) assigned in order, but as a resource for instructors, students, and aficionados of the musical and as a complement to other studies currently available. As well, scholars expert in one area of the musical might use our book as a first resource in coming to terms with other aspects of the art form less familiar to them and as an additional resource for courses on related topics, such as Tin Pan Alley or Popular Song.

Since the publication of *The Oxford Handbook of the American Musical* in 2011, the American musical continues to thrive, both reflecting and shaping cultural values and social norms, and even commenting on politics, whether directly and on a national scale (*Hamilton* [2015]) or somewhat more obliquely and on a more intimate scale (*Fun Home* [2015]). New stage musicals, such as *Come from Away* (2017) and *The Band's Visit* (2017), open on Broadway every season, challenging conventions of form and content, and revivals offer audiences a different perspective on extant shows (*Carousel* [2018]; *My Fair Lady* [2018]). Television musicals broadcast live, including *Peter Pan Live!* (2014) and *The Wiz Live!* (2015), at once hearken back to 1950s television's affection for musical theatre and aim to attract new audiences through the accessibility of television. Film musicals, including *Les Misérables* (2012) and *Into the Woods* (2014), capitalize on the medium's technical capabilities of perspective and point of view, as well as visual spectacle. Television has embraced the genre anew, and with unexpected gusto, not only devising musical episodes for countless dramatic and comedy series, but also generating musical series such as *Galavant* (2015-16) and *Crazy Ex-Girlfriend* (2015-). And animated musicals, such as Disney's *Moana* (2016), hail child and adult audiences with their dual messages, vibrant visual vocabulary, and hummable music.

The essays gathered in this book, Volume II of the reissued *Oxford Handbook,* are written by leading scholars in the field, and explore the American musical from the outside and from the inside. The first half collects articles that analyze various media in which musicals have been created. The second half is made up of articles that examine different components of a musical and the people who do the work to bring a musical to life.

The American musical appears in several guises: as a live stage event, as a film, as a television show, as an animated film, or as a cast album. Each of these media or formats employs specific technical and performance practices, and each engages its audience differently. All formats contain music—both orchestrated and sung—and lyrics, and all but the cast album feature bodies, whether live, filmed, or drawn, and include elements of design. The essays gathered in the first half of this book each focus on one media form and analyze its conventions. These pieces consider the dynamics of performance, the technical requirements of each media, and the history of each format, illustrated with many examples.

Whatever its media or format, the musical is perhaps the most intricately collaborative art and entertainment form in US culture. When audiences experience the emotional tug and infectious energy of a musical, they might not perceive the work of the many practitioners who contribute to the final production, including producers, directors, and orchestrators, among others. Importantly, the work of artists for the musical not only relies on their own areas of expertise, but also requires that they participate in art-making with others—sometimes a crowd of people who come to the table with different skills and speaking different artistic languages. Artists who enjoy making musicals appreciate the give and take of collaboration. The great composer and lyricist Stephen Sondheim told *Hamilton* creator Lin-Manuel Miranda, "Well, I collaborate with people. My spark often comes from collaborators. . . . I mean, I'm a collaborative animal. . . . I need the spur. And the spur and the boost comes [*sic*] from somebody else, generally."[4] The articles in this volume reflect Sondheim's comment by highlighting the complex collaboration that a musical necessitates.

Stacy Wolf

ACKNOWLEDGMENTS

Any book this complex—like the musical itself—has innumerable contributors beyond those headlined as editors and authors. The editors are extremely grateful for the abundant and varied support their scholarly communities have provided. On the institutional level, this included support, at UCLA, from the Office of Instructional Development, the Department of Musicology, and the Council on Research, along with a rich field of interactions among students and other faculty; we are especially grateful for insights that have found their way into this book from Juliana Gondek, Peter Kazaras, Elijah Wald, Sam Baltimore, Sarah Ellis, and Holley Replogle-Wong, and for Holley's exemplary work preparing and organizing materials for the book's Web site. At Princeton, we thank the Lewis Center for the Arts, especially Chair Michael Cadden. We thank Senior Production Editor Joellyn Ausanka for guiding us through the copyediting and proofing stages of the book. Norm Hirschy at Oxford University Press has been unfailingly, even brilliantly helpful, at every step of the process. And, for the reissued volumes, we have been blessed with the guidance, expertise, and patience of Lauralee Yeary.

Raymond Knapp, Mitchell Morris, Stacy Wolf

NOTES

1 Richard Dyer, "Entertainment and Utopia," in *Genre: The Musical*, ed. Rick Altman (London: Routledge and Kegan Paul, 1981); originally published in *Movie* 2 [Spring 1977]: 2–13.
2 Scott McMillin, *The Musical as Drama: A Study of the Principles and Conventions behind Musical Shows from Kern to Sondheim* (Princeton: Princeton University Press, 2006), p. 2.
3 See Stacy Wolf, "In Defense of Pleasure: Musical Theatre History in the Liberal Arts [A Manifesto]," *Theatre Topics* 17.1 (March 2007): 51–60.
4 Lin-Manuel Miranda, "Stephen Sondheim, Theater's Greatest Lyricist," *New York Times*, October 16, 2017. https://www.nytimes.com/2017/10/16/t-magazine/lin-manuel-miranda-stephen-sondheim.html?_r=0 Accessed November 25, 2017.

PART ONE

MEDIA

1

Theater

TAMSEN WOLFF

■ ◻ ■

THE POLISH DIRECTOR TADEUSZ KANTOR reportedly said that one of the main reasons people go to the theater is to sit down and stand up at the same time as other people. Certainly a defining aspect of theater is that it requires a group of spectators to come together in a room to watch performers. Live theater involves performer(s), spectator(s), and performance material; it is an immediate, transient, embodied, and unpredictable medium. The exchange between audience and performers has different dimensions for musical theater from those of straight theater. The relationship between an audience and musical theater is distinctive in at least two ways: in the communication, circulation, and shelf life of musical numbers; and in a pronounced focus in musicals on communal action, thematically, musically, and choreographically. Looking at these two features of musical theater and where they overlap helps illustrate what is unique about musicals in the theater.

If Kantor is right that people gravitate toward live theater because of a desire for a shared activity or to feel part of a group with a clearly defined role, then musical theater's regular use of ensembles reflects and magnifies that desire on the stage. A central question of musical theater is how do people come together? The question was integral first to the influential musicals of Rodgers and Hammerstein, in which the importance of community solidarity routinely outweighs individual concerns. Although romantic couples are at the heart of the narrative in most Rodgers and Hammerstein musicals, the couple's union is also a measure of the community's cohesiveness and usually, sooner or later, the chorus envelops individuals. In *Oklahoma!* (1943), the main couple, Curly, a cowboy, and Laurey, who belongs to a farming family, represent the two quarreling factions of citizens in the Oklahoma territory. When Curly and Laurey eventually marry, their union anticipates and parallels the alliance of the ensemble and formation of the state.[1]

Musical theater's thematic emphasis on community is inseparable from the most powerful expression of that community onstage: everyone's singing and dancing together. Ensemble singing and matching choreography are entrenched musical theater conventions. As Scott McMillin puts it in *The Musical as Drama*, "There is a drive toward ensemble effect in the musical dramatic form. . . . Legitimate drama has its large scenes, too, but the ensemble numbers of a musical do something that does not happen in legitimate drama. The characters express themselves simultaneously, and the build-up of a number to a simultaneous performance is often a dramatic event itself."[2] A crowded, synchronized musical number on stage is also different from the same big number performed on screen. In the theater, the physical proximity of the performers' bodies and their exertion is unmediated and unpredictable. Watching a large group of individuals performing in uncanny unison is often particularly thrilling for audiences, although it can just as easily be disturbing. Historically, large-scale simultaneous performance has been used to intimidate as well as impress spectators, especially in displays of military power—think of Stalin's processions of soldiers, or Nazi storm troopers' marches. Audience fascination with this kind of unified spectacle has deep roots, in everything from political rallies, to the chorus in Greek drama, to the apparently endless appeal of the Radio City Music Hall Rockettes.

Performers' singing and dancing skills are also exposed in the present tense, embodied theater. People may very well go to musicals for the same reason that they watch the Olympics: the stakes are high and live bodies can't fake the necessary effort. There's no logical explanation for what athletes and performers do, but both fulfill a human desire to test the limits and talents of the body, to see what it can do and what it can express. A performer can do the feat (the high dive, the javelin throw, the solo) only with a greater or lesser degree of proficiency. Singing ability is the first and most demanding requirement for musical theater performers. When a performer opens her mouth to sing, she can bomb. Singing and dancing are both measurable skills that always contain the riveting possibility of audible and visible public failure. Whereas on film and in recordings, singing and dancing can be edited and augmented in a variety of ways, this kind of intervention is harder, if not impossible, in live theater. Certainly performers can be miked and usually are, especially in bigger houses. This practice has generated plenty of controversy and has shifted the requirements for both the acting and singing skills of musical theater performers. Nonetheless, it hasn't changed the fact that performers reveal themselves when singing. It tends to be easier for audiences to agree on the quality of singing, even without a trained ear, than to do the same for acting, but audiences can see slips as well as hear them on stage—the wrong note, the dropped partner, the fudged line. The possibility of accidents or even fiascos in live performance, and the accompanying excitement for an audience, is raised exponentially in a musical, where such a wide range of skills—singing, dancing, and acting—are required.

The frequent movement among the basic dramatic elements of speech, song, and dance in musical theater not only underscores the many abilities of the performers on stage but also repeatedly reminds the audience that they are watching a performance. As McMillin argues, the unavoidable push-and-pull between elements on the musical theater stage creates a unique dramatic form and experience for the audience. The competition and contrast between the different elements means that songs and dance stand out in high relief from spoken dialogue on stage. This differentiation is further highlighted for the audience by the way in which speech, song, and dance often function in a hierarchy of authentic affect. A character becomes most articulate and emotionally truthful in song and dance (and characters are not necessarily in charge of their revealing, intuitive singing and dancing selves). This truth-telling convention dovetails with the exposure of a performer's ability, which is also revealed primarily in song. Songs that are characters' truthful asides or confessionals to the audience can allow audiences to feel closer to the characters and their dilemmas during musical numbers. The disjunction between song and speech doesn't exist on recordings (if there are snippets of dialogue, they usually occur during the lead-in to a song or as brief interjections) and it works very differently in film where there are multiple ways to suggest characters' emotional states and to gloss over or highlight shifts from speech to song to dance. In live theater, to watch performers jump between modes of performance is an exuberant, liberating exercise, one that audiences frequently celebrate by applauding at the end of numbers, which in turn reinforces the distinction between song and dialogue.

The relationships among song, dance, and book—the ways in which the elements collide and coexist in performance—mirror musical theater's common narrative focus on how characters come together to form a community and what kinds of communities they form. In many mid-twentieth-century musicals, the struggle to create a seamless community within the story corresponds to a structural effort to integrate song, dance, and book. Rodgers and Hammerstein's *Oklahoma!* is one of the most frequently cited examples of this development, in part because Rodgers directly and repeatedly addressed the aesthetic choices that the creators made. As he described *Oklahoma!* in his autobiography, *Musical Stages*, "No single element over-shadows any other. . . . It was a work created by many that gave the impression of having been created by one."[3] Not only do song, dance, and book complement one another, but this harmony merges with the narrative focus on the joyful integration of the farmers and the cowmen (and, eventually, the merchants).

At the same time, musicals that devote themselves to the question of a community's coming together by way of singing and dancing include a wide range of works that offer diverse representations of communities. *West Side Story* (1957) marked a shift in musicals' portrayals of communities by focusing on society's outsiders who want in as opposed to social insiders solidifying their base. If in *Oklahoma!* territory folks stick together because they know they belong to the land and the land they belong to is grand, in *West Side Story*, the socially marginalized warring groups of the Jets and Sharks are deeply ambivalent about whether this land is grand, and they know for sure that they don't belong to it. This doesn't stop their fighting over it, but their failure to come together in *West Side Story* is depicted as society's failure and raises the question of how, whether, and what groups are brought together by singing and dancing.

This darker take on social harmony appears in musicals as dissimilar as *Assassins* (1991), and *A Chorus Line* (1975). *A Chorus Line* is a self-referential ode to performers auditioning to join a musical kick line while *Assassins* is an episodic, vaudeville-inspired, trans-historical story of assassins and would-be assassins of United States presidents. Both depict makeshift communities of outsiders looking for social inclusion. In *Assassins* and *A Chorus Line*, the route to social inclusion is through performance, celebrity, or public recognition. The stakes are higher than getting the girl or the boy. The minor love plot in *A Chorus Line* between the director, Zach, and his ex-leading lady, Cassie, is displaced by her focus on joining the chorus. The only semblance of a love plot in *Assassins* lies in John Wilkes Booth's wooing Lee Harvey Oswald to join the group of assassins. *Assassins* in particular offers what Raymond Knapp refers to as a "counter-mythology" to the romantic unification myths about America that are generally promoted in Golden Age musicals.[4] Community formation is still central, but now it is identified as deeply troubling, if not downright dangerous. Indeed, both "Another National Anthem" from *Assassins* and the musical number "One," in *A Chorus Line* offer cautionary comments on what is compromised when individuals join forces.

A number of contemporary musicals explicitly challenge the value of community. In *Parade* (1998) a community in Georgia in 1913 functions as the terrifying antagonist— eventually transforming into a lynch mob—that threatens the central romantic couple, Leo and Lucille Frank. Here the ensemble's collective force is meant to disturb the audience. The story is a direct inversion of the traditional communal embrace of the main couple. But it's not an exclusively new idea. Arguably, the classic *Music Man* (1957) also presents the couple of Harold Hill and Marian Paroo as unassimilated outsiders. Hill is a peripatetic con artist and Marian is a freethinking librarian at odds with her hometown in River City, Iowa. The romantic connection between Hill and Marian emerges in the linked melodies of "Seventy-Six Trombones" and "Goodnight My Someone," Hill's need to complete the duet of "Til There Was You" and the shared music of the "Trombones/Goodnight" reprise, but their union is not about their integration into the larger community. They remain individuals uniquely matched to each other and set apart from the general population of River City. The community itself is revealed to be a sham, a group formed only as a result of Hill's con game and united in fantasy rather than in reality.[5]

Already in the sentimental celebration of like-minded community that characterizes many of the musicals from the mid-twentieth century, happy unity frequently occurs at the violent expense of characters who threaten it for any reason. In the case of *Oklahoma!*, Jud Fry, the farmhand who repeatedly comes between the main couple of Curly and Laurey, is finally killed, conveniently falling on his own knife. But his death is only the most obvious instance of the violence necessary to create a unified community. Much of *Oklahoma!* is informed by fear of violence connected to romantic coupling, either comically (when Ali Hakim is threatened at gunpoint to marry) or potentially less so (when Aunt Eller points a gun at both the cowboys and the farmers, who will need to make a symbolic shotgun marriage of their own in order to form the titular state). Indeed, this element was even more pronounced in the original play (*Green Grow the Lilacs*, by Lynn Riggs), where Laurey's fear of the shivaree is given more play (Riggs at one time planned to title the play "Shivaree"). Thus, even within an early classic, jubilant promotion of community, cohesiveness is more complicated than it might appear.

The problem of representing the simultaneous pleasure and difficulty of community formation is well suited to live musical theater. Theater allows for unfixed, here-and-then-gone interpretations, which have the potential to challenge and reinvigorate individual shows and the whole form.[6] This can happen in a single actor's performance, in a musical number, or in a whole production. For example, the grand finale of *A Chorus Line*, "One," in which the individual dancers join the kick line and become indistinguishable, can be dehumanizing, but it can also be passionate and emotional, revealing the human beauty and power of both dance itself and the chorus line as a miraculous, organic, living being. While this contradiction is built into every performance of *A Chorus Line*, revisionist revivals tend to expose the underbellies of traditional musicals. An extreme example of this is Anne Bogart's unauthorized, revisionist 1984 production of Rodgers and Hammerstein's *South Pacific* (1949). Bogart set the show, one of the most popular romantic musicals of all time, in a disturbing, clinical rehabilitation facility for shell-shocked war veterans who were acting out the show as a kind of behavioral modification therapy. The production was almost entirely faithful to the score, but the setting and approach upended the original sentiments. In one instance, during the famous—and famously lighthearted—number "I'm Gonna Wash that Man Right Outa My Hair," the inmates got stuck on the line, "I'm in love I'm in love I'm in love I'm in love I'm in love" like a broken record, until romance looked and sounded like mental illness. Even highly restrained individual performances can illuminate productions. In the 2001 London revival of *My Fair Lady*, Nicholas Le Prevost's affectionate and understated portrayal of Colonel Pickering left no doubt that Pickering was gay. This choice—never clearer than when Pickering took charge of dressing Eliza for the ball—subtly reconfigured the relationships among the three central characters.

Because theater comes and goes so quickly and allows for play in interpretation even within every performance, more varied—if not always more daring—versions of musicals have the potential to show up on stage. While creative and revisionist interpretations are certainly possible on film, the movie market won't bear multiple versions of the same show, whereas revivals are the mainstay of the musical theater business. This gives directors and performers the opportunity to try new approaches to the same shows. It means, too, that audiences are often repeat customers who can anticipate the score with a thorough knowledge of the songs and of the songs' histories in multiple productions. What's more, these audiences can develop their own layered relationship to the songs and the characters.

Musicals often have built-in singing lessons, inducements to sing, and examples of how singing can open up unlikely lines of connection, all of which work together to strengthen an audience's understanding of and pleasure in what they are watching. Songs that explain within musicals either explicitly how music works or how it could work, simultaneously suggest to an audience what and how to think about music and how to respond to what they are hearing. These strategies can be straight-forward and practical, as is true of the unambiguously named *The Sound of Music* (1959). Maria, as a new governess to the seven Von Trapp children, wins them over with song but also breaks down the basics of music for them and teaches them to sing with the number "Do-Re-Mi." *Floyd Collins* (1996) offers another way of thinking about the singing voice and its powers. Floyd uses the echoes of his voice to sound out caves in Kentucky. In the dark he tests his voice and its ability to reach across undefined distances. Later when he is trapped in a cave, he makes the imaginative leap to connect to the outside world through singing. Many of the songs in *Floyd Collins* emphasize vocalizing and mouth noises, as well as call-and-response. For an audience, these musicals extend an invitation to make any kind of noise, test the vocal waters, chant a musical scale, harmonize, and sing in order to open up space and reach out to people and places that are unseen, or even unknown.

One of the most important measures of the success of a musical—if not the only truly vital measure—is the power of the music onstage to inspire imitation. The longevity of a musical has a lot to do with how singers put over songs—how they communicate them—and whether those songs are then sung again offstage. This may mean that an audience member sings along with performers in a production, but certainly that the audience *wants* to sing along then, and will sing the songs at some point. At the 2001 London revival of *My Fair Lady*, a woman sitting behind me sang every number, mostly quietly. (She hit top volume on "I Could Have Danced All Night," which was a high point of the show.) Twice she apologized and whispered, "I can't help it." But her response was a testament to the show's achievement, and the relative equanimity of her neighbors suggested that they sympathized with the urge. The pervasiveness of this impulse is recognized in a number of different forums, including "musicals" karaoke and piano bars, and screening sing-alongs like *The Sing-Along Sound of Music*. Since film doesn't allow for literal audience-performer interaction, *The Sing-Along* goes a little way toward reinserting a live exchange into or alongside viewing the film of *The Sound of Music*. Audience members wear costumes from the movie, are provided with props, are coached in ensemble responses (booing the Nazis, cheering Maria), and sing along with the subtitles on the screen. *The Sing-Along Sound of Music* shares ground with a number of hybrid, interactive events, most obviously *The Rocky Horror Picture Show*, as well as TV shows like *Sing Along with Mitch, Mystery Science Theater 3000*, and, most recently, the online event of Joss Whedon's *Dr. Horrible's Sing-Along Blog* (2008).

Musical theater frequently holds out an appeal, not only among characters within the musical but also to the audience to participate. When the chorus sings, "Join us!" in *Pippin* (1972), this is not only a direct invitation to the audience to witness Pippin's journey but also an indirect invitation to keep that story alive by singing the songs again. Consider the difference with straight plays: we generally do not expect a play to inspire the desire to act or to prompt an imitative response (a more common expectation might be that a good play will inspire an empathetic or critical response). Not everyone can be Hamlet—or would want to be—but anyone can sing in the shower or to a child. While all theater is transient, musical theater is different because the music is the most memorable part of the show and the transmission of that music keeps the show alive. Participating is possible even for people who don't own or play cast recordings and for people without anything reasonably considered a passable singing voice. Since a show's survival depends on the audience's desire to sing its songs, quantity and not quality of participation is what matters most offstage.

Musical theater's democratic, open-ended invitation to audiences is not simply to sing along, but even more to imagine themselves in any of the roles of the often dramatic, expressive characters who populate musicals. This extends the continued life of musical numbers because many people respond to the idea of imagining themselves in the role of the singer, publicly or privately. Musical theater circulates through offstage communities in ways that are at once unpredictable and surprisingly constant. This movement and maintenance relies on recordings, TV and film versions, reality TV shows about stage productions, and Internet versions of musicals. Nonetheless, the experience of singing musical numbers and thus spreading the music around is an embodied experience that originates in and is sustained by live performance. Musical theater has particular weight and currency in certain communities, notably among gay men, as has been insightfully detailed by D. A. Miller in *Place for Us*, and John Clum in *Something for the Boys*, among others.[7] But its circulation is not limited to any one demographic.

The movement of songs from musicals across generations, for instance, is also unexpectedly consistent. Students routinely mention being exposed to musicals by their parents' singing the songs to them at an early age. (This transmission can happen unwittingly. Once, when my eighteen-month-old daughter was attempting to hurl herself out of her high chair, I said, "Sit down," and she immediately chanted, "*Sit down, sit down, sit down, sit down, sit down, you're rocking the boat!*" I must have sung her the line from *Guys and Dolls*, but I had no memory of doing so. She latched onto the call-and-response gospel-inspired rhythm and repetition, as well as onto my pleasure in it, and sang it right back at me.) The practice of musicals being passed down through generations seems to be reflected in the omnipresence of nostalgia in musicals themselves. Musicals are notoriously backward looking in settings and stories, from *Oklahoma!* (1943), which is nostalgic for 1906 Oklahoma Territory, to *Grease!* (1972), which embraces the fifties, to *Hairspray* (2002), which grooves to the rebellious sounds of 1962 from a safe distance. Very few musicals are set in their present moment. The cross-generational pull is also present in the eruption of jukebox musicals, which cater to an audience's familiarity with previously recorded soundtracks and established recording artists, from Frankie Valli and the Four Seasons (*Jersey Boys*, 2005) to ABBA (*Mamma Mia!* 2001). Even satirical contemporary musicals with fantastical or futuristic story lines—*Bat Boy* (1997) or *Urinetown* (2001) for instance—hearken back to and play with musical theater's own history.

One musical that exemplifies the intersection of the issue of community, onstage and off, and the communication and circulation of musical numbers, is the rock musical *Rent* (1994). *Rent* is, in part, a retelling of Puccini's *La Bohème* set in the early 1990s in the East Village in New York, which follows a group of socially marginal, idealistic young people, who come together to deal with poverty, AIDS, heroin addiction, romantic difficulties, and homelessness. The cast of the initial workshop at New York Theater Workshop, who went on to Broadway, was made up of almost entirely unknown young actors. The musical and the production embraced cheap bohemianism, and a clever, similarly minded marketing campaign sold cheap tickets to anyone who wanted to camp out on the street outside the run-down Nederlander Theater, which is right up the street from the gritty Port Authority Bus Terminal and was frequently populated by homeless people at the time. An astonishing number of young audience members enthusiastically took up the challenge, often sleeping on the street all night, and often for a remarkable number of repeat visits. According to Elizabeth Wollman, the marketing campaigns for rock musicals often have to be particularly innovative because of the difficulties of selling this kind of musical, and *Rent* was no exception.[8] But the invitation to join the onstage community of *Rent*—the invitation for the audience to imagine themselves as the offstage counterparts to the characters—was an easy leap. That invitation is built into the story, the lyrics, and the performance style of the songs in the show, which were sung either directly to the audience, at standing microphones set downstage left and right, or into the obvious radio microphones the actors wore on their heads, with the accompaniment of an onstage rock band.

Before embarking on multiple national and international tours, *Rent* ran for twelve years on Broadway, the eighth longest run in Broadway's history. The die-hard fans of the show who helped sustain its run, self-named Rentheads, formed Internet groups based on, among other things, the camaraderie that resulted from the ticket buying on the street; the number of times people had seen the show, in how many cities and countries; and quizzes devoted to all the lyrics and music of the show.[9] This community's delight in the show was bound up in their lived experience of going to the theater and in their understanding of themselves as an extension of the show's characters.

Rent answers the question of how people come together this way: through shared hardship, a message of the story that was readily adopted by the show's most dedicated audiences. All theater brings people together in a room, but musical theater regularly brings people together to contemplate the spectacle of people coming together, in book, song, and dance. Musical theater also encourages and relies on the audience's desire to perform the songs that they have heard performed, and to form communities based on that desire. In its examination and staging of the problems and pleasures of community on stage to a group of people offstage, live musical theater offers an experience unlike anything else.

NOTES

1 This device, termed the "marriage trope" by Raymond Knapp, has been described by Rick Altman as a fundamental structure of musicals: "The marriage which resolves the primary (sexual) dichotomy also mediates between two terms of the secondary (thematic) opposition"; see Rick Altman, *The American Film Musical* (Bloomington: Indiana University Press, 1987), p. 50, and Raymond Knapp, *The American Musical and the Formation of National Identity* (Princeton, NJ: Princeton University Press, 2005), p. 9 and elsewhere.
2 Scott McMillin, *The Musical as Drama* (Princeton, NJ: Princeton University Press, 2006), pp. 78–79.
3 Richard Rodgers, *Musical Stages: An Autobiography* (New York: Random House, 1975; reprinted New York: Da Capo, 1995, 2000), p. 227.

4 Knapp 2005, 162–76; see also his *"Assassins, Oklahoma!*, and the 'Shifting Fringe of Dark around the Campfire'" (*Cambridge Opera Journal* 16 [2004]: 77–101).
5 For a related discussion, see Scott Miller, *Deconstructing Harold Hill: An Insider's Guide to Musical Theatre* (Portsmouth, NH: Heinemann, 2000), ch. 5.
6 For an extended discussion of this dynamic, see Bruce Kirle, *Unfinished Show Business: Broadway Musicals as Works-in-Process* (Carbondale: Southern Illinois University Press, 2005).
7 D. A. Miller, *Place for Us (Essay on the Broadway Musical)* (Cambridge: Harvard University Press, 1998), and John Clum, *Something for the Boys: Musical Theater and Gay Culture* (New York: Palgrave, 1999).
8 Elizabeth L. Wollman, *The Theater Will Rock: A History of the Rock Musical, from Hair to Hedwig* (Ann Arbor: University of Michigan Press, 2006), p. 174.
9 Regarding the growing importance of Internet groups to sustaining a fan base for individual shows, see Stacy Wolf, "*Wicked* Divas, Musical Theater, and Internet Girl Fans" (*Camera Obscura* 65 22.2 [2007]: 39–71.

2

The Filmed Musical

RAYMOND KNAPP AND MITCHELL MORRIS

■ □ ■

INTERACTIONS BETWEEN STAGED AND FILMED musicals have, since the beginning of commercially viable synchronized sound, been thoroughgoing and powerful, shaping the development of both. Given the longer existence of stage musicals, filmed musicals would naturally seem to be the derivative genre. Yet for the *American* musical, this "natural" understanding is dubious, since almost all staged musicals that still hold significance for American audiences were created within film's "sound" era. Whether it was due to coincidence, kismet, or some complex causal web, 1927 saw the births of both the "sound era" in film (with *The Jazz Singer*) and, by some reckonings, the "Golden Age" of American musicals on stage (with *Show Boat*). Later developments of either type require some consideration of the other.

Despite this intertwining of intimately shared histories, most studies consider staged and filmed musicals as separate genres, an academic habit bred more by the drawing of disciplinal boundaries than anything else. Thus, scholarly engagements with the former mostly ignore the latter (or consign it to secondary status through token consideration), whereas Rick Altman's *The Film Musical*—the landmark monograph on its topic—although full of insight and valuable readings of particular films, virtually ignores all relevant staged versions and models.[1]

In this chapter, rather than focus narrowly on the filmed musical's specific historical contributions, which would reinforce the filmed musical's "token" status, we examine selected areas of intersection between stage and screen, as sites where fusions and fissures between them have enlivened or beset one or the other (or both). We begin, after a brief exposition of some vocabulary essential to the study of film musicals, by addressing a set of practical issues related to race, stars, and adaptation, as grounded in the commercial realities of the film industry. We then proceed to a consideration of the separate and sometimes interactive worlds created by film musicals, choosing to focus on three specific aspects of those worlds: (1) modes of evoking the "real" (and the "artificial"), (2) the presentation of song, especially when tending toward the intimate, and (3) the specific role of camp, both in presentation and reception.

THE MUSICAL AS FILM

Because of the ubiquity of blends, hybrids, and fusions that compose the filmed musical, an acquaintance with basic stylistic concepts used in cinema studies is crucial to their formal analysis and interpretation.[2] Four domains seem most immediately relevant:

Mise-en-scène. This term, derived from theater criticism, encompasses all aspects of the "look" within the film's frame: setting, whether specially constructed or found in the everyday world; lighting, both artificial and "natural"; costumes and makeup; special effects (if any); and all modes of actorly performance such as gesture and stance, speaking, and singing. All of these aspects tend to combine, with greater or lesser success, with the others, and to acquire additional significance through the way their changes are articulated through performance time. In sum, mise-en-scène refers to how the scene is "staged." And in the case of musicals, the mise-en-scènes appropriate to theatrical productions are often apt to play an important role in the structuring of their films.

Cinematography. A film is always shot in a particular way that shapes the affective charge of particular moments and their combination into the whole. Analysis of cinematography typically attends to three things: (1) photographic qualities of the "shot" such as color, hue, speed, perspective, focus, and field depth; (2) framing, or the way that the borders of the particular image focus viewer attention, particularizing the image; and (3) duration, or "take," the length of the camera's view of a specific scene before cutting to another. Each of these factors can be broken down into many subcomponents in the course of an analysis, and more detailed study of the particulars of filmic language is invaluable in consolidating interpretations.

Editing. A film comprises a series of shots, and the way that these are combined (montage) decisively shapes viewers' interpretations.[3] Shots may be joined by devices such as fade-outs and fade-ins, dissolves and wipes, and most commonly by cuts—the direct juxtaposition of two shots. Qualities of the mise-en-scène and cinematography, the rhythmic play that comes from lengths of shots, and the spatio-temporal relations that they may imply are all relevant to a consideration of the editorial process, not least because they help determine a viewer's sense of the degree of continuity and discontinuity present in the narrative.

Sound. A film musical's numbers are generally recorded separately before they are shot and are thus subject to alterations that are difficult or impossible to make in live performances. Before the advent of amplification and the widespread use of prerecorded music in live theater, this was one of the most distinctive features of film musicals. The production of *My Fair Lady* (1964), where almost all of Audrey Hepburn's songs were "dubbed" by Marni Nixon, and Jeremy Brett's by Bill Shirley,[4] illustrates this difference well. But more subtly, the necessity of recording sound for film musicals meant that performers who did not sound well in live theaters could more easily participate in film musicals, whereas performers who flourished before the coming of the microphone (Ethel Merman comes to mind) arguably found themselves disadvantaged in film by the very skills that served them well in the theater. The expansion of studio techniques of sound manipulation in the 1960s as well as the rise of cinematic sound design at the end of the 1970s, coupled with the introduction of amplification in live musical theater from the 1970s on have further complicated analysis of both live and filmed musicals, as people bring expectations fostered by one venue to the other. In any case, the particulars of a filmed musical's sound design—the timbres of voices, their relationship to the arrangements they inhabit, and their place in the overall sound design—are perhaps best analyzed as working synergistically with the more visually oriented aspects of the overall work.

MANAGING RACE AND STARS

As discussed more extensively in this book's companion volumes (see especially chapter 5 in *Histories* and 1 in *Identities and Audiences*), race has played a huge role in the history of the American musical, especially regarding the black/white "color line" and the practices of blackface. The latter helped launch the sound era, figuring prominently in *The Jazz Singer*, and continued to play a part in filmed musicals until well into the 1940s—long after its use in Broadway musicals had waned—with a few stars specializing in blackface and many others taking at least an occasional turn in blackface.

Perhaps the most startling example of the latter is Fred Astaire's "Bojangles of Harlem" in *Swing Time* (George Stevens, 1936; ◉ Example 2.1). Because it pays specific homage to a then still-active screen star, Bill "Bojangles" Robinson, the usual signifying elements of blackface have a specific point of reference rather than functioning as a generic mask. Yet several things complicate this number and contemporary reactions to it. As Todd Decker has shown, in other films Astaire took box-office risks in his forthright integration of black musicians into his musical numbers, making it difficult to cut them out of the picture for distribution in the American South (a standard practice for musical numbers performed by blacks).[5] Astaire's decision to "honor" Robinson with a number that not only uses blackface but also partakes of other stereotypical race-based images and emphases, then, seems odd. Especially problematic is the doubly offensive opening visual joke, when a large caricature of the blackface persona, with cheap bowler hat and exaggerated painted lips, turns into a pair of exaggeratedly large feet—a visual reference, perhaps, to the "educated feets" of minstrel performers. The centrality of race to the number is reinforced by stark oppositions of black and white throughout the scene (and elsewhere in the film), as in the contrasting outfits of the dancers, who alternately evoke segregation and miscegenation in their deployments, and in the giant black shadows of Astaire dancing, eventually recreating a kind of "challenge" dance evocative of early minstrelsy. Further, his dance, while overtly an homage, comes across quite differently, especially in his free use of hands, arms, and upper body, contrasting vividly with Robinson, who was criticized (reportedly by Astaire himself) for dancing only from the waist down. Intriguingly, Astaire's blackface resonates with Ginger Rogers's entrance in "The Way You Look Tonight," when she appears, distracted by Astaire's song, in a whitening shampoo lather (▶ Example 2.2). While it is possible to trace a liberating narrative in the mixing of races and Astaire's dismissal of the shadows in "Bojangles," and to understand the parallel scene with Rogers as part of a coordinated claim that color is only skin deep, it is just as easy, and probably more common, to take the references at their offensive (black)face value, especially as they are reinforced by the sprinkling throughout the film of such elements as "jungle" drumming and a brief "indefinite talk" routine (with sidekick Victor Moore).

Astaire's struggles to make good on a debt he and many other white dancers felt toward a systematically excluded population of black performers—given that tap dancing was grounded in black and blackface traditions—found institutional echo in the war years, when *Stormy Weather* (Andrew Stone) appeared as one of two all-black musicals produced by major Hollywood studios in 1943. While its central story line falls flat, based on the unconvincing romantic pairing of an aging Bill Robinson with an oddly restrained Lena Horne, the trajectory of its musical numbers, as with Astaire's blackface number, points both to a tainted legacy in minstrelsy (thus the cakewalk, indefinite talk, and jungle numbers) and the evolving makeover of these elements, especially in Cab Callaway's "Jumpin' Jive" and its climactic dance turn by the Nicholas Brothers (▶ Example 2.3).[6] If such gestures were inadequately reparative and largely ineffective in changing Hollywood race-based practices, in *Singin' in the Rain* (Stanley Donen and Gene Kelly, 1952) those practices could nevertheless be brushed aside as period curiosities, with Donald O'Connor's brief reference to Jolson's "Mammy" number in *The Jazz Singer* and Kelly's throwaway greeting to a white actor whose elaborate jungle makeup makes him unrecognizable.

Singin' in the Rain and *Stormy Weather* are each concerned with enacting a specific historical moment within the context of a "backstage" musical, and so, naturally enough, each strikes a particular attitude toward "stars" and the "star system." While stars and teams (usually comic or romantic) were common enough on Broadway, and perhaps even more common in vaudeville and related venues, they were still more important in Hollywood, where they were aggressively marketed as such by the studios. Like most backstage musicals, the narratives of both of these films center on the prospects of an unknown "making it" and becoming a star. And because they are adult-oriented musicals, that quest combines easily with a romantic quest, in which the other half of the romantic pair is already a star and serves emblematically as stardom itself, with success in both realms achieved at one stroke.

While star teams were often the preferred marketing tool of the studios because of their multiple points of appeal—offering two or more stars individually and a familiar interactive dynamic—many stars tried to break away from this sometimes limiting pattern, with differing degrees of success. Judy Garland, for example, was effectively paired, as a "juvenile," with Mickey Rooney and struggled for years to emerge as an adult star in her own right. Ironically, *The Wizard of Oz* (Victor Fleming, 1939), in which she played a girl younger than her actual age, probably held up this process somewhat; five years later, in *Meet Me in St. Louis* (Vicente Minnelli), she was still playing "young," although in many respects more mature than her romantic partner, "The Boy Next Door" (played by Tom Drake).

Among the most successful star teams of the 1930s was that of Fred Astaire and Ginger Rogers, who enjoyed considerably more success together than either seemed destined to achieve individually in Hollywood (although each achieved individual success as their pairing played itself out). *Swing Time*, filmed at the height of their partnership, with songs by Jerome Kern and Dorothy Fields, and often cited as the most satisfying overall, exemplifies how their films tended to work. Astaire was easily the better dancer and, although rather thin of voice, more capable of "delivering" a song. Yet in both song and dance they proved both compatible and effectively complementary. It was thus in their musical numbers that their romance evolved, overcoming the frictions established by plot situations and their wise-cracking personae. Ironically, while *Stormy Weather* attempts something like this strategy, the crackling energy of its "real-life" partners and ensembles—especially in the case of the Nicholas Brothers—easily overwhelms the film's "official" center of interest.

ADAPTATIONS

Adaptations represent the most direct point of contact between Broadway and Hollywood and have been a mainstay of the latter ever since *The Jazz Singer* first showed the potential for sound film to bring a Broadway star in a Broadway show to a wider public. Critical views of adaptations depend on the perspective taken, on whether the resulting artifact is regarded as a filmed *version* of a stage show, or as a *film musical* that happens to derive from a stage show. We will consider these somewhat opposed perspectives in order.

While audiences have tended more often to see film adaptations as *versions* of the stage show, there are often large differences between them. Until the 1940s, for example, song substitutions and omissions were not only common but rampant, before the growing popularity of show-based albums after *Oklahoma!* (1943) made audiences invest more heavily in a stage show's specific song list and come to expect a more faithful version of the show on screen. Apart from this basic difference in song content, Hollywood was always eager to emphasize differences, often specifically cinematic; thus, they relied on naturalistic settings, added songs, larger-scale dance numbers, more fluid scene and act structures, and established film stars, among other strategies, to provide "more" than the stage version could and to compensate for the absent vitality of live performance.

The Music Man (Morton DaCosta, 1962) is a classic example of a film that remains fairly faithful to its stage predecessor, although it interweaves a new song and strives to create a fuller sense of the town of River City. But its train sequence illustrates the limitations of taking staged material to a "naturalized" screen. Here, the signal triumph of the stage's patter number, "Rock Island," depends on the actors bouncing in rhythm to create the illusion of a train's motion. This technique, though blatantly artificial, is brought intact to the screen, despite the "naturalized" setting of a "real train" emphasized by occasional cuts to train wheels (▶ Example 2.4). Just as this scene is thus so clearly about reproducing a *stage* effect, filmed musicals in general, and especially adaptations, must often deliberately forgo the cinematic in order to provide adequate space for the artificialities of stage musicals. *Guys and Dolls* (Joseph Mankiewicz, 1955), another fairly faithful adaptation, is perhaps more forthright in mixing the artificial and the real, adding actual cars and pavement to what is clearly a stage set, and recreating much of the stage choreography for the screen. The latter film also exhibits other—to some, more transgressive—differences: using film star Marlon Brando despite his limitations as a singer, redistributing songs to accommodate the demands of Frank Sinatra, and dropping "Marry the Man Today" and "Bushel and a Peck" to make room for new songs.

Considered more distinctively as films, adaptations lie on a continuum between poles: filmed versions of theatrically staged productions, and versions that translate stage works into more distinctively cinematic styles. The first of these poles is not as straightforward as it has often seemed, which is an important consideration since for a significant number of musicals it creates a primary object of study. One of the challenges that a filmed staging presents arises from its apparent documentary function: the film can seem implicitly to claim the status of an "innocent eye," offering simple secondary reportage of the genuine primary staged event. As such, the filmed staging is a surrogate for the theatrical performance, and the film itself might be taken to be interpretively transparent, with the particularities of its realization irrelevant to any close study of the show. But this is not true. A quick canvass of several filmed stagings will show that film as a medium exerts significant influence over the shaping of our experience of a staged work through the placement of shots, the choice and pacing of cuts, and other technical devices. Even the most minimal apparatus (such as a single camera aimed at center stage and including the entire stage picture in the frame) by its fixed point of view and exclusion of subsidiary senses such as touch and smell, frames the work in a way that does not occur in staged performances. Thus, Stephen Sondheim's *Passion* (1994), which was filmed and first broadcast on the PBS series "American Playhouse" in 1996, assumes a largely documentary point of view with respect to the way that it is filmed. But again, any form of cinéma vérité is always a necessarily stylized sampling of live performance, evident especially in the film's use of dissolves that superimpose images of the show's writers and recipients of letters as they share the dramatic act of singing them. However valuable the filmed staging may be in providing details of the theatrical performance, it is not identical to the theatrical work and must be treated as a work in its own right.

At the other pole lie films that create versions of musicals in which the theatrical apparatus is wholly absent. In a case such as *The Sound of Music* (1965), for instance, the picturesque environs of Salzburg are instrumental in creating a mise-en-scène of realism within which the song-and-dance of von Trappish courtship-and-politics takes place. That is, when songs are not in play, the film operates as a standard sound film shot on location, with interactions between characters managed largely as they would be in any nonmusical film of its period. The musical's status as a theatrical object is largely irrelevant to the shape of its filmic realization. In other films, such as *Cabaret* (1973) and *Chicago* (2002), nearly the reverse happens, as montage during songs allows realms of cinematic reality and fantasy to permeate more explicitly what was originally a theatrical space. But even in this regard, the montage sequences in *The Sound of Music* ("Do-Re-Mi") provide common ground between otherwise disparate approaches.

Especially in the case of musicals, a large number of intermediate forms between these poles loom large in the film tradition. They do not seek the modified cinematic realism of a film such as the *Sound of Music* nor the strictly theatrical milieu of *Passion*, but rather blend cinematic realism with various forms of stylization. The subgenre of the "backstage musical," for instance, establishes a stage world and a "real world" so that it can play on the difference between "life" and "performance" (but in backstage musicals such as *Broadway Melody of 1936*, or a more recent example such as *Fame* [1980, remade in 2009], performances end up occurring offstage as well as on). A particularly interesting case of a middle ground can be found in the film version of *South Pacific* (1958), which was shot in Technicolor, an intense process that amplifies color past the standards of realism in the late 1950s. In order to vary the intensity of the color, director Joshua Logan sought to use color filters during the performance of songs (this was a technique directly borrowed from the lighting effect used in the stage production). The process was enormously time-consuming, however, and Columbia Pictures refused to allow time to adjust the color from its lurid original. The result is spectacularly unrealistic, all the more so because of the role given the on-location sites of Kauai and Fiji. Thus, the visual aspect of *South Pacific* has been a source of critical dispute ever since the film's release and unquestionably exerts pressure on the ways that viewers understand the relationship between the musical numbers and the rest of the narrative (⊙ Example 2.5).

The increasing tendency to adapt films to the musical stage intertwines with the parallel rise in revivals and "revisals," and speaks also to the importance of film adaptations in building audiences for the latter. This co-dependency is especially evident when "revisals" are remade to resemble more closely the film versions, as in the 1998 Broadway staging of *Cabaret*, which incorporated many elements of Bob Fosse's 1973 film, or in revivals and repertory performances of *The Rocky Horror Show* that accommodate audience predilections to "call back" and otherwise participate in the show, continuing practices that bloomed during the film version's run at New York's Waverly Theater and other venues (*The Rocky Horror Picture Show*, Jim Sharman, 1975). In such cases, the filmed version effectively becomes the definitive version, a claim that may also be made for other filmed adaptations, even when, as in *Gentlemen Prefer Blondes* (Howard Hawks, 1953), song omissions and substitutions are more the rule than the exception.

THE WORLDS OF FILMED MUSICALS

Cinematic Realism and MERM

Narrative sound film typically maintains what André Bazin terms "the illusion of reality" through deploying its combination of images and sounds so as to seem natural to audiences, whether by directly simulating experienced reality or by following familiar conventions of cinematic storytelling. In classic Hollywood film and its derivatives, this mode of cinematic realism depends on such things as continuity (a consistent look and feel to the filmic world), maintaining a consistency of acting styles across the field (tending mainly toward restraint, so as not to seem to be playing to an audience), an aspect of cinematography that Bazin calls "cinematic tact" (maintaining a close relation to the human perspective), a seeming naturalness in the structure of narrative events, and the general subjugation of montage (especially associative montage) to a unity of space created through mise-en-scène.[7]

Musicals adjust the default aesthetic of cinematic realism at nearly every turn, because—on the most obvious level—in musical numbers characters appear to sing and dance their feelings in open violation of the restrained acting fostered by cinematic realism. Although these behaviors are often naturalized in various ways (particularly in backstage musicals), they nevertheless routinely depart from "the natural" in key respects. Thus, even if a character has a legitimizing reason to sing or dance, doing so brings into play a number of familiar tropes from musicals, such as the conceit that while singing in a musical number, a character is more honest than normal, more intensely present, more capable of interpersonal connection, more empowered, more empower*ing*, and generally better able to effect transformative change. Musical numbers, however they might be justified in terms of cinematic realism, thereby invoke what has been termed MERM (Musically Enhanced Reality Mode; see Knapp, 67–70 and *passim*), which is both a matter of the associated psychological dimensions of musical numbers and actual enhancements to the visual and aural experience of musical performance that have become typical of musical numbers in film.

MERM derives from stage musicals, where it has a similar profile in reception, but it has become even more vital to film musicals, because of both its challenges to cinematic realism and the capacity of film to intensify the presentation of musical numbers. Thus, regarding the latter, filmic MERM almost always includes lipsynching to prerecorded, studio-based singing, with non-diegetic instrumental and/or vocal support (that is, music that has no apparent source in the film's world). Through the device of performing to "playback" (the prerecorded track), not only might characters seem capable of singing effortlessly, regardless of how strenuous their physical activity might be, but the sound we hear will also remain uniformly good however the setting and positioning of the actor might change during a number: even a number filmed outdoors will, by default, have the focused, well-rounded sound of the studio. MERM might also include post-production manipulation of the performance's audio field—for example, through overdubbing taps to a dance routine, or by adding Foleys (sound effects) to enhance the cinematic reality of the scene, but which also (if they are done well) make the performance itself seem more immediate, if not fully believable as a filmed live performance. Other cinematic techniques may also be deployed more extravagantly to align with MERM (especially but not only in the work of Busby Berkeley). These might involve more elaborate camera positioning (crane shots and the like); montage; overt violations of the film's mise-en-scène (as when an actual stage mutates invisibly into an enormous sound stage in *42nd Street*, 1933); broader acting styles; otherwise unexplained adjustments to costume, sets, and lighting; an increased use of closeups; or other enhancements to the presentation whether or not an audience might be expected to notice them. Paradoxically, despite the blatant artificiality of the world created by and in coordination with MERM, the result is usually designed to create a heightened sense of reality, giving an extra charge to the performance of a musical number. This paradox provides the means by which MERM, especially through its capacity to highlight performance as such, might serve as a gateway to camp, allowing it to acquire a secure foothold in film musicals.

The differential between cinematic realism and MERM heightens the potentially difficult "reality" threshold that must be crossed to enter or leave the musical number. This threshold exists also in stage musicals, between the spoken play's dialogue and the sung (and/or danced) number, and it has been much discussed in that context.[8] But its disruptive capacity is even greater in its filmic form, with many possible consequences. Most common, perhaps, is the intensification of the pleasures afforded by the musical number's excursions from cinematic realism, perhaps releasing overtly into camp but in any case often veering toward the immoderate in both gesture and duration. More unusually, the threshold between cinematic realism and MERM may involve a collision of sensibilities or worldviews sufficiently extreme that it can overturn the genre itself. In some cases, "reality" becomes, in a sense, too "real" to support escape into a musical number, so that a film musical stops being a musical; examples include *The Wizard of Oz* (1939), where the last song, "If I Were King of the Forest," occurs just before Dorothy and her cohort have their audience with the Wizard, and *Meet Me in St. Louis* (1944), which stumbles forward with only an occasional song after Alonso Smith's announcement that the family will soon be moving to New York. (Notably, parallel examples for this phenomenon in stage musicals are extremely rare.) On the flip side of this phenomenon are traditionally narrative films that suddenly become musicals (generally, at or near the end). In one familiar example, *The Life of Brian* (1979), "Always Look on the Bright Side of Life" is sung by a hillside of crucifixion victims, culminating the film's long series of outrages against cinematic realism. But there are more subtle examples, as well, such as *Bagdad Cafe* (1987) and *Bread and Tulips* (*Pane e Tulipani*, 2000), in which the final song-and-dance number both surprises and confirms the element of fantasy that has underwritten each film from the outset, however it may otherwise have behaved according to the conventions of cinematic realism.[9]

Sung Intimacy

Musicals on both stage and screen try to do two sometimes contradictory things through their musical numbers: to be intimately revealing of a character's inner life, and to indulge an audience's taste for opulent spectacle on a large scale. Although musicals on film lose the edge of immediacy and risk-taking that can add excitement to both intimacy and spectacle on the stage, film offers compensating opportunities to both realms. MERM, for example, can be used to augment both extravagant and intimate dimensions in a film's musical numbers. This is perhaps more obvious with the former; spectacle has from the beginning been a Hollywood specialty, and its capacity to indulge that predilection has been steadily enhanced by technology. In filmed musicals, there are few restraints on what might be used to pump up the (mostly non-diegetic) aural dimension of a large production number or to make a more modest number come across as "big"—although in their eagerness to outdo stage musicals, some films too readily abandon the framing that can make a full-scale ensemble number seem overwhelming on stage. Because MERM's capacity to enhance intimacy may on the other hand often pass unnoticed, we will focus here on the "small" rather than the "big."

In *Singin' in the Rain*, Don Lockwood overtly highlights the capacity of MERM to manage and enhance the expression of inner feelings by adding lighting effects, mist, and wind to the set as he prepares to sing "You Were Meant for Me" to Kathy Selden. But what may well pass unnoticed in this sequence is the way musical underscore and orchestration support these and other intimately drawn visual moments as the song and dance number gets under way, since orchestral underscore has long been a central device of Hollywood films, as dependable as lighting as a means to enhance intimacy (or withdraw from it, as when we pan out during the dance number for a breakout passage; ▶ Example 2.6). That we are more likely to notice this manner of scoring when it is absent than when it is present is deftly exploited to comic effect in *Moulin Rouge* (2001); thus, we may not even notice the faint musical background that continues to support Christian and Satine's moment of intimacy just after "Your Song"—until it is audibly "turned off" (that is, imitating the effect of stopping a record turntable) with the revelation that he is not a duke.

Even more subtle, and probably more common than not, is the effect of sudden intimacy that will accompany the movement into song on film (unless it is deliberately counteracted), as we leave the world of set- or location-generated sound (even if Foleyed in after the fact) for the world of prerecorded studio sound. In "Somewhere Over the Rainbow" in *The Wizard of Oz*, for example, the studio recording gradually eclipses the background sounds of the farmyard as Dorothy begins the number, helping to effect the transition into Dorothy's inner world from the annoying, oblivious bustle of everyday reality (only to be displaced immediately after the song by a return to the mix of leitmotivic and familiar/generic "background" music provided by journeyman operetta composer Herbert Stothart, as the film cuts to Miss Gulch on her bicycle; ▶ Example 2.7).

Musically framed intimacy has become the special province of film, always ready to be exploited by filmed musicals, especially in duet numbers. A particularly good example of the latter—even if, in sung terms, it is not exactly a duet—is "Over the Bannister" in *Meet Me in St. Louis*, which moves an increasingly intimate post-party progression from bustle to quietude as the guests leave, from light into shadows as Esther dims the lights, and from separation to proximity as, during the song, Esther descends the stairway to face John Truitt within a single frame. John has been our proxy until this moment, stammeringly in awe of Esther's beauty—her face lit by each dimming lamp in turn, the reduced lighting then circling around her auburn hair, creating a double halo for her softly bedimmed features—and cajoling her into prolonging the moment through song. Although one is likely to remember "Over the Bannister" less as a song and more for its surrounding qualities and John's comic inability to follow through, its somewhat stilted lyric and sweetly arched melodic lines fully support those qualities, especially by providing Judy Garland's voice and exquisitely nuanced visual delivery the opportunity to provide the aural equivalent for the caresses John is too timid to offer (▶ Example 2.8).

Camp

The term "camp" has been used since the early twentieth century to refer to a style of performance and reception that favors the ostentatiously theatrical, the gaudily stylized.[10] As an attitude toward art, it may be understood as a democratization or carnivalization of the stance of the late nineteenth-century "dandy." In England, particularly, the Aesthetic movement, with its public relations slogan of "Art for Art's sake," was commonly equated with the complex associations of artists and attitudes that often carried labels such as "Symbolist" or "Decadent" in their French incarnations. In any case, in these cultural styles we typically find a rarefied attention to aesthetic nuance and detail coupled with a canny sense of public effect; consider the arch pronouncements of such fin-de-siècle figures as James Abbott MacNeill Whistler, Aubrey Beardsley, and especially Oscar Wilde. A sampling of Wilde's aphorisms points our attention toward the characteristic flavor of camp: "Music makes one feel so romantic—at least it always gets on one's nerves—which is the same thing; Illusion is the first of all pleasures; If you want to tell people the truth, make them laugh, otherwise they'll kill you." The role of paradox in these pithy one-liners translates into camp taste's preference for highly artificial "performances" that fail in one respect or another. For instance, if a style of theatrical acting prizes "realism," a camp point of view might tend willfully to elevate an instance of realism that has somehow gotten away from itself. Virtuosic skill in musical performance, for instance, is best for camp listeners if it is joined with completely implausible acting, or ludicrously inappropriate body type, or an unexpected and hilarious failure of costuming, scenery, or stage business.

The point of camp is not mockery by itself, but mockery that actually disguises an enormous tenderness toward the object or event under consideration. A camp appreciation of a great performer such as Ethel Merman, for instance, will probably pay special attention to Merman's well-known habit of moving to center stage and facing the audience directly whenever she was singing: dramatic plausibility, interactions with other performers, all such details of "realism" tended to be jettisoned in the interest of hurling that formidable sound toward the audience as overwhelmingly as possible. It seems likely, from Merman's own comments, that she saw this performance choice as a question of "giving the audience their money's worth." But for many listeners, the full-frontal sonic assault seems a capitulation to a spectacular narcissistic complex—and it's that very narcissism that wins the affection and sympathy of an audience predisposed to camp.

The example of Ethel Merman also raises the question of performers' intentions. In critical writings on camp, a distinction frequently appears between nonintentional and intentional camp. The nonintentional camp object is camp because a particular audience says it is, not because the creator strives to make it so. Intentional camp arises when the performer, clued into the interpretive practices of the specific marginal audience, deliberately plays to them. In-jokes and sly subcultural references are thickly constellated around an ostensibly "straight" performance.

Whether intentional or not, such modes of performance and appreciation operate by projecting a dualistic structure that distinguishes between essences and accidents, that is, between "real interiors" and "artificial exteriors." In musicals, for instance, there is "the character" being performed, but there is also a "real person" playing that character, and a camp moment represents the place where the concerns of the "real person" suddenly override, and hilariously sabotage, the decorum of performance that allowed "the character" to be formulated in the first place. Thus, the "failure" of performance represents on another level the triumph of the "true self" that crafted that performance. This also helps explain the preference of camp attitudes for styles of presentation and performance that are just slightly outmoded: when a hairstyle, for instance, is just beginning to be out of date, it looks silly, but when it has been out of date for a significant period, it tends to look merely "historical." What is happening in this case has to do with conventions and stylizations—they begin to seem passé because the fashion shifts, but they cannot go along for the ride. Thus, the very details that once passed unnoticed, because they merely seemed to be "natural," begin to become uncomfortably apparent and anything *but* "natural." The revelation of forgeries by the passing of time has become something of a cliché in art connoisseurship, primarily because it depends upon this consensus understanding of conventions' historical nature. But unlike the dubious objet d'art, which becomes less valuable because its failed conventions expose its meretricious "inner nature," the camp artifact becomes all the more funny and yet touching because its inadequacies seem like deeply human failings. Nearly everyone has at one time or another experienced an embarrassing failure of what the sociologist Erving Goffman called "impression management"; camp tastes tend to take such failures as the very incarnation of the values they hold most dear. As the façade cracks open, we may have a chance to glimpse the truth of interiority.

Not surprisingly, these modes of representation and interpretation have been especially appealing to stigmatized social groups who were able to "pass." Since the very notion of passing posits a "real self" that is prior to, more important than, and more vulnerable than the social self, the dualistic structure outlined above models the tensions and embodies the risks inherent in such social strategies. Jews and especially homosexuals, as the exemplary passing minorities of twentieth-century America, tended to adopt camp positions as a form of "in-house" culture-making. But with all due respect to Susan Sontag, whose famous essay "Notes on Camp," asserted a contrast between "Jewish moral seriousness" and "homosexual aestheticism and irony," these two "forms of modern sensibility" turn out to overlap in remarkable, intricate ways that would require a separate study to discuss.[11] For our purposes here, what matters is the imbrication of aesthetico-political concerns especially poignant for Jews and for queer folks in the texts and performances that constituted the musical as a genre. "Realism," to the extent that it underwrites a tendency to regard cultural norms as "natural," is the enemy of all marginal(ized) social groups and identities; and because the musical gave only lip service (at best) to the practices and moral commitments of "realism," it was one of the most hospitable of genres to camp styles and receptions. And to the degree that audience members who occupied less socially marginal positions accommodated themselves to the characteristic practices of the in-house audiences, they became proficient at camp reception as well. And the camp reading practices thus absorbed were relevant to film and stage musicals alike.

A striking example of intentional camp in film musicals is MGM's 1948 vehicle *The Pirate* (produced by Arthur Freed, songs by Cole Porter, directed by Vincente Minnelli, starring Judy Garland and Gene Kelly).[12] From the film's first frames, the musical sets up a spectacle of marvelous visual and sonic gaudiness. Technicolor was always the most strenuously vivid of the color film processes, but everything in the mise-en-scène—especially the crazy costumes—amps up the chromatism. The arrangements of the songs, too, are timbrally polychromatic, especially to the degree that Latin influences enfold themselves into the score. Both Garland and Kelly are terrifically sly about the details of performance: pacing and intonation of lines, gestural complexes and postures (especially facial ones—viewers may often note a tendency for different parts of the actors' faces to express opposed emotions, a sure tip-off to their performance of serious frivolity). That is, at nearly every level of the film's construction, there is a bias toward anti-realism—a kind of anti-realism, moreover, that was by 1948 distinctly on the wane.[13] To add to the contexts of reception, the audiences who were "in the know" at the time of the film's premiere would have been aware of some off-camera details about the lives of the film's creators—Freed's taste for hiring gay men to work in his MGM production unit (Freed's Fairies), the complicated sexual orientations of Porter and Minnelli, Garland's evolving status as a gay icon—that would likely have facilitated camp readings of the film (▶ Example 2.9; ▶ Example 2.10). The case was otherwise with audiences not-so-marginal; *The Pirate* met with mixed critical reactions and tepid box office, and its reputation has improved only gradually.

But it would be a mistake to assume that camp practices of presentation and interpretation maintained themselves unchanged over the course of the twentieth century. Sontag's 1964 essay, along with the critical treatment of the work of avant-garde filmmakers such as Jack Smith or Kenneth Anger, and most important, nearly everything associated with Andy Warhol, reveal the translation of camp stances into a more mainstreamed cluster of interpretive attitudes. This could be considered typical of the ways mainstream commercial culture harvests motifs, styles, and attitudes from various American subcultures over the course of the twentieth century.[14] But in the wake of the Stonewall Rebellion in 1969, when a more active and confrontational phase of gay politics began to exert major pressure on the customary social arrangements of American society, the mainstreaming impulses that in Sontag or Warhol seemed avant-gardishly rarefied were brought to a much wider public.

One of the most influential post-Stonewall musicals to articulate a camp point of view is *The Rocky Horror Picture Show* (1975). Although space does not permit a detailed analysis, a number of its aspects that attract camp can be observed. The film begins with a nostalgic recollection of 1950s science fiction films—by the beginning of the 1970s, a kind of film that would be available only as a late-night film or a television rerun. In either case, such science fiction films were, even when first released, relatively low in status,[15] and, especially because the genre is so preoccupied with technology, the mise-en-scéne of science fiction films erodes more quickly than in almost any other genre. The rapid obsolescence of these films, together with the second-rate status of their later broadcastings, made science fiction an ultra-powerful camp-magnet (⏵ Example 2.11). Similarly, the musical style, which tends toward the démodé (most overtly in the song "Hot Patootie—Bless My Soul," but in numerous less foregrounded musical details as well), attracts campish attentions and affections. The generic and musical framework of recycling resonates strongly with the frequent reference in the plot and dialogue to precedents from 1950s films ("normal, healthy kids," "juvenile delinquents," and so on), but just as strongly with the peculiar erotic bricolage of the Transylvanians, eventually revealed to be space aliens passing as humans.

The most critical difference between the camp attitudes of *The Pirate* and those of *The Rocky Horror Picture Show* have everything to do with the vast amount of social change that separates their periods of genesis. Dr. Frank-N-Furter can flash his corset and fishnets, and serially seduce everyone who takes his fancy, because by 1975, a panoply of tastes and styles that were unrepresentable even a decade before had become public and voluble. By contrast, the exotic desires expressed in *The Pirate*—especially the marvelously steamy dance-dream sequence—had to be expressed mostly by connotation. For that matter, the number "Voodoo" was famously cut by Mayer because it was far too overtly sexual for his sense of what the censor would allow.

But in both cases, the central point remains: by their affection for conventions—those agreements of social style that seem so powerful until toppled, as they inevitably are by their inherent weaknesses—camp attitudes make up one of the most powerful modes of interpretation in the musical, especially the musical film. Though Hollywood may thunder, "Pay no attention to the man behind the curtain," the musical on film is prone to pull the curtain back. And to the extent that we experience camp as one of the central possibilities of the musical on film, we can respond to its pleasures in toto, too.

NOTES

1 Rick Altman, *The American Film Musical* (Bloomington: Indiana University Press, 1987); a similar narrowness of focus may

be found in Jane Feuer, *The Hollywood Musical*, 2nd ed. (Bloomington: Indiana University Press, 1992), among other studies.
2 A useful guide to these and other elements central to the study of film is David Bordwell and Kristin Thompson's *Film Art: An Introduction*, 8th ed. (Boston: McGraw-Hill, 2008).
3 *Montage* can refer in general terms, as here, to the assembly of shots (or cuts) within a film, although it has a number of more specific applications as well. Soviet filmmakers in the 1920s (e.g., Lev Kuleshov, Vsevolod Pudovkin, and Sergei Eisenstein) practiced and theorized montage as a means for creating filmic meaning through the juxtaposition of images, often in violation of continuity. And montage, used as a singular noun, is frequently used to refer to a filmic sequence (a "montage sequence") in which a quick succession of images suggests the passage of time, or a series of simultaneous occurrences, often to the accompaniment of music. A "musical montage" uses a musical number (song and/or dance) to frame a montage sequence, whether temporally based (as in a classic montage sequence) or associative (as in Soviet montage). The final reprise of "Let Me Entertain You" in the stage show *Gypsy* (1959) offers an example of musical montage, as a device, being imported to the stage, reminiscent of "Fit as a Fiddle" in *Singin' in the Rain*, among others.
4 While this process of substitution is often called "dubbing"—which would mean recording elements of a soundtrack to add to (or replace) the soundtrack of an already edited film, as is common with sound effects, or as an alternative to subtitles in foreign-language films—it is almost always used inaccurately when applied to musical numbers (the central plotline of *Singin' in the Rain* notwithstanding).
5 See Todd Decker, *Music Makes Me: Fred Astaire and Jazz* (Berkeley: University of California Press, 2011). Decker details Astaire's role in shaping the number, citing Kern's lack of affinity for the type of rhythm number Astaire wanted in this spot ("Bojangles" was a late addition to the score), and Astaire's lack of real involvement with choreographing the song itself, focusing instead on his own dance, in which Kern's "Bojangles" song plays no part.

6 For more on this dimension of *Stormy Weather*, see Raymond Knapp, *The American Musical and the Performance of Personal Identity* (Princeton, NJ: Princeton University Press, 2006), pp. 79–94.
7 Although the list of attributes here is of our own devising, they overlap with many described and discussed by Bazin in a series of seminal essays, including "The Evolution of the Language of Cinema" (1950, 1952, and 1955), "The Virtues and Limitations of Montage" (1953 and 1957), and "An Aesthetic of Reality" (1948). See André Bazin, "The Evolution of the Language of Cinema" and "The Virtues and Limitations of Montage" (*What Is Cinema? Essays Selected and Translated by Hugh Gray*, Vol. 1 [Berkeley: University of California Press, 2005, originally published 1967], pp. 23–52), and "An Aesthetic of Reality: Neorealism (Cinematic Realism and the Italian School of Liberation)" (*What Is Cinema?: Essays Selected and Translated by Hugh Gray*, Vol. 2 [Berkeley: University of California Press, 2005, originally published 1971], pp. 16–40).
8 See especially Scott McMillin, *The Musical as Drama: A Study of the Principles and Conventions behind Musical Shows from Kern to Sondheim* (Princeton, NJ: Princeton University Press, 2006).
9 For more on the phenomena described here, see Raymond Knapp, "Getting Off the Trolley: Musicals *contra* Cinematic Reality" (*From Stage to Screen:Musical Films in Europe and United States (1927-1961)*, ed. Massimiliano Sala, vol. 18 of *Speculum Musicae* [Turnhout, Belgium: Brepols Publishers], 2012, pp. 157–72).
10 The term is popularly supposed to derive from slang usage of the French verb *se camper*, "to encamp, plant onself; *slang*—to pose in an exaggerated fashion," but this is not very well supported by research.
11 Sontag's often-reprinted essay probably owes much of its fame to the way that it turned one of the major cultural practices of a then-despised minority culture into a tool of high modernist critical scrutiny. This is not to say that the essay was generally welcomed by the gay people whose sensibility was being characterized.
12 Regarding the camp dimension of *The Pirate*, see also Richard Dyer's "Judy Garland and Camp" (*Heavenly Bodies*,

New York: St. Martin's Press and Basingstoke: Macmillan, 1986, pp. 178–86); Steven Pysnik's "Camp Identities: Conrad Salinger and the Aesthetics of MGM Musicals" (Ph.D. dissertation, Duke University, 2014) and "Musical Camp: Conrad Salinger and the Performance of Gayness in *The Pirate*" (*Music and Camp*. Ed. Christopher Moore and Philip Purvis. Wesleyan Unviversity Press, forthcoming); and Raymond Knapp's "The Musical Faces of Pirate Camp in Hollywood (Part I)" (*Music and the Moving Image* 7.2 [Summer 2014]: 3–33) and *Making Light: Haydn, Musical Camp, and the Long Shadow of German Idealism* (Durham: Duke University Press, 2018), chapter 4.

13 The way that Kelly manages a waggish version of Errol Flynn's swashbuckling, even more than the vaudevillian orientation of the film's musical numbers, aims to establish the prevailing mood of hilarious anachronism. The creak of the conventions is not only deliberate but it is also central to the film's overall aesthetic.

14 Queer styles, black styles, and Jewish styles have historically been the most frequently exploited resources for mainstream renovation, though other liminal types (Latinos, poor Southern whites) have also come in for a degree of appropriation as well.

15 The genre's prestige rose dramatically after the 1977 release of *Star Wars*.

3

The Television Musical

ROBYNN J. STILWELL

■ □ ■

THE MUSICAL IS A GENRE split between two dominant media, theater and cinema. While the dialogue and lead sheets may be nearly identical between the two, the differences are stark and can significantly effect the *affect* for the audience. Those medium-specific differences are highlighted by the fact that theatrical musicals tend to be studied by theater and performance scholars, cinematic musicals by film scholars; the creative heart of the genre, the music, is studied by musicologists, if at all—that in itself is a recent development, and all these groups are only just beginning to talk to each other.

One of the manifestations of the musical that has been left out of the discussion almost entirely is the television musical. The reasons for the relative neglect are manifold, interlocking, and conditioned by disciplinary boundaries. In addition to the strong divide that has existed between the studies of film and theater (and music), television has been largely the province of communications, in which interest was significantly slanted away from textual analysis toward institutional structures and ethnography.

Television musicals have also been a relative historical blip, at their most pertinent in the 1950s and into the 1960s.

Many of the original broadcasts during the 1950s were either not recorded or are too inaccessible for most scholars, let alone for a casual audience; moreover, they increasingly became targeted toward children, based on fairy tales, often starring performers familiar from Hollywood musicals like the *Pied Piper of Hamelin* (1957) starring Van Johnson, or *Jack and the Beanstalk* (1967) starring and directed by Gene Kelly. The musical, across all media, receded in importance to the mainstream of entertainment[1]—although that impression has been amplified because of the amount of attention given to the rise of rock music and youth culture in the media of the time and certainly in the scholarship since, a tendency only now beginning to be redressed.

Television was also a new medium in the 1950s, and in terms of its own specific qualities, it was still finding its way. Like many new technologies, particularly those that were in some way in a circular/spiraling relationship between perception and representation, television began by mimicking older technologies;[2] though photography emulated painting and cinema emulated theater and photography, television had at least three primary antecedents: live theater; film, which had developed its own language in the half-century before the widespread embrace of television; and, as is often lost in the discussion, radio. Television is as at least as much an audio medium as it a visual one.

The presentation of musicals on television began by most closely mimicking live theater. Within a decade, the development of videotape and more fluid camera technique led to a distinctive television language. Over time, television became more and more like film in many respects, while still retaining some native elements, and by the 1980s, the techniques of music video were the cutting edge of cinematic language, infiltrating film from television. Arguably, such television shows as *Miami Vice* and *Moonlighting* are more uniquely television musicals than the more obvious *Cop Rock, Ally McBeal, Scrubs,* and *Eli Stone,* or special "musical episodes", particularly those in such late 1990s fantasy fare as *Xena: Warrior Princess* and *Buffy the Vampire Slayer.* However, no single television musical better allows us the opportunity to explore a developing medium than Rodgers and Hammerstein's *Cinderella*, first produced as a major event in 1957 starring a rising young singer-actress, Julie Andrews. It was revived twice, once with Rodgers's participation, in a 1965 televised performance that was repeated annually for a decade; and in a 1997 version for Disney television, as part of a cycle of revivals that also included *Annie*.[3]

The three different versions of *Cinderella* offer a chance to look not only at the specificity of a musical made for television but also at the medium as it changes over the forty years between the first and third—and indeed, perhaps even more significantly in the seven years between the first and second.[4] A case study such as this demonstrates some of the key questions that may arise when dealing with a television musical.

THE THREE PRODUCTIONS: AN OVERVIEW

Cinderella was part of a cycle of televised musicals in the 1950s, whether versions of Broadway musicals (*Annie Get Your Gun, Kiss Me Kate, Peter Pan*) or newly composed (1956's *High Tor* starred Bing Crosby and a pre-*My Fair Lady* Julie Andrews). Richard Rodgers and Oscar Hammerstein II were the reigning kings of Broadway, and the initial production was a significant prestige event, broadcast on CBS in 1957.

This first version was performed live in a complex soundstage set. The liveness and the integral set meant that the performance was closest to a theatrical production (although the use of cameras also meant that the audience was moved around several "fronts" on the stage). The actors were primarily from Broadway, though some supporting actors (notably stepsisters Kaye Ballard and Alice Ghostley) also became important players in the new medium. The acting style is theatrical, slightly restrained to the small scale of the television screen, particularly the small screen of the 1950s. The story is the spun-sugar fantasy of a classic fairy tale. The King and Queen, played by Broadway veteran couple Howard Lindsay and Dorothy Stickney, are benevolent monarchs, but also recognizably a middle-class, middle-American, middle-aged couple. Edie Adams is a young fairy Godmother who straddles the theater, television, and popular recordings/nightclub singing. All of the supporting characters have more delineation than the central couple; Julie Andrews's Cinderella is clearly the antecedent of Disney's searching Belle from *Beauty and the Beast*, but she is also much more demure and composed. Jon Cypher's Prince is commonly tagged with the obvious "cipher," but, well . . . it's true. He is so generic as to be almost invisible; the couple does not meet until the ball, and the love-at-first-sight plot is acceptable as a fairy tale.

The 1965 version was shot on soundstages, with much simpler and more spacious sets. While the 1957 version has a rococo design aesthetic, the 1965 is a combination of the modern and the medieval. The minimalist sets are clearly artificial and in some cases simply flat cut-outs. The designs recall less Charles Perrault than the Brothers Grimm. The older cast members are movie stars—Walter Pidgeon and Ginger Rogers play the King and Queen, Celeste Holm is the Fairy Godmother, Jo Van Vleet (also, of course, a theatrical actress) is the Stepmother, and television actresses Barbara Ruick and Pat Carroll play the sisters. Newcomers Lesley Ann Warren and Stuart Damon are at the beginnings of lifelong careers in (mostly) television. Unlike in the 1957 production, we get a sense of both Cinderella and the Prince; they meet and connect early in the plot, and therefore the falling in love seems much more plausible.

The Disney version is strongly centered on the voice. The property was purchased by Whitney Houston as a starring vehicle for herself; by the time it went into production, she was in her early thirties and looked to find another Cinderella while she herself took the role of the Fairy Godmother. As a consequence, the latter role is more prominent in this version than in the other two. The casting of Brandy (Norwood) further emphasizes the voice, as she was primarily identified as a singer (though also the star of the sitcom *Moesha*), and Paolo Montalban (the Prince) is a Broadway performer. The role of the Prince is considerably more "generic adolescent" than the Prince of the 1965 version, while not being quite as much of a cipher as the 1957 Prince. Compared to the 1965 version, the relationship between the Prince and Cinderella is both more and less developed: in terms of musical theater convention, their sense of being destined for each other is strengthened structurally by a parallel introduction; unlike the Prince and Cinderella in the 1965 version, however, they are introduced more as a couple and less as two individuals: instead of each getting a song, they perform a duet across a crowded market square, creating their bond through the voice.

BOOK

Hammerstein expressed respect for the classic fairy tale, but a number of 1950s stereotypes appear in his teleplay, most notably in the "comic" supporting characters: the King and Queen are a typical middle-aged, middle-class mid-century couple familiar from the family sitcom of the era—he is vaguely oblivious to the family dynamics and his expanding waistline, she is seen mending his trousers and tidying the ballroom with a feather duster and a kerchief tied around her hair beneath her crown while worrying about her dreamy son; the stepsisters are less mean than stupid and thoughtless.

The characterization of these two pairs of characters changes perhaps most in the three versions; the King and Queen move with the times, not least in the portrayal of their relationship to one another and the expectations of middle-aged love. If Lindsay and Stickney are an old married couple, Rogers and Pidgeon (appropriately, given their status as beloved romantic movie leads of an earlier era) are nostalgic and romantic; and Whoopi Goldberg and Victor Garber have a bantering affection with glimpses of actual sexual attraction. Goldberg's Queen is the flightiest and most comic of the three, and yet she seems to want her son's happiness the most. The stepsisters have a simpler trajectory, becoming increasingly comical and ridiculous through the three productions. Veanne Cox's gawky Calliope and Natalie Desselle's enthusiastic Minerva are superficial and exaggerated, more broadly comedic. Pat Carroll's Prunella and Barbara Ruick's Esmeralda are almost as exaggerated as Cox and Desselle in their character traits, but both also betray a humanity that stands out in relief to their more cartoonish aspects. This is particularly notable in the post-ball kitchen table scene, in which Prunella admits that the Prince danced with her only for a moment, and Esmeralda admits the same: in both other versions, the stepsisters claim that they each danced with the Prince for an hour or more. While Ghostley's Joy and Ballard's Portia also have their moments of vulnerability, they somehow seem more beaten down and pathetic. Robert L. Freedman's 1997 script, particularly in dealing with the Stepmother and Stepsisters, combines a number of lines of dialogue from both earlier versions, leaning more heavily on Hammerstein's in terms of word count, but hewing closer to Joseph Schrank's 1965 version in emotional tone.

The 1965 version is, arguably, *more* fairy tale–like than Hammerstein's book. In design and mythology, it is medieval in setting. And in perhaps the most drastic difference between the original and the 1965 version—and indeed, the 1997 version—this Prince Charming is a genuine character with a sense of humor and more concrete desires. Stuart Damon's Prince (the only one never called Christopher or Chris in the dialogue) is not a courtier or a student, but a knight. He's been off slaying dragons and rescuing damsels and is bored.

Schrank's book makes the story less about Cinderella than about this couple, as is evident from the beginning. We actually meet the Prince first, returning from a year of travel. Tired and thirsty, he stops by a thatched cottage, and a shy girl peeks out the window, her face smudged with soot—our first glimpse of Cinderella. Despite her fear of her Stepmother's retribution, she offers the Prince a dipper of cool water, and their dialogue is echoed throughout at structural moments:

PRINCE: "Thank you most kindly."
CINDERELLA: "You are most kindly welcome."

The exchange is a moment of connection between them at the ball, when he thanks her for the dance, and at the end when he has come with the glass slipper and she again offers him water.

This structural rigor—conventional, yes, but narratively powerful in creating a relationship in only an hour and twenty minutes—is fleshed out with parallel scenes. After the Prince leaves Cinderella's cottage, he pauses to sing the interpolated "The Loneliness of Evening" against the stylized backdrop of a ruined church in the distance. The placement, and Damon's fervent performance, recall "Something's Coming" in *West Side Story* combined with the "I wish" song familiar from the later Disney musicals. Thus, this Prince has an identity, a personality, and, most important, a *song* the equal of Cinderella's.

Because it comes first, its relative shortness (two choruses) is not immediately noticeable, even though Cinderella's "In My Own Little Corner" (the opposite of an "I wish" song, in a way) runs to several choruses and an in-scene reprise. At the end of the musical, each lead also has a solo that features a non-diegetic reminiscence of the other, as is discussed in more detail later in the chapter.

This structural bonding between Cinderella and the Prince is used efficiently (if perhaps not as substantially) in the 1997 version, where the leads meet through Richard Rodgers's "The Sweetest Sound," interpolated from *No Strings*. This choice may have been cued by a line in the original Hammerstein book, in which the Prince says that Cinderella's voice is the sweetest sound he's ever heard (Block 198). The relationship between the Prince and Cinderella is still the catalyst of the plot, but more attention is given to other characters, particularly the Fairy Godmother, the Stepmother, and the major-domo of the castle, Lionel—undoubtedly a function of casting Whitney Houston, Bernadette Peters, and Jason Alexander, respectively. Perhaps due to casting, perhaps due to changed sensibilities, the romance between the Cinderella and the Prince in this version seems more youthful; at the end, the procession to the castle seems less like going to a wedding and more like going to the prom. While less of a fairy tale, it is also a more realistic contemporary depiction of young love.

MUSIC

Cinderella is a late Rodgers and Hammerstein show, their last but for *The Sound of Music* (1959), and while distinct Rodgers fingerprints exist in the score ("In My Own Little Corner" is first cousin, if not sibling, to "Whistle a Happy Tune"; the big love song is a waltz), it is also a bit less lush and romantic harmonically than previous scores, leaning toward the more astringent and linear harmonies of Rodgers's later scores, notably 1962's *No Strings,* Rodgers's first post-Hammerstein musical and source of "The Sweetest Sound," with its minor key and downward chromatic motion, easily interpolated into the 1997 version.

The songs of *Cinderella* seem to have a delicacy quite different from the bumptious Americanness of "Kansas City" or "I'm Gonna Wash That Man Right Outa My Hair," or even "Shall We Dance." The Fairy Godmother's "Impossible" has a trotting rhythm like that of "The Surrey with the Fringe on Top," but with a large leap down on the downbeat ("Impossible!"), rather than the upward escape at the end of the phrase ("scurry"). That melodic profile gives a very different feel, as does the inflection of the rhythm: whereas "Surrey" has a relaxed sway, "Impossible" pushes forward, creating anticipation. The melodic curve of "Impossible" reflects the lyrics' emotional progression remarkably well: "Impossible!" is an emphatic denial; the diatonic downward march "for a plain country bumpkin and a prince to join in marriage" over steady V–I repetitions composes a statement of inexorable logic; then, as "folderol" and "fiddle-dee-dee" are called on repeated notes, the pitch creeps upward chromatically at the ends of phrases, suggesting doubt, before "impossible!" asserts the new tonic. The bridge likewise stresses repeated notes on the tonic (G) which is now the dominant of a plagal-side excursion that oscillates between C major and minor—those "who don't believe in sensible rules" keep building up hopes in driving phrases of repeated pitches that eventually rise up and break through the B♭ B♮ in the tonic major (G) of the title phrase. All this resistance to the pull of the tonic seems like hesitation, doubt, even sarcasm in "Impossible," but inexorability and exhilaration in the reprise, "It's possible."

Cinderella's two primary solo songs are "In My Own Little Corner" and "Lovely Night," Both have a light but emphatic duple rhythm and balance strong diatonic grounding with playful chromatic lines that add both wistfulness and intensity to the songs (🔊 Example 3.1; 🔊 Example 3.2; (🔘 Example 3.3)). While it is entirely possible that this chromatic tendency, especially toward the flat side, was an emerging trait of Rodgers's late style, it makes the interpolation of "The Sweetest Sound" all the more appropriate. The striking A section of the song relies heavily on emphasized dissonances that fall on ♯4 and ♭2/♯1. The melody descends chromatically, decorated by escape tones, but is otherwise very similar to the whole-tone descent in the coda-like extension of "Lovely Night," giving coherence to the interpolated duet while emphasizing Cinderella as a character. The chromatic sliding is a long-standing sign of feminine sexuality, and these short strands emerging out of a largely diatonic context may be a symbol of Cinderella's awakening yearnings out of innocence.

The major song for the Prince generates excitement in another, more linear fashion, remaining a "masculine" diatonic even in the context of a waltz, normally heard as a feminine rhythm (the Prince is a bit of a "new man," particularly in the later two adaptations; Jon Cypher's Prince doesn't have enough of a personality to tell either way). While not as famous as the elegantly balanced, chromatically inflected *Carousel* Waltz, "Ten Minutes Ago" is arguably one of Rodgers's finest moments as a dramatic composer.

The A section starts with a quiet, narrow, rocking melody under "Ten minutes ago, I saw you," which repeats, then sequences up a third. It feels like a much larger leap, in part because the harmony shifts from a solid tonic-dominant to a descending sequence, initiated with a secondary dominant.[5] Additionally, the melody does not take the balanced pause of the first half of the period—the rocking motion swings through the expected break (rather like the extended sequence of the A" of "Lovely Night"), creating a greater forward impetus. In the second repetition of A, this sense of swinging motion is emphasized, rather than impeded, by a sudden rest after the word "bells," allowing the word to "peal" out through the sudden cessation of accompaniment and sharpening of the rhythm. It is also a foreshadowing of the dramatic B section which sweeps up to "I have found" with a similar emphatic rest afterward, emphasized by the fall down to "her," a sixth lower, a phrase then sequenced downward on "she's an angel." The repetition gives similar emphasis to "danc-" and "fly-" while the drops on the "ing" part of the gerundial verb form keep the movement sailing across the rest. As with "Impossible" and "Lovely Night," the large leaps over a driving rhythm have a sweep that not only mimics the Prince's elated feelings but can also invoke them in the listener.

The songs are undoubtedly the focus of musical energy of the three versions, but other musical aspects also shape the productions. As much as the sets, the musical direction reflects the medium-specific aspects: the 1957 version is very close to a stage production, with a small, wind-heavy pit orchestra and little underscoring. The 1997 version has a full orchestra, lush orchestration, and a heavily leitmotivic underscore; very little is *not* underscored. The 1965 version is somewhere in between, with a pit orchestra but also more bridging cues and underscore than 1957.

CASTING AND PERFORMANCE

Casting can be crucial in any production, and the approach to casting in each of the three versions of *Cinderella* changed with the times, influencing the effect of each adaptation. The cast of the 1957 version is primarily from the stage; the cast of the 1965 version blends a leading couple new to television with an older generation from the silver screen; the 1997 version features singers above all, some from the stage but more significantly from popular music.

Cinderella was part of the constellation of roles that would, within a decade, make Julie Andrews an icon. At only twenty-one, she came to *Cinderella* as an established Broadway leading lady. The *My Fair Lady* original cast album had been a huge hit in 1956, and the roles of Eliza, Cinderella, Mary Poppins, and Maria von Trapp together created a strong star text by mutually reinforcing several qualities: a good heart, an impish sense of humor, and slightly varying rebelliousness, all nonetheless correct, polite, always easily contained in the socially acceptable. Andrews's voice is extremely precise in pitch, timbral clarity, and diction, strongly reinforcing the impression/illusion that she is a "good girl," not least because it betrays a training that is tinged with class privilege.[6]

Is it coincidence or a direct influence that the unknown chosen to play Cinderella in 1965 looks so much like Audrey Hepburn, the actress who controversially was cast instead of Andrews in the film version of *My Fair Lady*? Although slightly more robust than Hepburn in frame, Lesley Ann Warren is also a dancer and has the same triangular face, pointed nose, and large dark eyes. The resemblance is certainly emphasized by the parallel scenes in which Hepburn as Eliza and Warren as Cinderella appear at the ball—both are wearing empire-waisted gowns of ivory with touches of gold that emphasize their long necks, and their hair is wound on top of their heads inside a tiara (see Figure 3.1). Warren's imperfect voice (and teeth) and her obvious youth give us a heroine whom audiences might more readily recognize as a teenager, where Andrews seems already a grown woman (see Figure 3.2).

THE TELEVISION MUSICAL | 67

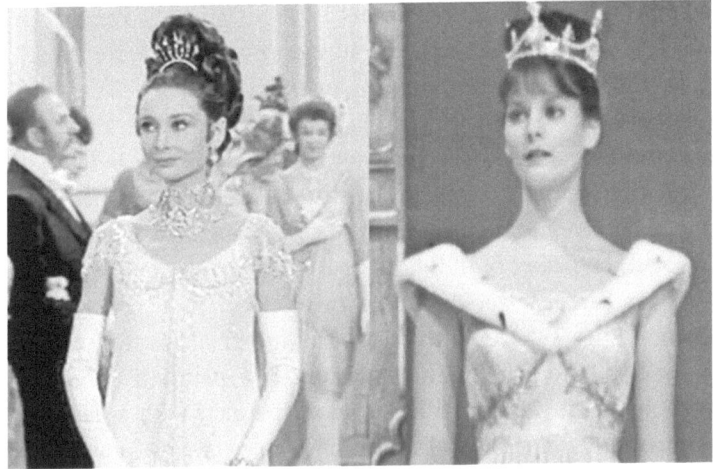

FIGURE 3.1 Audrey Hepburn as Eliza Doolittle; Lesley Ann Warren as Cinderella

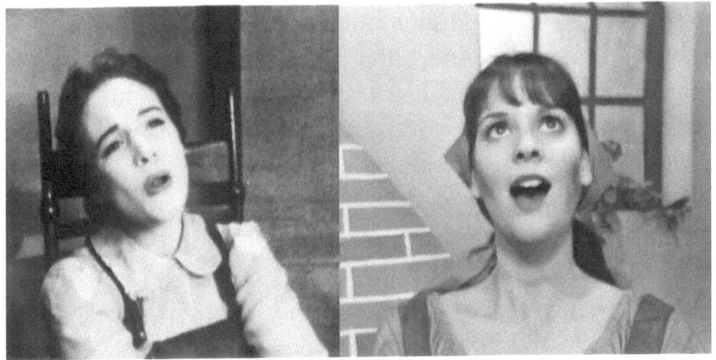

FIGURE 3.2 Julie Andrews and Lesley Ann Warren as Cinderella

Warren and Norwood were both eighteen, though the difference in experience is significant. Compared to newcomer Warren, Brandy was already a pop star and had starred in two sitcoms, including her title role in *Moesha* (1996–2001).[7] The sitcom quality of Brandy's acting is obvious in her version, in overreactions and arch line readings, as if they were punch lines rather than emotionally generated phrases. The 1997 version is of a piece with the Disney animated musicals of the era, and Brandy's Cinderella is very much more like Belle than either of her predecessors, thoughtful and self-determined. Her most effective moments as an actress are when she asserts herself and the power of individuality.

The Princes were all unknowns when cast, but Stuart Damon has subsequently had the most successful career, in British and American television. His prince is practical and obedient, though still a bit of a dreamer, with a deadpan humor that carried over into his later roles. He has a stronger, better-trained voice than Warren's, but as with her, his acting penetrates his voice, something that happens with neither other central couple. This is notable, for instance, in the first bridge of "Ten Minutes Ago," when his joy at finding his love stretches his vowels and adds a slightly tremulous undercurrent to his baritone, broadening and flattening the vowels. You can hear the exhilarated laughter trapped just beneath his larynx, pushing to escape, and it adds impetus to the releases on those high points in the B section in a melding of performance and song. The song hints at that performance, even encourages it, but neither of the other princes pull it off in the same way (▶ Example 3.4).

The performances of Norwood and Montalban are slightly more stilted, and they have less obvious chemistry—those nuances of body language and timing that are perceptible but hard to quantify or describe. They are primarily singers, performing for an audience most familiar with animated Disney musicals and music videos. A duet is a stronger choice than the paired solos in this version, lessening the burden on their simple screen presence and adding to the attraction of their voices. Unlike the live 1957 version or the half-playback (recorded backing track, live-recorded voices) of the 1965 one, the highly produced recordings of the 1997 version were made first and played back for filming. Brandy's relatively fragile voice can thus be boosted, particularly in duets, although it is also evident that Montalban is restraining his stage belt on occasion (◉ Example 3.5).

As mentioned earlier, the supporting casting causes shifts in the various productions: as King and Queen, Stickney and Lindsay bring solidity and gravitas as old Broadway pros, whereas Rogers and Pidgeon recall the romantic films of the classical Hollywood period. Comedienne Whoopi Goldberg and versatile singer-actor Victor Garber create a more modern couple of two individuals, with both shifting power relationships and a spark of sexuality. The Stepsisters are always comic relief and become more exaggerated with each iteration, but certainly Alice Ghostley's dithering, glum Joy and Kaye Ballard's distinctly New York-Jewish Portia are recognizable manifestations of their individual personae.

Of the Stepmothers, Bernadette Peters has by far the biggest role, not surprisingly, given that she is the dominant Broadway musical star of her generation and well known to television audiences. She is given her own comical romantic partnering with Lionel—a part that *becomes* a part for sitcom and Broadway star Jason Alexander—and her own song. Another interpolation, Rodgers and Hart's "Falling in Love with Love" might seem an odd choice historically, given that it comes from an earlier stage of Rodgers's career, but it makes some musical sense in the fast waltz tempo that has the same anticipatory urgency as "My Own Little Corner" and "Lovely Night," but with more drive, as is appropriate for a conniving Stepmother who knows what she wants. Likewise, the Fairy Godmother role, for producer Whitney Houston, is strengthened, giving her a status recalling such interactive narrators as the Stage Manager in Thornton Wilder's *Our Town* or Che in *Evita*.[8]

The performances reflect their times and the media that shape the performers. While Cypher and Andrews perform like operetta stars—their body language at times strongly recalls Jeanette MacDonald and Nelson Eddy, stylized, conventional, polite (▶ Example 3.6)—and Norwood and Montalban perform like pop stars in a rock video that looks like a musical, with a mobile camera and multiple quick cuts, Warren and Damon perform like *actors*. Damon in particular looks at Warren with such intense adoration, more Gene Kelly and Judy Garland than MacDonald and Eddy. They remind us of the shifting terrain of musical production between the first two productions—without doubt, both are possessed of the talent and star quality to succeed in film musicals, but the genre is dying. And the subtlety of their performances, the flickers of emotion across their faces and the engagement of their eyes, together with the slight imperfections of their vocal performances, made them weaker candidates for the stage. They are meant to be seen on camera.

TECHNOLOGICAL FRAMES AND LENSES

The first, live broadcast version was preserved on a kinescope, though widely unavailable until the 2004 DVD release. Because it was a live broadcast, it has many of the same constraints as a live performance—quick changes, entrances and exits that have to be blocked and timed, a set that is constricted in space, for instance. The difference is that while the camera is not particularly mobile in 1957—dollies in and out are the major form of "camera movement" that are used, and those sparingly—the production employed multiple cameras, which allow different angles, and "editing" occurs live in a control room, as the director switches from one camera/set-up to another.

The camera does allow for a more three-dimensional set than would be possible on a stage. Some of the larger sets—the ballroom, the village square, the royal chambers, the palace gardens, and the downstairs area of Cinderella's home—allow a fairly fluent application of the multiple camera technique, deploying large master shots of the entire area with cuts in to individual close-ups and two-shots. Other areas (the gallery/balcony area of the ballroom, the tops of staircases) are cramped and often demand odd, high-angle shots that do not accord to the conventions of "film" cinematography of the era. To a modern eye, given the placement of most security cameras and the prevalence of their use by such filmmakers as Alfred Hitchcock and Michael Mann, they elicit an odd feeling of disruption or even surveillance. Another common feature of the camera technique demanded by the set and the live broadcast is efficient but can come off as blocky and clumsy to a modern viewer: in some of the larger ensemble numbers, notably the first iteration of "The Prince Is Giving a Ball," the wide shots are mingled with cameo-esque shots of soloists (for instance, the girl who sings "And me, I'm in the second grade"—another example of Hammerstein's book being not only modern but also American in slant). The direct address of the "Stepsisters' Lament" is mediated by an ornate frame which suggests that they are looking in a powder-room mirror. Special effects are limited primarily to the superimposition of a sparkler over "magical" elements, such as the fairy godmother's transformation of Cinderella's dress (in one of the better examples of a quick change, the camera starts on her feet and pans up over a large wrap coat that could have been easily flung over Andrews, finally arriving at the tiara that could have been put on as the camera moves up her body). Andrews's dress looks very much like a contemporary 1950s "deb" dress—of course, the ball is essentially a debutante ball sans escorts.

The 1965 version has one great technical advantage—videotape. Gone are the spatial and temporal demands of live broadcast; this opens up the sets, and the cameras themselves are more mobile. Post-production editing allows for more fluency. Most important, the odd camera angles are smoothed out, and the somewhat jarring "cameo" close-ups in the ensemble numbers are handled by panning the camera across the characters in rhythm to the music. (It could be argued that the earlier cameo close-ups are more strongly rhythmic and create a stronger impression, but the converse is that they are choppy and impede the forward momentum that the pans actually amplify.) While the non-diegetic voices could have been managed technically in a live broadcast by an offstage microphone, they are undoubtedly easier to deal with on videotape.

The special effects in 1965 aren't much more sophisticated in concept, mostly the superimposition of a spinning sparkly effect (not unlike the "ruby slippers" effect for *The Wizard of Oz* from 1939) for magic and a cut-out animation of the horse and carriage carrying Cinderella to the ball during the reprise of "It's Possible." A simple cross-fade takes care of the transformations of pumpkin to carriage and bumpkin to princess.

By 1997, the technical differences between television and cinematic filming are minimal. The production is shot on film with more subtle special effects, and it certainly has the best choreography of the three, provided by Rob Marshall (later to direct and choreograph *Chicago* [2002]). The only element that really betrays the confines of television is the slightly cramped feeling of the sets, crammed onto a soundstage—although clever camera angles often minimize this, it's more obvious in the wide shots. The camera movement shows the influence of Gene Kelly's mobile, "dancing" camera as well as the faster cutting rhythms from music video, which also eases the possible "cinematic" anxiety of direct address. The Fairy Godmother opens the film with a sparkly wave of her wand, singing "Impossible" to the camera, which multiplies her functions: she's theatrical onstage narrator, television host, and music video performer, the role with which Houston is most strongly associated.

A quick look at the same moment in the three different productions—the beginning of "Ten Minutes Ago"—can illustrate how performance and technology meld with conventions of the distinct media over time (see Figure 3.3; see also ⬤ Examples 3.4, 3.5, and 3.6).

In 1957, technological limitations are exacerbated by the logistics of the cramped set. Although clearly blocked for the camera, the performers are in theatrical mode, projecting to the audience more than to each other or even to the camera. Cypher is singing for the back of the hall, and even though Andrews's bashful flirtatiousness is more natural in front of the camera, she is angled more toward the camera than him, and their interaction is almost contrapuntal, with moments of eye contact functioning like a higher-level harmonic rhythm that keeps them engaged with each other and carries across the more outward-projecting moments.

By 1997, the prerecorded music allows more freedom of movement and exertion without loss of vocal quality, so that Norwood and Montalban can converse and sing while in a

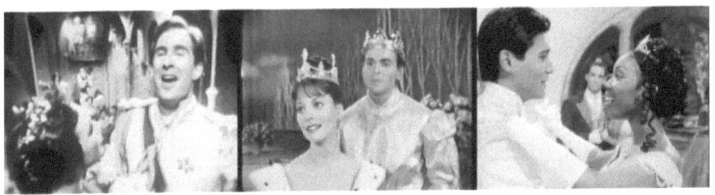

FIGURE 3.3 The camera frames Cinderella and the Prince in "Ten Minutes Ago"

conventional dance hold. Their focus is entirely and naturalistically on each other, while the camera whirls vertiginously around them.

Although traces of both theatrical and cinematic modes are evident in the 1965 version, I would argue that it is "televisual" as well as "teleauditory." Some of that is technological—the "look" of videotape, the resultant openness of the sets and camera movement, and the half-playback, which allows the security of the prerecorded orchestra as well as the immediacy of the live vocal performance, a kind of vocal "close-up" that captures Damon's above-mentioned acting-through-singing. Warren's performance is captured by the visual close-ups; where Andrews's nervousness is projected primarily by "business"—looking away, touching her hair—Warren's is in her body language and facial expressions. The counterpoint of touching and parting that we saw with Andrews and Cypher is still there, but the blocking is simpler, more open, and seemingly more naturalistic because their relationship to one another is always direct, even if not direct to the camera. They are moved onto the oblique of the shot-reverse-shot cinematic convention so that when she turns away in shyness, both of them are clearly and closely framed.

The 1965 version also has a structural feature that is highlighted by its cinematically influenced televisual production. A pair of scenes bonds Cinderella and her Prince even at a distance. As Cinderella and her Stepmother and Stepsisters talk about the ball, an instrumental reminiscence of "Ten Minutes Ago" is interpolated, and unique among the versions, Cinderella moves out into the garden to sing "Lovely Night" alone, highlighting Warren's dancing. Then the scene shifts to the Palace, where the Prince is wondering "Do I Love You," while his parents express concern about his sincerity. But as he moves outside (in parallel to Cinderella), he hears Cinderella respond to him in a non-diegetic reminiscence of the previous night, balancing her recall of "Ten Minutes Ago." A hint of echo on her voice invokes disembodied presence, and Damon's angle toward the left of the screen recalls their previous position. On a large-scale model of parallel editing, where two scenes in succession are read as simultaneity, these two scenes suggest that they are dueting across their physical (and temporal?) divide.

"DO I LOVE YOU BECAUSE YOU'RE BEAUTIFUL? OR ARE YOU BEAUTIFUL BECAUSE I LOVE YOU?"

I have wondered, as I return over and over again to the 1965 version—for which I'm sure you've noticed a decided bias—do I love it most because it was the one I saw every year as I grew up? Or is it really the best one? Of course, that depends upon your criteria for "best." I don't think there's a right or wrong answer; however, it does make us think more specifically about what elements influence our reactions.

There's no doubt that the 1957 version is closest to the "authorial intention" of Rodgers and Hammerstein; on a sheer technical level (most especially the quality of the choreography and camera work), there's no doubt that the 1997 version is superior. These are certainly valid criteria on which to judge. So why do I overlook the dated color schemes and cut-out sets of the 1960s design? The flip answer would be that I *like* those cut-out sets. Which I do. I've always been fond of the mid-century tendency toward schematic sets, like Isamu Noguchi's sparse sets for Martha Graham—but then perhaps that's because some of my earliest "design" memories are this production of *Cinderella* and the odd, spare (and false) false-front designs for the OK Corral dreamscape in the *Star Trek* episode "The Spectre of the Gun" (1967). It's distinctly possible those shaped my taste. But a more affective answer is that Lesley Ann Warren and Stuart Damon have a chemistry that neither of the other couples do—when it comes down to it, if there's a love story, I think it helps if the lovers convince me that they *are*. There's an energy and excitement in the performances that bubbles over into natural smiles and laughter in the singing, a balance of nostalgia and possibility in the casting, and a technology likewise poised between the past and the future.

The musical is a fascinating genre across which to consider those elements that are specific to the distinct media of theatrical performance, television, and cinema; television also offers us the opportunity to compare iterations. In the theater, challenges include not only the multiplicity of stagings and revivals but also the finer distinctions of re-castings and each individual performance—eight performances a week, even for a modest run, is an amazing amount of material, and there is still work that could and should be done about the mounting of a musical, including out-of-town try-outs and revisions. In cinema, musicals are a genre in which remakes are relatively rare; Rodgers and Hammerstein's own *State Fair* is a significant exception, as is Hammerstein's earlier, seminal *Show Boat*, which has been filmed three times in substantially different forms. And cinema is a medium in which the "text" becomes frozen on film but not necessarily in performance: Gene Kelly's version of "Singin' in the Rain" may differ from Cliff Edwards's, Judy Garland's, and Jimmy Durante's, but it is always and forever the same Gene Kelly performance—although one could argue that the self-same recording playing over the end of *A Clockwork Orange* (Kubrick, 1968) is a different "performance" of the song because of its context.

These television performances give us a middle ground. The iterations are closest in tone to a revival, taking into consideration changes of technology as well as in musical style and cultural sensibilities.

NOTES

1. Since the original writing, there has been a resurgence in live musicals on television (starting with *The Sound of Music* in 2013 and continuing at a pace of one or two per year), and musical situation comedies like *Crazy Ex-Girlfriend* (2015–) and *Galavant* (2015-16) have been moderately successful broadly, while finding fervent niche audiences.
2. Rick Altman counters the conflation of technology and technique: "In order to represent properly, each new technology must therefore succeed in representing not reality itself, but the version of reality established by a previously dominant representational technology. In other words, there is no such thing as a representation of the real; there is only representation of representation." See "Toward a Theory of the History of Representational Technologies" (*Iris* 2.2 [1984]: 111–25), p. 121.
3. The all-black television musical *Cindy* (1978), although fascinating in itself, is an original production set in Harlem in 1943, not an adaptation of Rodgers and Hammerstein.
4. Geoffrey Block compares the three versions extensively in *Richard Rodgers* (Yale Broadway Masters Series, New Haven, CT: Yale University Press, 2003); my analysis does not disagree with his so much as stress other aspects.
5. I-III^7-vi-iv-ii^7—while this progression is not technically to the flat side, the prevalence of minor subdominant-function chords gives a similar impression.
6. For more extended discussions of this constellation of roles, see Stacy Wolf, *A Problem Like Maria: Gender and Sexuality in the American Musical* (Ann Arbor: University of Michigan Press, 2002) and Peter Kemp, "How Do You Solve a 'Problem' like Maria von Poppins," in *Musicals: Hollywood and Beyond*, ed. Bill Marshall and Robynn Stilwell (Portland: Intellect, 2000), pp. 55–61.
7. Norwood became a pop star under her single first name, "Brandy."
8. Block questions the multicultural casting of the 1997 version in terms of genetics—was Cinderella's father black? Were the two stepsisters fathered by different men because one is white and one is black? How do a black Queen and white King produce a Filipino

son? While these questions are logical in reality, they are out of step with modern practices of race-blind casting. (Block himself asks "Should we not ask questions like this?" [199].) In an era when the American president is himself biracial and Disney has been seen as perpetuating racial and ethnic stereotypes in its animated films, it seems a positive step to present a multiracial cast as "natural."

4

The Animated Film Musical

SUSAN SMITH

■ □ ■

CONSIDER THIS SEQUENCE, ARGUABLY ONE of the most moving in the history of animation...

Dumbo has just been taken by his friend Timothy Q. Mouse to visit Dumbo's mother in the cage where she is being held in solitary confinement, branded mad for protecting her son from a boy's taunts about his outsized ears. On glimpsing Dumbo's little trunk through the bars of her window, Mrs. Jumbo moves toward him only to be held back by the shackles around her legs. As Dumbo looks up at her window, her trunk appears through its bars and, feeling around for him, touches the top of his head. The emotional force of this moment—as their trunks then meet and intertwine—is accentuated by the emergence on the soundtrack of the initial strains of "Baby Mine," sung by a female chorus in hushed tones. Following a shift to a closer view of Mrs. Jumbo's trunk lovingly caressing Dumbo's head while tears well out of his eyes, Betty Noyes begins her heartrending rendition of the lyrics of the song ("Baby mine, don't you cry/Baby mine, dry your eyes"). To Dumbo's delight, Mrs. Jumbo curls her trunk into a loop for him to sit in, and then rocks him gently from side to side while the lyrics offer reassuring testimony to her ability to soothe her child ("Rest your head close to my heart/Never to part, baby of mine"; ▶ Example 4.1).

Consider also the "Little April Shower" sequence from *Bambi* (Hand, 1942) . . . Brilliantly encapsulating the film's "circle of life" theme in microcosm, this begins with the young deer being surprised by the sound of raindrops (rendered on the soundtrack by a series of single clarinet notes) tapping out a tune as they splash onto the leaves around him while a chorus of female (and, later, male) voices sings the lyric ("Drip, drip, drop/Little April shower/Beating a tune/As you fall all around"). The shower accelerates its pace, prompting the forest animals to scuttle for cover, eventually turning into a full-blown thunderstorm (accompanied by cymbal crashes)—only to return to a gentler mood as the storm dies out and nature emerges glisteningly refreshed by the rain, its drops gradually coming to a stop as the last three fall with a tinkling musical flourish onto a pool of water (▶ Example 4.2).

It's worth beginning with a discussion of these two sequences, since in different ways they raise important questions concerning what constitutes an animated film musical and how it may be considered distinct from its live action counterpart. Moreover, they also illustrate how Disney animated films in particular often contain songs that, while absolutely essential to the emotional fabric of their narrative worlds, wouldn't necessarily be considered musical numbers in the conventional sense. All of these factors suggest the value of making this studio's work a focal point for this chapter.

In the case of the "Baby Mine" sequence in *Dumbo* (Sharpsteen, 1942), much of its emotional richness stems precisely from the fact that Mrs. Jumbo doesn't perform the song as she would in a traditional number in a musical; indeed, her lack of access to the music and the latter's status outside of the diegesis reinforce her helplessness within the narrative and her physical separation from her son. Yet in resisting the temptation to have Mrs. Jumbo sing, the film exhibits a delicacy of restraint that enables her to express her feelings for her son on her own terms, as she uses the tactile properties of her trunk to overcome the physical confinement of her cage and reach out to her son. At the same time, there is also a sense in which the song *is* giving voice to Mrs. Jumbo's otherwise silent, soothing invocation to her son, and this intimacy of connection between song and character is suggested not only by the directness of address inherent in the lyrics themselves (which means that Mrs. Jumbo *could* have sung this song if the filmmakers had so chosen), but also by the manner in which the female chorus starts up just as mother and son's trunks intertwine for the first time.

In creating this harmonious fusion of tactile and vocal forms of expression, the sequence thus brings diegetic and non-diegetic layers together in a way that suggests some form of utopian bonding not just between mother and son but between human and animal sensibilities, and thereby provides a strong counterpoint to the more dominant view (expressed by one of the clowns moments later) that "elephants ain't got no feelings." Indeed, what we have here, arguably, are two parts of one overall musical performance, with the song bringing out the natural lyricism of the mother elephant's wordless lullaby and the gentle swaying of her trunk offering something analogous to the graceful movements of a dancer's body.

With *Bambi*'s "Little April Shower" sequence, the song is also non-diegetic but again there is a strong sense of its being intimately involved with the narrative world. Here, though, the song is not expressive of the animal characters' feelings in the way that it was for Mrs. Jumbo, but, rather, it acts as a kind of lyrical evocation of the music made by the sound of the raindrops falling. The non-diegetic song that we hear on the soundtrack is thus not construed as the *source* of the music as such but instead as a reflection of a natural musicality that, as the words themselves make clear, is already inherent within the narrative and superior to its own ("Drip, drip drop/Little April shower/What can compare to your beautiful sound?"). What we have here, in effect, then, is "Singin' in the Rain" but without Gene Kelly. In that live action number, Kelly both sings and dances while the rain functions more subserviently as the trigger and background for his character's expressions of joy, but here it is the raindrops themselves that dance across the screen, tapping out their own musical rhythms as they fall to the ground. The song, lacking a human figure to perform it, is projected instead onto the non-diegetic layer of the soundtrack, yielding to the rain itself as the main site of performance and focus of celebration.

What these two sequences suggest, then, is that the specific conditions of the animated film may require us to be more flexible in the way we think about the relationship between song and dance, performer and song. Indeed, the frequency with which these films have animals or some other nonhuman character at their center indicates that the animated film employs a much broader notion of performance and a greater range of performer types, some of whom (as in the case of the "Little April Shower" sequence) may not even have the kind of bodily presence that one takes for granted in the delivery of a live action musical number. When considered in relation to animation's ability to bring the inanimate to life, then, this makes it possible for anything to become endowed with a musicality of movement and expression all its own (something that Disney's first sound cartoon, *Steamboat Willie* [Disney and Iwerks, 1928], delights in right from the start; ▶ Example 4.3; ▶ Example 4.4). The presence of the human voice on the soundtrack pulls against any more radical decentering of the human figure from the field of performance, although the pairing of this with the animated body engenders further complexities specific to the animated musical genre. Thus, while some might argue that the "Baby Mine" sequence is not a musical number by virtue of the voice's non-diegetic status on the soundtrack, in animated films no voice ever really belongs to the performer we see on the screen, since the figure we see has no living entity outside of the text and its movements have no direct ontological equivalent in real life. The actions that constitute the performance (with the notable exception of the voice) are instead created through the manipulation of a set of drawings or other inanimate shapes and forms outside of the filming process, rather than from any physical action performed within the frame. As Hamilton Luske observes with regard to the cel-based form of animation that Disney developed and which became the dominant model against which other forms of animation were defined:

> Our actors are drawings. We cannot work on the inspiration of the moment as an actor does, but must present our characterizations through a combination of art, technique, and mechanics that takes months from the conception to the finished product.[1]

Animation's roots in the inanimate in turn raise the question of whether onscreen performance is actually a viable concept with this form, leading some to locate the identity of the performer outside of the film itself. Thomas and Johnston argue:

> Basically, the animator is the actor in animated films. He is many other things as well; however, in his efforts to communicate his ideas, acting becomes his most important device. (18)

They go on to highlight some of the special difficulties involved in trying to create a performance under such conditions:

> But the animator has a special problem. On the stage, all of the foregoing symbols are accompanied by some kind of personal magnetism that can communicate the feelings and attitudes equally as well as the action itself. There is a spirit in this kind of communication that is extremely alive and vital. However, wonderful as the world of animation is, it is too crude to capture completely that kind of subtlety. . . .
>
> The live actor has another advantage in that he can interrelate with others in the cast. In fact, the producer relies heavily on this. When he begins a live action picture, he starts with two actors of proven ability who will generate something special just by being together. There will be a chemistry at work that will create charisma, a special excitement that will elicit an immediate response from the audience. The actors will each project a unique energy simply because they are real people.
>
> By contrast, in animation we start with a blank piece of paper! Out of nowhere we have to come up with characters that are real, that live, that interrelate. We have to work up the chemistry between them (if any is to exist), find ways to create the counterpart of charisma, have the characters move in a believable manner, and do it all with mere pencil drawings. (18)

While these challenges are common to animation as a whole, they are particularly an issue when it comes to thinking about this form in relation to the musical, given the musical's heavy reliance on the abilities and charisma of its star performers, together with its investment in notions of spontaneity and improvisation. In this context, one could argue that what the voice brings to the animated performance is a complexity and subtlety of expression that may be difficult to achieve through the visual dimension of animation alone, while at the same time having the potential (not always realized) to free the human actor from the constraints of her or his body and even prompt a reconfiguring of the relationship between voice and star image. But this reliance on the human voice has at times been considered a threat to the creative potential of animation's visual dimension, owing mainly to the influence that a well-known star may be deemed to have in over-determining the look and personality of the character he or she is voicing. Even here, though, the voice's associations with a star personality can endow a character's otherwise entirely fictional status with a quality of emotional reality that may be crucial in overcoming the sense of implausibility arising from the sight of an imaginary figure bursting into song and dance; in doing so it highlights the special capacity of the singing voice to breathe life into the inanimate.

This power to bring the inanimate to life[2] is something that Sergei Eisenstein, the Soviet filmmaker and writer, found fascinating about animation as an art form, particularly the early short cartoons of Disney. What intrigued him most was their capacity to enact a modern-day version of animism, namely, "'The belief [which goes back to early forms of human thought] that all objects possess a natural life or vital force, that they are endowed with an indwelling spirit.'"[3] Indeed, for Eisenstein, "The very idea . . . of the animated cartoon is like a direct embodiment of the method of animism" in the sense that inherent in its process is the "supplying of an inanimate object with life and a soul" (44). Eisenstein sees both forms of animism (the physical and the spiritual) operating in Disney's animated shorts, observing that not only are they "animated drawings" (41) brought to life but they also have a tendency to invest ordinary objects within the films with human traits and emotions (43). The latter is something that, according to Eisenstein, extends beyond animism to Disney's depiction of animals, this humanizing of them being evidence of a totemistic belief in "the unity of man and animal" (49) and something that Disney shares with other forms of art through the ages. As in other cases, this "'flight' into an animal skin and the humanization of animals" functions in Disney's work as "a displacement, an upheaval, a unique protest against the metaphorical immobility of the once-and-forever given" (33).

According to Eisenstein, this revolt against the fixity of one's human status also manifests itself in what he refers to as the "plasmaticness" of Disney's animated cartoons, which he defines as follows:

> We have a being represented in drawing, a being of a definite form, a being which has attained a definite appearance, and which behaves like the primal protoplasm, not yet possessing a "stable" form, but capable of assuming any form and which, skipping along the rungs of the evolutionary ladder, attaches itself to any and all forms of animal existence. (21)

This elasticity of form is something that Eisenstein considers capable of evoking an almost primordial state akin to what existed prior to the stabilization of human form and the fixing of boundaries between different species, containing within it a sense of endless possibility. The affective outcome of all this is one of "pure ecstasy" (42), which he defines as "a sensing and experiencing of the primal 'omnipotence'—the element of 'coming into being'—the 'plasmaticness' of existence, from which *everything* can arise" (46).

For Eisenstein, these traits of animism, totemism, and plasmaticness all contribute to what he calls the "pre-logical attractiveness" of Disney's work (41), a quality that he explains in terms of an investment in an "infantile, pre-human realm" (64) that allows Disney to create on a "conceptual level . . . not yet shackled by logic, reason, or experience" (2). He contrasts this with Chaplin's approach, which, while also infantile in nature, results in "a constant, agonized and some-where at its core, an always tragic lament over the lost golden age of childhood" (2). For Eisenstein, Disney's infantilism is infinitely more hopeful and liberating, one that—in offering "a revolt against partitioning and legislating, against spiritual stagnation and greyness" (4)—allows the films to create a sense of "Paradise Regained," something that is otherwise "Unreachable on earth" and "Created only by a drawing" (2).

Eisenstein is extremely useful in helping us understand the potential of the animated film musical to offer something distinct from its live action counterpart. His use of the term "ecstasy" certainly suggests an affective dimension to the animated film that is compatible with the utopian sensibility of the musical. And his claims that Disney's cartoons convey a sense of "Paradise Regained" gestures toward the animated film's capacity to offer a more satisfying sense of what that utopia would look like, not just feel like (as Dyer famously contended).[4] The idea that an animistic impulse underpins the creative process of animation also seems absolutely crucial in understanding the special kind of utopian sensibility associated with this branch of the genre and helps explain why so many animated film musicals often find themselves devoted to expressions of joy at the bestowal or rediscovery of life, for in doing so they are celebrating something fundamental to the form itself.[5] Indeed, it is possible to see the relationship between animation and the musical as mutually enhancing, with the former's capacity to invest the inanimate with life finding its ultimate means of realization in the heightened physical vitality and emotional intensity of the production number, and the joyful spirit of the genre's utopian sensibility reaching its satisfying extension in the life-giving, not just life-affirming, nature of animation as an art form. It is important to acknowledge this compatibility, since in other respects animation's reliance on the painstaking manipulation of drawings, models, and other inanimate objects for its effects pulls against those notions of spontaneity of movement and expression on which the live-action musical depends.

Jane Feuer argues that the Hollywood musical is a capitalist, mass, prerecorded form of entertainment seeking to pass itself off as folk art through attempting (among other things) to create the illusion of spontaneity and improvisation in the performance of song and dance routines.[6] But this is difficult to sustain against the specific conditions of the animated film musical. This is especially the case in the field of stop-motion animation, where (as in the case of *The Nightmare before Christmas* [Selick, 1993]) it is possible to see the blatantly stitched-together nature of the characters' bodies, and where (depending on the sophistication of the technology) these figures' movements often have a jerky, unreal quality. It is precisely our awareness of such conditions that makes Jack Skellington's ability to achieve an Astaire-like grace of movement during his solo numbers seem all the more remarkable (▶ Example 4.5). Rather than relying on an effacement of its constructedness for its effects, then, or on an audience's forgetting the time and effort that goes into the production of its song and dance routines, the utopian pleasures of this branch of the musical seem more plausibly rooted in a self-conscious delight in animation's capacity for bringing things to life.

The other elements Eisenstein identifies can also enhance and extend the animated film musical's utopian sensibility. Plasticity offers unique opportunities in performance terms, with the animated human body (or human skeleton, as in the case of Disney's first "Silly Symphony," *Skeleton Dance* [Disney, 1929]), being capable of stretching, compressing, and changing shape in response to the rhythms and patterns of music to a degree that is impossible in the live-action musical (▶ Example 4.6). Totemism invests the utopianism of the animated film musical with another distinctive dimension, the potential freedom it offers being one of escape not just from the restrictions of ordinary society (as in the live-action musical), but also from the constraints of human identity itself, through a merging with animals and reconnecting with nature.

The "Pink Elephants on Parade" sequence in *Dumbo* demonstrates how all three of these elements may combine in an animated musical number. A tour de force of animation that has no equivalent in live-action musicals, it seems unhampered by the kind of conservative ethos and realist codes of representation that Disney has been criticized for. The fact that Dumbo is mute throughout the film (so that the singing must again be displaced onto the non-diegetic area of the soundtrack) makes him an unlikely figure to have at the center of a musical, yet it is precisely this that gives "Pink Elephants" its special rationale as a production number. Following soon after the "Baby Mine" sequence, its impact is heightened by that juxtaposition. Thus, whereas the soothing rhythms of the lullaby and Mrs. Jumbo's rocking of her son had earlier reinforced his child-like state of dependency on her, this gives way here to a much more unsettling realm of surrealist-inspired, free-form animation. It is this shift that allows Dumbo (now inebriated as a result of having unwittingly drunk from a bucket of water into which a clown has just accidentally knocked a bottle of champagne) to discover a newfound creativity and independent sense of self. Such a change is evident in the contrasting use made of the elephant's trunk: from Mrs. Jumbo's cradling of Dumbo in hers to his playful blowing of an assortment of bubbles of various shapes and sizes through his, at one point (egged on by Timothy) even molding it into a square concertina-like instrument in order to produce the desired effect, before finally blowing a giant bubble that suddenly morphs into a "live" pink elephant (▶ Example 4.7). This form of creative expression links Dumbo with the life-giving powers of animation itself, as his trunk, functioning in analogous terms like an animator's pencil, projects onto the blankness of the night sky a circular shape that, in morphing into a moving elephant image, seems to enact the coming to life of the animator's drawing.

The malleable nature of the outline shape that Dumbo creates also exemplifies the "plasmatic" quality that Eisenstein valued in Disney's work. In exploiting this to the full through the morphing, dancing elephants that follow, the sequence can be understood to offer, from this infant protagonist's point of view, an imaginative release of all those feelings that he otherwise can't express. Branded a freak because of his oversized ears, Dumbo is able to explore here a much more liberating version of his own sense of difference, with the imaginary elephants' constant morphing—expanding, shrinking, and changing into different shapes and forms—constituting an extreme display of bodily deviance that is now defined in terms of creativity and freedom of expression rather than ugly abnormality or social failure. Early on, the free-form animation also gives vent to his feelings of oppression, as the bizarre image of a large elephant stamping on the head of a much smaller one renders literal Dumbo's own downtrodden state. Subsequent images enact a rebellion against such power structures, however, as the smaller elephant is shown kicking the large one from behind before responding to the four elephants that materialize in front of him by expanding into a giant version of his former self and crushing them between a large pair of cymbals.

Above all, the "Pink Elephants" sequence offers Dumbo an empowering release from the containing environment of the circus, as the entrapping, degrading forms of performance that both he and the other animals are forced to undergo there are replaced by more liberating ones. The fluidity of the elephants' movements and the plasticity of their bodies thus enable them to morph into a whole range of different animal and object forms while also appropriating, in the process, various human forms of dance, including Indian belly dance, classical ballet, ice skating, and Latin American rhumba. In also showing the elephants adapting their bodies to suit (dancing on two legs while retaining their trunks and other familiar features), this number pushes the "Baby Mine" sequence's idealized fusion of human and elephant forms of expression in other, more daring directions. Exploiting the plasticity and anti-realist properties of the form, "Pink Elephants" manages to generate a highly fluid, less representationally hidebound vision of totemistic union, one that involves the elephants "skipping along the rungs of the evolutionary ladder" (Eisenstein, 21) and exhibiting the skillful grace of a human dancer's body. It isn't just that elephants appropriate human forms of dance, moreover, as the hybrid nature of their physical features also gestures toward a more disruptive crossing of bodily boundaries. This finds its most disconcerting vision in the menacing image of a figure advancing toward the audience whose outline conforms to the human form but whose torso, head, and limbs are entirely made up of differently colored elephants' heads (◉ Example 4.8). It is an image of totemistic union that inverts the power structure of the narrative's circus world, departing markedly from the cozy, sentimental forms of anthropomorphism for which Disney has so often been criticized. The unsettling nature of this effect is accentuated all the more by our awareness that such a vision has purportedly emerged out of the mind of one of the studio's most genuinely cute animal characters.

Given how this surrealist sequence suddenly erupts out of an otherwise fairly conventional child's narrative, it is possible to regard this number as offering release not just for Dumbo but also for the animators themselves who, freed from the constraints of the narrative feature film, are able to give vent to a more anarchic style of animation, closer in spirit to the innovative earlier phase of Disney's work. Indeed, the sequence almost feels like an animated short interpolated into a feature, although both the film and this surrealist-inspired piece gain much from their interaction. Dumbo's gradual recedence from view as the sequence progresses is suggestive of this fantasy sequence's increasing capacity to take on a life of its own. Yet what the closing segment goes on to imply is that what we have been witnessing all along is some form of hallucinatory buildup to—or even enactment of—Dumbo's first, undisclosed act of flight, the creative freedom of its images thus constituting a surrealist flight of fancy that on some level seems to enable the discovery of his own ability to fly. The final sequence, showing the elephants morphing into cars, trains, dinghies, and rollercoaster cars, rushing chaotically across the screen, appears especially evocative of the chaos and excitement of those first few moments of flight. This is followed by the dream-like image of the imaginary pink elephants floating down and morphing into clouds that hang in the sky next to the tree where Dumbo and his friend are found sleeping, the effect of which is to negotiate the transition from number to narrative with an effortlessness that encapsulates the naturalness of their connection (▶ Example 4.9).

The pastoral nature of this new setting highlights the impact of the "Pink Elephants" sequence in opening up a more utopian sphere, and this finds its culminating expression in the film's final number, "When I See an Elephant Fly." Initially performed by the crows as a jovial putdown of Timothy's claims regarding Dumbo's ability to fly, it first functions as an expression of the birds' resistance to the kind of deviant animal behavior that "Pink Elephants" wholeheartedly embraced. But this is completely reversed in the two reprises that follow, when the crows sing it in outright celebration of Dumbo's newfound abilities.

"Pink Elephants" thus seems to epitomize the qualities that Eisenstein extols in Disney animation, with its plasmatic, animistic and totemistic tendencies helping to pave the way for the film's utopian resolution. But Eisenstein's appreciation of Disney's films along such lines has not been echoed by many subsequent critics. In construing those aspects that Eisenstein so admired in entirely negative terms, their accounts are symptomatic instead of a growing application of media and cultural studies approaches to Disney's work, approaches that tend to seize upon what some regard as an increasing conservatism in the Disney studio's postwar era (which Eisenstein hints at himself). Thus, whereas Eisenstein celebrates Disney's innovative early animated films, seeing a direct causal connection between their formal creativity and their ability to offer a release from the standardization and mechanization of American capitalist society, more recent critics such as Jack Zipes have condemned the studio, as a corporate organization intent on maximizing profits, for its own standardization of the animated film and the fairy tale form on which it frequently draws. Any technical innovations are seen by Zipes as operating rather emptily, either as a means of promoting the Disney label or in the service of a deeply conservative ideological vision.[7] Eisenstein's extolling of the "plasmatic" quality of Disney animation for its ability to offer freedom from conventional modes of representation also finds its inverse reflection in the more common tendency nowadays for Disney to be criticized for not deviating enough from traditional live action codes of realism, and for thus stunting the development of animation as an art form (Wells, 21–28). Eisenstein's delight in Disney's totemistic outlook has similarly been supplanted in recent years by the view that Disney imposes its values on animals by anthropomorphizing them. And—most notably of all—whereas Eisenstein revels in what he sees as the socially liberating effects of Disney's investment in a child-like, prelogical form of thought, Zipes and others accuse Disney of trading in a sentimental, regressive form of infantile escapism, diverting audiences from more radical utopian longings by encouraging them "to long nostalgically for neatly ordered patriarchal realms" (Zipes 1995, 40).

One of the challenges we face when studying the Disney animated film musical, then, is the need to be alert to these ideological issues while at the same time remaining open to the possibility of the films offering pleasures rooted in their animation and musical aspects, which may not be accessible through approaches based in a political or "representations" style of analysis. The crows' sequence in *Dumbo* offers a case in point. Labeled racist by some for its coding of these characters as African Americans, much of the controversy has centered upon the actors' use of an inaccurate black dialect, the naming of the lead bird "Jim Crow," the sequence's deployment of familiar racialized stereotypes such as preacher and jazz musician, and its borrowing of conventions associated with the popular 1940s' TV show *Amos and Andy*.[8] Considering *Dumbo* in terms of its musical and animation pleasures may produce a useful counterbalance to this kind of reading, prompting consideration of how the crows in fact occupy a privileged generic position as the only animals to perform a full-blown production number, the two reprises of which function as the defining expression of the film's utopian sensibility. The crows' privileged status in musical terms seems linked to their place outside of the circus environment, the freedom this grants them from the exploitative strategies and demeaning rituals of performance demanded from the other animals that work there enabling them (in a surprising inversion of the more typical containment of blacks and exclusion of them from the utopian spaces of the Hollywood musical) to engage in a number full of wonderful fluidity and jazz style inflections. The syncopated movements of two of the crows as they shimmy toward each other from opposite ends of the frame, together with the rousing harmonies achieved by the Hall Johnson choir and accompanying singers on the final two lines of the song, combine to convey a wonderful sense of brotherhood and communal spirit quite different from the (white?) middle-class snobbery and prejudice previously displayed by the adult elephants. The dynamic poses displayed by the lead crow, as he scats and struts his way across the screen, also exude an exuberant self-confidence and vitality of spirit refreshingly at odds with the film's earlier images of animal enslavement (⏵ Example 4.10). The lyrics, too, are infused with an intelligent, inventive form of wit that pulls against the more stereotypical, folksy dialects used by the crows. In destabilizing the fixed meanings of certain words they even manage to display a plasticity of form and animism of spirit that are capable of transforming nouns into verbs and objects into active, sentient, musical beings ("I've seen a peanut stand/ And heard a rubber band/I've seen a needle that winked its eye/But I be done seen about everything/When I see a elephant fly...."; ⏵ Example 4.11).

Compared to the crows' sequence in *Dumbo*, the "I Wanna Be Like You" number from Disney's *The Jungle Book* (Reitherman, 1967) has been viewed by some as more irredeemably racist. As Susan Miller and Greg Rhode argue:

> Once we make the obvious connection between King Louie and African Americans—at least the African Americanism dear to white bourgeois liberal culture—the lyrics of his song become a humiliating revelation, for King Louie sings of his desire to be a man "and stroll right into town . . . ooo I want to be like you."[9]

The question arises again, though, as to whether such a reading is able to capture the full scope of the animated characters' performances (which arguably have a much greater degree of fluidity than Miller and Rhode seem prepared to allow) and the range of pleasures that these might in turn offer the film's audiences. A more rounded approach might begin, for example, by noting Louis Prima's initial scatting play with the opening line of the song ("I wanna be a man-man, mon-mon, lorang orangutango jango"), which immediately destabilizes these categories of racial difference by running the words together and bringing out their rhyming properties (▶ Example 4.12). This fluidity of performance continues in the next phase of the dance as King Louie's expressed desire to attain human status finds its inverse reflection in Mowgli's emulation of the orangutan's style of movement, as he slaps his hands down on the ground in delight and then uses his left hand to lift himself off the ground (▶ Example 4.13). Mowgli's performance both here and during the main body of the number, where he is shown joining in with the other monkeys' dance around the ancient ruins, consequently becomes expressive of *his* resistance to his *human* destiny, forming part of a series of numbers in the film where he is shown trying on different animal identities (emulating elephants during "Colonel Hathi's March" and a bear while performing "Bare Necessities" with Baloo; ▶ Example 4.14; ▶ Example 4.15). Baloo's own entry into the dance poses another disruption to the jungle's carefully demarcated boundaries, his appearance dressed in a grass skirt and wearing a coconut over his mouth signaling a mode of performance that is capable of crossing both gender and species lines. The full impact of this is realized later on in the delightful scatting exchange that takes place between Baloo and King Louie and, as they begin to dance in lindy hop style, it is the orangutan who then takes on the female role by allowing Baloo to swing him between his legs (▶ Example 4.16).

When considered in relation to the full range of the number's performance elements, the song's title thus becomes expressive not just of King Louie's aspiration to achieve human status but of a collective desire of all characters to break free from the restrictions of their fixed identities. What we are being invited to share in here is some kind of ultimate musical celebration of those totemistic and plasmatic impulses that Eisenstein deemed essential to the utopian spirit of Disney animation. The fact that Bagheera the panther is the only one of the main characters not to give in to the flow of the music during this number thus acquires a deeper logic, for although he may well be given a voice of authority within the narrative, and while he may exemplify how "the film invariably endows regal mannerisms and posh British accents to characters with power" (Miller and Rhode, 92–93), his well-spoken authoritarianism, like that of Colonel Hathi, is associated with a rigidity and inflexibility of approach that is presented as quite at odds with the "plasmatic" freedoms and animistic impulses of the animated film musical. This is depicted nowhere more clearly than when, just before a disguised Baloo bursts onto the scene, Bagheera attempts to hide from King Louie and his entourage by freezing suddenly, emulating the stone statue of a cat standing on the other side of the doorway. In adopting this static pose, he resists the music in a way that also constitutes a rejection of the life-giving powers it offers to him as an animated character—the "beat" of the music that Baloo so readily succumbs to being the very pulse of life that Disney animators used to time the movements of their characters' actions. His transformation of himself into a stone statue amounts to a symbolic death, in animation terms, as he allows himself to revert to the very condition of inanimate object from whence he came (◉ Example 4.17).

I have tried—unlike Bagheera—in this essay to respond to the special properties of the animated film musical, so as to help open up for further study an area of the genre that has rarely been given the attention it deserves. There are, in particular, many subdivisions of this field still to explore, such as the short cartoon's role in the development of the animated film musical; the different effects that can be achieved through pairing the musical with non-cel-based forms of animation;

and the significance of the practice, in recent years, of adapting Disney animated musicals for the stage. The complex question of how one thinks about performance or the relationship between body and voice within the animated film musical also warrants much further consideration. In pointing toward some of the issues raised by this and other areas, this chapter has sought to establish a creative platform on which to build.

NOTES

1. Quoted in Frank Thomas and Ollie Johnston, *Disney Animation: The Illusion of Life* (New York: Abbeville Press, 1981), p. 113.
2. As Paul Wells observes, "To animate, and the related words, animation, animated and animator all derive from the Latin verb, *animare*, which means to give life to, and within the context of the animated film, this largely means the artificial creation of the illusion of movement in inanimate lines and forms" (Paul Wells, *Understanding Animation* [London: Routledge, 1998], p. 10). Wells also cites Norman McClaren's definition of animation, namely, that it "is not the art of drawings that move, but rather the art of movements that are drawn. What happens *between* each frame is more important than what happens *on* each frame" (quoted in Wells, 10).
3. Quotation attributed to Webster's *Dictionary*, in Sergei Eisenstein, *Eisenstein on Disney* (London: Methuen, 1988), p. 95.
4. See Richard Dyer, "Entertainment and Utopia," in *Genre: The Musical*, ed. Rick Altman (London: Routledge & Kegan Paul, 1981), p. 177. Originally published in *Movie* 2 (Spring 1977): 2–13.
5. For a more melancholy meditation on the paradoxes involved in being an animated character, consider Emily/Helena Bonham Carter's moving rendition of the song "Tears to Shed" in Tim Burton's *The Corpse Bride* (2005).
6. Jane Feuer, *The Hollywood Musical*, 2nd ed. (Bloomington: Indiana University Press, 1992).

7 See Jack Zipes, "Breaking the Disney Spell," in *From Mouse to Mermaid: The Politics of Film, Gender and Culture*, ed. Elizabeth Bell, Lynda Haas, and Laura Sells (Bloomington: Indiana University Press, 1995), pp. 21–40; and Jack Zipes, *Happily Ever After: Fairy Tales, Children and the Culture Industry* (New York: Routledge, 1997), pp. 89–95.
8 See, for example, Mark I. Pinsky, *The Gospel According to Disney: Faith, Trust and Pixie Dust* (Louisville, KY: Westminster John Knox Press, 2004), pp. 43–45.
9 Susan Miller and Greg Rhode, "The Movie You See, the Movie You Don't: How Disney Do's That Old Time Derision," in *From Mouse to Mermaid: The Politics of Film, Gender and Culture*, p. 92.

5

The Evolution of the Original Cast Album

GEORGE REDDICK

■ □ ■

"When you listen to Pinza, you can only describe his voice—now silken is too weak. Velvet. Plush. . . . When there is that rare combination of all the essentials of person and character and beauty and voice and image that you accept entirely as being true and real—those moments, whether in opera or in theatre, are treasured. And if one is fortunate enough to have experienced them, to have been there when it happened, I guess that's what life is made up of. Of moments."

As Saul waxed philosophical, I asked if his stereo system had been mainly a time machine designed to recapture those moments. "Oh no," he said. "It was not intended to recapture any of these, because it couldn't. It was parallel but separate. In other words, the pleasure I derived from recordings was independent of any pleasures I may have derived from the real thing. But I'm fortunate in having experienced so many real, that I can sort of trade off against what I enjoy from recordings. Because it's the real that stay. They are indelible. I don't know if I ever had any indelible recordings, do you follow me? . . . The beauty of listening to a recording is you doooon't see. . . . You only hear and feel."[1]

—EVAN EISENBERG, *The Recording Angel*

Otto Baensch wrote: "A work of art that gives eternal form to a feeling thereby accomplishes its task, and thus fulfills its function, no matter what kind of feeling it is that figures in this fulfillment."

Eternal is surely a big word, and phonograph records make no pretense to that. But they are, at least, a step in the right direction;

and one hopes that these records will serve as a means by which the future listener will be able to sense not only the accomplishment of the author and performers, but the mood of the time in which they wrote, and acted, and lived.[2]

—GODDARD LIEBERSON

IN THE MIDDLE OF THE twentieth century, the cast recording enjoyed popularity so widespread that of all the long-playing records released in the 1950s, the second highest-selling album of the decade was of a Broadway musical. Though thousands made the trip to New York to see *My Fair Lady* in person during its six years on Broadway, millions who experienced it as a cast recording would never see it on stage. But while its sophisticated music and witty lyrics appealed to a large market in the 1950s, within a decade, cultural tastes had so radically changed that the cast album went from one of the most popular forms of entertainment in the world to a small niche market that was often considered "out of touch." In this chapter, I explore the development of the cast album, its rise to popularity, and its sudden and seemingly permanent loss of cultural currency.

DEVELOPING TECHNOLOGY AND THE FIRST ORIGINAL CAST ALBUMS

At the beginning of the twentieth century, the burgeoning American music industry was heavily influenced by musicals appearing on stages in New York. Many of the hit songs of the day, sold as sheet music throughout the country, came from song-writers in New York, and many directly from shows being performed on Broadway. The development of new technologies that made it possible to record and distribute those hit songs on records began to revolutionize the way the country received its music. By 1920, when broadcast radio began another revolution of the music industry, songs from Broadway hits were regularly being recorded and broadcast for an even larger audience. Suddenly music and performances that had once been accessible by only relatively small numbers of people could be experienced by almost anyone.[3] Moreover, performances that only a few years earlier would have survived only in the memories of audience members at a particular performance could now be relived over and over again.

These technological advances did not make everyone happy. The American Federation of Musicians (AFM) was growing increasingly anxious during the 1920s and '30s that the work of the musician would become obsolete. Once a musician had recorded a single live performance of a work, that recording could go on to be used hundreds of times, across the country and even across the world, calling the value of live performance into question. Yet many consumers and critics felt that the recording age could provide a wide national audience with unprecedented access to good music. As early as 1924, Pauline Partridge wrote in the housekeeping journal *Sunset*, "The gracious response of the phonograph is untiring. No cajolery is necessary to persuade it to give of its richest treasure, it is never temperamental, needs no thanks, wishes no praise." Perhaps most important, the phonograph could bring "music, real music, good music, into the American home for the first time in history."[4] In a study of the integration of the phonograph into American culture in the first thirty years of the twentieth century, Mark Katz finds that Americans at the time did indeed seek to gain access to music of a higher cultural value, finding themselves lacking knowledge of "good" music and seeing the phonograph as the means through which they could acquire the "good" and "important" music their

European counterparts took for granted. R. D. Darrell, critic for the *Phonograph Monthly Review*, wrote in 1926 that "the phonograph will in time do more for the cause of music than concert hall performances can ever do," concluding that "the phonograph is in the home," and "the home in which there is a phonograph is potentially a musical one."[5]

Meanwhile, James Caesar Petrillo, who had led the Chicago Federation of Musicians (CFM) in successful strikes for better terms regarding the broadcast and recording of musicians in Chicago in the 1930s, was strongly opposed to the idea that any phonograph could replace a live musician. "Since when is there any difference between Heifetz and the fiddler in the tavern? They're both musicians," he said.[6] Petrillo's past was a checkered one; he was connected with organized crime in Chicago and had once been kidnapped by the mob. Nevertheless, largely on the strength of his successes for the CFM, Petrillo was chosen as the new president of the AFM in 1940 (Anderson, 237–40).

As the possibilities offered by recorded music continued to appear, Petrillo led the AFM in a crescendo of protests that eventually resulted in the first of two major recording bans, beginning in August 1942. Musicians were on strike from that point, effectively banning any new music from being recorded. The record labels had stockpiled as much music as possible in the weeks before the ban took effect and as a result were able to hold out for a remarkably long time as musicians continued to perform only live or in live radio broadcasts. However, while records of classical music could be doled out over time, popular music had to be recorded and released in a relatively short period to capitalize on current trends and standards for popular music. Eventually, a series of pioneering records reintroducing popular music to the recording industry would contribute to the end of the strike.

Decca's 1943 cast recording of the original Broadway production of *Oklahoma!* is often cited as the first original Broadway cast album (⊙ Example 5.1). This claim is also often disputed, since recordings of music from musicals performed by members of the stage cast had been heard on records since at least the turn of the twentieth century when Emile Berliner, inventor of the gramophone, recorded songs from *Florodora*, featuring members of the London cast.[7] *Oklahoma!*, however, in addition to its being a milestone in the development of the musical as an art form, was also a major landmark in recording history, since the success of its album release established the original cast recording as a staple element of the Broadway musical.[8]

Although many recordings of Broadway material appeared before *Oklahoma!*, they largely consisted of songs recorded by studio singers rather than by cast members of stage productions, and usually with different arrangements and different orchestras. Stars such as Ethel Merman and Gertrude Lawrence recorded songs from hit shows in which they had appeared, including *Panama Hattie* and *Lady in the Dark*, respectively.[9] Some scores were represented in studio-assembled recordings such as those of the Victor Light Opera Company, which released choral renditions of songs from a given score, including most of Jerome Kern's Princess Theatre musicals (Grant, 203–4). Several early British productions of musicals had been recorded in the early part of the century, and by the 1930s a few Broadway musicals received significant recordings, including a 1932 *Show Boat* recording featuring two members of the Broadway revival cast, and Victor's 1935 recording of *Porgy and Bess* featuring the Broadway chorus and orchestra and soloists Lawrence Tibbett and Helen Jepson from the Met.[10]

There were also a few musicals that actually received recordings of the original cast singing most of the songs of the show. Marc Blitzstein's *The Cradle Will Rock* (1937) was preserved on record with its original cast members accompanied by piano (as they had been in the first public performances).[11] However, Blitzstein's work did not appeal to a mainstream audience. The 1943 Decca *Oklahoma!* was a milestone in the history of the genre not only because it was essentially the first cast album to feature cast, chorus, and orchestra as heard in the theater, but also because it preserved what was, at that time, one of the biggest hit musicals in Broadway history.

Prior to the release of the cast album, several of *Oklahoma!*'s songs had already gained popularity, though its book writer and lyricist Oscar Hammerstein II apparently had attempted to promote the show and score as a whole and was not interested in pushing hit singles. The 1942 recording ban meant that while pop singers and other artists could perform songs from the show on the radio, they were prevented from recording pop "covers" with instrumental backing. Nevertheless, both Frank Sinatra and Bing Crosby got around the ban by recording two of the most popular songs, "People Will Say We're In Love" and "Oh, What a Beautiful Mornin'" in the summer of 1943 by using vocal, rather than orchestral, accompaniment.[12]

During the negotiation period prior to the end of the ban, Jack Kapp at Decca had taken advantage of a notable exemption. Petrillo effectively lifted his ban on any recordings made for servicemen,[13] so Kapp had recorded Irving Berlin's *This Is the Army*, serving as another early example of a cast album. With that success behind him, *Oklahoma!*, the biggest hit show of the year, must have seemed like an irresistible follow-up, and Kapp struck a deal with Petrillo in late summer of 1943 to allow the original cast album of *Oklahoma!* to be made that fall.[14]

In 1943, when *Oklahoma!* premiered, the recording industry was facing difficult challenges in addition to the recording ban. Wartime shortages were cutting into the availability of materials to produce records, and experimentation with new formats and technology was intensifying competition among record labels. At the time, records were generally ten- or twelve-inch discs that rotated at 78 rpm. Each side could yield between two-and-a-half and four minutes of music. A group of related records could be sold together in an album—literally a bound book in which paper sleeves held separate records, much like a photograph album. The principal raw material used to make 78s was shellac, a resin secreted by an Asian tree insect. The war cut off supplies from the East, so records had to be rationed. In order to buy a new record, in some cases music lovers were required to turn in an old record to be reused (◉ Example 5.2).[15]

As a label primarily known for popular recordings, Decca had weathered the recording ban less well than its competitors, who had been able to fall back on stockpiled recordings of classical titles. With the stunning success of *Oklahoma!* on record, Decca quickly capitalized on its exclusive deal with Petrillo and began to record and release other cast recordings, including *One Touch of Venus, Bloomer Girl, Song of Norway*, and *On the Town*. The other labels did not cave to the pressures of the ban until 1944, a full year after Decca's initial agreement,[16] and did not fully engage in the field of cast recordings until 1946 when Capitol released *St. Louis Woman* and Columbia entered the arena with its recording of Hammerstein's revival of *Show Boat* from that year, followed by *Street Scene* in 1947, the same year as Victor's first entry, Lerner and Loewe's *Brigadoon*. But Columbia would soon surpass Decca as the premier label for cast recordings.

GODDARD LIEBERSON AND THE LONG-PLAYING RECORD

During this time, cast albums consisted of cumbersome, weighty books binding several records together, and listening to the entirety of a show necessitated the constant changing of records after every couple of songs. In 1948, however, Columbia introduced a technological innovation that had been in development in different forms for years. The long-playing (LP) record could hold over twenty minutes on each side, allowing an entire cast album to fit on one record, about the same size as one 78.[17] The vinyl material used for the LP was also more durable and provided better sound than 78s (Elborough, 19–40). It was a watershed change for the recording industry.

The LP introduced a new era in music listening for 1950s America. Jazz artists were able to capture the elusive and ephemeral nature of a long improvised set in a format that anyone could revisit after that one single performance. Lengthy classical works that had previously existed in complete form only in a concert hall could now be heard in their entirety in one manageable set of LPs. John Culshaw's Decca recording of Wagner's *Der Ring des Nibelungen*, the first recording of the score in its entirety (released in installments between 1958 and 1966), eventually took up nineteen records.[18] Culshaw estimated that the same recording would have required 112 records on 78s (Elborough, 47).

Cast recordings were perhaps the ideal product for the LP. While a symphony or improvisational jazz performance could be almost any length, the approximate forty-five minute playing time of an LP, separated like acts into two sides, perfectly reflected the average amount of music in a two-act musical. At Columbia Records, where the LP was born, Goddard Lieberson eventually became recognized as a leader in the field of cast recordings, particularly with the release and wide success of *South Pacific* on LP in 1949. *South Pacific* was one of the earliest and most successful LPs of any kind and while *Oklahoma!* and *South Pacific* would have to wait almost a decade to be released for mass consumption as Hollywood films, these hugely popular musicals were by then already well known through their original cast recordings.

Goddard Lieberson became president of Columbia Records in June of 1956, just two months after producing the most successful cast album of all time, the original Broadway cast recording of *My Fair Lady* (◉ Example 5.3). Lieberson is frequently credited, if not with the creation of the cast album, then with the promotion and solidification of the art form. In a 1973 tribute to Stephen Sondheim, when introducing Lieberson as a speaker, Leonard Bernstein described him as "the man who has done most to preserve and perpetuate the music of shows. Of course, that's only fractional. He is also the man who invented perpetuating the music of shows."[19]

Lieberson came to Columbia in 1939 as the assistant to the director of the Masterworks Division, eventually becoming the head of the division and vice president in charge of Masterworks artists and repertoire. He had attended the Eastman School of Music and had composed many of his own works; he even found time to write a novel, *3 for Bedroom C,* which was adapted into a Hollywood film starring Gloria Swanson.[20] Lieberson saw much of the popular music of the late '40s and '50s as a fad, and was at first reluctant to record rock-and-roll music during his tenure at Columbia. Lieberson saw the LP as a tool to bring "the university lecture hall, the theatre and the concert hall into the intimate possession of many who had never known them," establishing "a new consciousness in the art of listening" (Elborough, 68). Some of Lieberson's decidedly highbrow recordings included the works of Schoenberg, an extensive series of recordings featuring Igor Stravinsky conducting his own works, and the first recording of a stage play on LP, Shaw's *Don Juan in Hell,* directed by Charles Laughton. Other plays would follow, including the Broadway production of *Waiting for Godot* in 1956, which he not only produced for records but also provided what he called in the album notes "invented sounds of a more or less abstract nature."[21]

Lieberson's greatest legacy, however, lies with the musical cast recording. Lieberson saw the genre as an opportunity to bring the theater into the home, but he often required changes and alterations to scores of musicals in order to make the album work for the listener who would not have access to the show as it appeared on stage. By the time of his retirement, Lieberson claimed to have changed the "quality and style" of cast recordings:

> I'd usually be with a show since its inception, I'd go out of town two or three times, and by the time it came for the recording session, I'd know it pretty well. I sometimes changed the arrangements and tempos for the record—not always pleasing the arranger—but the sound you write for in the theater is quite different from the sound you need on an album. . . . Another thing I did away with was dialogue lead-ins for songs unless they were absolutely necessary. I would have to explain patiently to the librettist and the composer and lyricist that you could listen to a song on a record forty times, but to hear some banal, spoken introduction to the song drives you nuts after the third time. [22]

Every album required some adjustment to make the album work for the home listener. Lieberson was interested in preserving Broadway scores which would otherwise disappear after their Broadway productions ended, but from the changes he made, we can infer that he did not see his role as a documentarian or historian, attempting to recreate shows exactly as they appeared on stage. Instead, he attempted to give the wider American public the best possible experience of a Broadway score through only its LP.

Lieberson dominated the era when original cast albums were popular. In the years he was regularly recording Broadway

THE EVOLUTION OF THE ORIGINAL CAST ALBUM | 111

musicals, the practice became so common that fewer and fewer musicals went unrecorded. Some seasons, such as the 1957–58 and 1958–59 seasons, saw virtually no new book musicals that went without a recording (Mordden 1983, 199). Additionally, from the earliest days of the LP era, Lieberson, in collaboration with conductor Lehman Engel, began to record the scores of classic shows that were not tied to any production. Studio recordings of songs from shows were not a new idea. Popular artists had often recorded several tunes by a specific composer or from a specific show. But the Lieberson/Engel studio recordings were a new idea in that they began to take the scores of shows seriously as musical compositions. Some were recordings of shows that had pre-dated *Oklahoma!* and had not received original cast recordings, such as *Pal Joey*. Others were recordings of scores that had been previously taken down, but incompletely, such as *Porgy and Bess*.

The LP was a perfect new cultural product for an era in which the suburban lifestyle became the preferred choice for many Americans—the first time in the country's history that as many people lived in suburbs as in cities.[23] New York musicals were for them sophisticated cultural products that were not easily available, except through cast recordings on LP, which allowed access to thousands of people who might never see a Broadway show in New York. Like the earlier part of the century's interest in "good music," Americans in the late 1940s and 1950s began to be interested in status items, and Broadway musicals eventually came to be regarded as must-have items for what Ethan Mordden calls "the Informed Middle Class" (Mordden 1999, 261). Musicals became so popular with the general public outside of New York that when, in 1954, General Foods celebrated Rodgers and Hammerstein with a television salute, all three networks broadcast the show to 70 million viewers (Grant, 1). Three years later, when Rodgers and Hammerstein's television musical version of *Cinderella* premiered starring Julie

Andrews, already a household name in large part due to the ubiquitous *My Fair Lady* LP, the viewership was 107 million.[24]

These telecasts made it possible for millions of people to experience Broadway talent in their own homes, and the cast recording on LP allowed constant in-home access. By the 1960s, however, a major sea change was afoot in the recording industry. Up to this time, the LP had represented largely contemporary "adult" tastes. Broadway cast recordings (most notably the original LP of *My Fair Lady*) were among the most popular LPs of the decade. Rock-and-roll was of course present and gaining popularity by then, but it was still dismissed by many critics and recording industry moguls as a passing fad, and relatively few recordings of the genre were widely popular on LP during the first years the format was in existence. But this was to change in the 1960s.

THE CONCEPT ALBUM AND POPULAR MUSIC ON LP

By the mid-1960s, the Beatles and other groups were beginning to have an impact not only with hit singles but also with LPs. By the end of the decade, the format that only ten years earlier had been almost totally dominated by show music and soft "adult" fare was now taken over by the country's "new" music. Between 1959 and 1970, the percentage of "rock" or "rock and roll" music sold on LP increased from below 10% of all LPs sold to over 50%.[25] Much of this radical change in music listening happened in the latter half of the decade. In 1968, the Beatles released *Sgt. Pepper's Lonely Hearts Club Band*, now often cited as the first "concept album." As *Reading the Beatles* authors Kenneth Womack and Todd F. Davis see it, the album suggested the idea that "the songs of an album [could] add up to a unified and coherent whole."[26] Paul McCartney would later suggest that he had no memory of an overt decision to write songs with a particularly "Northern" sound,[27] although the idea that the album consisted of songs by another group—alter egos for the Fab Four—gave the album a conceit, and the inclusion of a reprise of the title song gave it a cohesiveness that suggested a connection between all of the songs. Other popular artists would soon create even more elaborate "concept" albums, including The Who's 1969 double album, *Tommy*.

Of course, the idea of a group of interrelated songs, including reprises, was hardly something new for the LP. Besides Broadway show recordings, many artists had released albums of songs on a single theme or all by one composer. Sinatra is often given credit as the first artist to use the LP format to create an overall experience; as early as 1938, Sinatra's *The Voice*, released in an album of 78s, reflected an overall mood, and by the LP era, Sinatra began to make more complex choices, using his albums to portray himself as a character, described by biographer Chris Rojek as "the Zen master" of the game of love, with Sinatra "the very generalissimo of rejection."[28]

Other artists and genres also suggested the idea of a concept album long before the release of *Sgt. Pepper*, including jazz and comedy LPs all on one theme, but cast recordings and movie musical soundtrack albums were the most natural contributor to the form. There had also been Broadway-related concept albums since at least the 1940s—albums that would appear to represent a cast recording of a show but that had not yet appeared on stage; in some cases such albums actually did result in Broadway productions. The 1959 album *Clara*, for instance, starring Betty Garrett and James Komack, was produced on Broadway the next year as *Beg, Borrow or Steal*, a flop that lasted five performances.[29] But with the radical changes in popular culture during the 1960s, the idea of a concept album by a group like the Beatles was new. While most popular artists up to that time had found their widest audience through hit singles, the Beatles led the way for popular artists on LP. Though they continued to release singles after *Sgt. Pepper*, we as a culture, as Womack and Davis suggest, "came to recognize their albums as their principal form, as the ultimate goal for their artistic output" (16).

Changing ideas of what an album could be during the late 1960s had a profound effect on the role of Broadway cast recordings. At that time, a very young Andrew Lloyd Webber was attempting to break into the commercial theater as a composer. His collaborator and lyricist, Tim Rice, had begun his career working for EMI, which gave them an "in" with one of Great Britain's leading record companies.[30] At EMI, they released several songs together and in 1969 released a recording of their first larger work, a short musical originally written as a children's entertainment, *Joseph and the Amazing Technicolor Dreamcoat*. Their next collaboration would also materialize first on LP, though this time it would not be the small curiosity that the original *Joseph* recording had been.

Though Lloyd Webber later stated that it was always his intention for *Jesus Christ Superstar* to be a live theater piece,[31] the material was decidedly controversial. To test the waters, Lloyd Webber and Rice produced a single, "Superstar" (with "John 19:41" as the "B" side). The success of the single led to the recording and release of a double-LP concept album that became a phenomenon, particularly in the United States (◉ Example 5.4). The success of the album launched an unprecedented theatrical history for the show. Rather than an original production being captured first on record and later remounted in duplicate stagings in various cities, following its initial popularity as a record, *Jesus Christ Superstar* was seen in various concert and live stagings across the United States prior to its first fully staged, fully sanctioned production. Lloyd Webber actually became involved in legal battles attempting to shut down various stagings prior to its first official production. The original Broadway production, staged by Tom O'Horgan (who had directed *Hair* on Broadway) lasted two years but was disliked by Lloyd Webber and many of the New York critics. A much less elaborate production directed by Jim Sharman opened in London in 1972 and became the West End's then longest-running hit, lasting eight years.

Lloyd Webber and Rice's second major collaboration also premiered as an album. This practice allowed the material to become first and foremost the property of its writers before it became associated with any particular director or production (Walsh, 100). But unlike *Jesus Christ Superstar*, *Evita* would eventually become highly associated with a single staging, that of famed producer-director Hal Prince. Though the concept album had presented the raw material, it was the stage production that remained the property's most successful incarnation.

As Lloyd Webber's musicals were making influential changes in the development of and expectations for musicals and cast recordings in the '70s, Broadway musicals and the world they reflected were also changing. Nineteen years after becoming president of Columbia Records, Goddard Lieberson announced, one day after his official retirement, that he would produce *A Chorus Line* for Columbia, one of his two final cast recordings (Marmorstein, 289).[32] Musical Director Donald Pippin later stated that he felt the show was "a little too contemporary" for Lieberson, which he felt marred the recording.[33] Lieberson, who had been a pioneer in the 1950s of promoting the music that Cold War era Americans could relate to, was perhaps too bound to that earlier era to be entirely successful with a youthful, contemporary work that not only was innovative in its creation and structure but also reflected the immense cultural shift that had occurred since Lieberson's heyday in the 1950s and '60s.

In *A Chorus Line*, a previously successful featured dancer comes to an audition in hopes of returning to the chorus. She does not want to be a star, she merely wishes to work. Cassie is perhaps the polar opposite of *Gypsy*'s Rose, who epitomizes the post–World War II obsession with capitalistic success through the most glamorous of all forms, Show Business. *Gypsy* remains one of Lieberson's most acclaimed cast albums, capturing Ethel Merman's equally electrifying and terrifying performance of songs that portray a woman so desperate for a piece of American stardom that she pushes away everyone who loves her. In contrast, John Lahr sees Cassie's desire to return to the line in *A Chorus Line* as a "new sound—the post-Vietnam sound of retreat." In Cassie, Lahr sees a reflection of "the culture's nostalgia for a simpler, happier life, one undamaged by the nation's imperialism, one that would replace the destiny of me with the destiny of we."[34] Between Lieberson's recording of *Gypsy* in 1959 and his recording of *A Chorus Line* in 1975, the country had become a radically different place, and Lieberson's consumer-based middle-class culture had disappeared.

The recording of *A Chorus Line*, the biggest hit show of the decade, never rose above ninety-eighth best-selling album of the week on the charts, reflecting the era's diminishing interest in musicals on record. Music consumption in the years following would continue to develop further away from the standards set in the Lieberson era (Marmorstein, 291). The LP itself eventually gave way to the compact disc (CD) which remained standard format for music from the 1980s through the turn of the millennium. But in the 2000s, the iPod and the downloadable MP3 have once again changed the way consumers acquire music. In a sense, we have come full circle. In the '50s, with the advent of the LP, cast recordings, soundtrack albums, and musicians like Frank Sinatra and Elvis so popularized the idea of the "album" as a concept that it was perhaps inevitable that the Beatles and other popular recording artists would eventually adapt and take over the form. Today, however, we are back to a jukebox style of music consumption, where listeners can choose to download only the specific songs they want from any given album.

THE LEGACY AND FUTURE OF THE CAST RECORDING

In a recent discussion for the American Theatre Wing's "Working in the Theatre" series, Decca Label Group executive Brian Drutman stated that the majority of sales for cast recordings produced on the Decca label are sold "at the venue." Theatergoers who visit the show in person want to take the recording home as a souvenir, as part of the overall package they have purchased in going to see the show. Kurt Deutsch, a former actor who represents the small label Sh-K-Boom/Ghostlight Records, got started in the industry in part because the major record labels had become less interested in producing cast recordings, a largely money-losing venture. Deutsch states that many musicals on his label have done most of their business as digital downloads, including youth-oriented musicals such as *Legally Blonde*.[35]

With the current cost of creating a cast recording spiraling above $400,000 on average, the likelihood of making a profit becomes less and less. Few records sell the approximately 120,000 units necessary to recoup their costs. A new model for producing cast albums may be needed to make their future feasible. Mark N. Grant notes that musicals have rarely been recorded live in the theater, while there have long been live recordings of opera (204–5); however, this route might involve significant negotiations with the various unions involved.

Whether the cost of making cast recordings will ultimately result in fewer albums being recorded, their utility goes beyond their immediate uses in marketing a show and selling albums. Cast recordings of musicals are, among other uses, important tools for the thousands of productions of musicals that continue to appear throughout the United States and abroad. Ted Chapin, president and executive director of the Rodgers & Hammerstein Organization, notes that he has learned to be cautious when giving permission for new recordings of scores in the R&H licensing catalog, since new arrangements will lead producing groups to request to alter their own productions to reflect these later recordings ("For the Record").

John Yap at TER/Jay Records started his "Complete Original Masterworks Editions" (full-score recordings of Broadway shows) largely, he says, because he was "somewhat disappointed by the fact that a lot of the music and songs were cut and abridged for . . . original cast albums as opposed to opera recordings, where the works were not only recorded complete, they were always of the original orchestrations and there were multiple versions of each opera." But while Yap hopes these recordings will be embraced by the musical theater-loving public in much the way that opera devotees value complete recordings, he also admits to "an inkling that the series would be very useful and helpful to the likes of musical directors, choreographers, conductors, directors and perhaps some actors who wanted to get the measures of the characters" (private correspondence).

Since the decline of Broadway musicals within popular culture, the significance of the cast recording has changed. Once, the cast album was a product for home consumption largely for a public who would never witness the musicals from which the albums were derived. Today, new recordings of musicals are primarily souvenirs of a particular show for audience members who have seen it, or tools for young practitioners to use in the mounting of a show. But the Golden Age of cast albums— roughly the years Goddard Lieberson was recording musicals at Columbia, from the late 1940s to the early 1970s—yielded what amounts to a living history of the Broadway musical. Cast albums were not recorded as legacy items, but that is what they have become. They are important in preserving not only the music but also the actual performances of musicals. As the life of a show goes on, its score may be recorded many times. What the original cast recording can reveal is a sense of the production itself—what made the show what it was, live on stage in front of an audience. Particularly as we listen today to cast recordings from the 1940s and '50s, when Broadway musicals were at the zenith of their popularity, it is possible to detect living moments that would otherwise be completely lost to time.

Anyone who has attended a show on Broadway will know that many of the most thrilling moments come from the experience of witnessing the performance live in the theater. The experience of hearing live music accompanied by the performance of actors and dancers in front of you is vastly different from the experience of listening to a cast album of the same show at home. But while the thrill of live performance can never be duplicated on record or CD, the cast recording, across several decades, remains our most lasting documentation of performances on Broadway.

NOTES

1 Evan Eisenberg, *The Recording Angel: Music, Records and Culture from Aristotle to Zappa*, 2nd ed. (New Haven, CT: Yale University Press, 2005), pp. 180–81.
2 Goddard Lieberson, liner notes from *Who's Afraid of Virginia Woolf?*, an Original Broadway Cast Recording (Columbia Records Masterwork Series, Monaural DOL 287, 1963).
3 For more on the birth of commercial radio, see Kathleen Drowne and Patrick Huber, *American Popular Culture through History: The 1920s* (Westport, CT: Greenwood Press, 2004), pp. 238–42.

4 Quoted in Mark Katz, "Making America More Musical through the Phonograph, 1900–1930" (*American Music* 16.4 [Winter 1998]: 448–75), p. 453.
5 Katz, 453; see also Mark Tucker, ed., "RD Darell Criticism in the Phonograph Monthly Review (1927–1931)" (*The Duke Ellington Reader* [New York: Oxford University Press, 1995]).
6 Quoted in Tim Anderson, "'Buried under the Fecundity of His Own Creations': Reconsidering the Recording Bans of the American Federation of Musicians, 1942–1944 and 1948" (*American Music* 22.2 [Summer 2004]: 231–69), p. 237.
7 The first recordings were made of the London cast, followed by recordings of the American cast the following year; see Tim Brooks, "Early Recordings of Songs from Florodora: Tell Me, Pretty Maiden . . . Who Are You?—A Discographical Mystery" *(Association for Recorded Sound Collections Journal* 31 [2000]: 51–64), and Ethan Mordden, *Broadway Babies: The People Who Made the American Musical* (New York: Oxford University Press, 1983), p. 204. For blanket histories of the cast album, see Ethan Mordden, *Beautiful Mornin': The Broadway Musical in the 1940s* (New York: Oxford University Press, 1999), pp. 236–70, and Mark N. Grant, *The Rise and Fall of the Broadway Musical* (Boston: Northeastern University Press, 2004), pp. 203–7.
8 See, for instance, Leo N. Miletich, *Broadway's Prize-Winning Musicals: An Annotated Guide for Libraries and Audio Collectors* (New York: Haworth Press, 1993), p. 13, and Max Wilk, *Oh! The Story of Oklahoma! A Celebration of America's Most Loved Musical* (New York: Applause, 2002, 1993), pp. 240–41.
9 Mordden 1983, 217–19. Lawrence's recording is one of three early recordings of *Lady in the Dark*. RCA Victor released three ten-inch discs of Lawrence's six cuts, which featured a male quartet from the Broadway cast and mostly followed the score as it was performed on stage. Decca's preceding album of cuts featured Hildegarde, a popular radio singer, and Danny Kaye recorded six numbers for Columbia, including some of Lawrence's numbers, in pop arrangements. The show's composer, Kurt Weill, confided to Ira Gershwin (the show's lyricist) that he preferred Hildegarde's recordings to Lawrence's. See Bruce D. McClung.

Lady in the Dark: Biography of a Musical (New York: Oxford University Press, 2007), p. 106.
10. Edward Jablonski, *Gershwin: With a New Critical Discography* (New York: Da Capo Press, 1998), p. 291.
11. Geoffrey Block, *Enchanted Evenings: The Broadway Musical from Show Boat to Sondheim* (New York: Oxford University Press, 2004), pp. 117 and 365. Block argues that the 1938 recording of *Cradle* was "the first Broadway cast album, a historical distinction almost always invariably and incorrectly attributed to *Oklahaoma!*" (117). For a fuller history of *The Cradle Will Rock*'s first public performances and the use of piano accompaniment instead of Blitzstein's original full orchestration, see, for instance, *John Houseman, Run-Through: A Memoir* (New York: Touchstone, 1980), pp. 242–81.
12. Tim Carter, *Oklahoma! The Making of an American Musical* (New Haven, CT: Yale University Press, 2007), p. 226.
13. Wanda Martin, "V-Disks Help Hasten V-Day" (*The Billboard 1944 Music Year Book* [Sixth Annual Edition]), p. 148.
14. Mordden 1999, 239. The album was recorded in October and released in December. It was so popular that three additional songs from the show were recorded the following May, released in January 1945, effectively creating an album with every major number from the show, excluding only dances and reprises (Carter, 227).
15. Travis Elborough, *The Vinyl Countdown* (Berkeley: Soft Skull Press, 2009), p. 25.
16. Gary Marmorstein, *The Label: The Story of Columbia Records* (New York: Thunder's Mouth Press, 2007), p. 120.
17. With the LP, most record "albums" were in fact no longer albums in the literal sense, since most releases consisted of single discs, which eliminated the need to set multiple discs into individual sleeves. But the term stuck to LPs that were collections of shorter numbers (such as original cast albums) by analogy and by habit, whereas the term was only rarely applied to recordings of longer works (opera, symphonies) even though these, too, were released in album form before the advent of the LP.
18. J. K. Holman, *Wagner's Ring: A Listener's Companion and Concordance* (Pompton Plains, NJ: Amadeus Press, 1996), p. 428.

19 Leonard Bernstein, unreleased segment of *Sondheim: A Musical Tribute* (Warner Brothers, LP No. 2WS 2705, 1973).
20 "Lieberson Sees A&R Exec as 'Heart' of Record Business" (uncredited, *Billboard* [August 4, 1956]: B-21).
21 Quoted in William Hutchings, *Samuel Beckett's Waiting for Godot: A Reference Guide* (Westport, CT: Praeger, 2005), p. 18. Lieberson had previously produced an eighteen-record set of 78s of the 1943 Broadway production of *Othello* starring Paul Robeson, José Ferrer, and Uta Hagen. Widely regarded as a landmark production for its casting of an African American in the title role, it was also one of the first full-length recordings of a Shakespeare play. It was also a result of the then-current recording ban; as a spoken word album, it required no musicians; see Barbara Hodgdon and William B. Worthen, eds., *A Companion to Shakespeare and Performance* (Oxford: Blackwell, 2005), p. 424, and Marmorstein, 117.
22 Quoted in Craig Zadan, *Sondheim & Co.*, 2nd ed. (New York: Perennial Library, 1989), p. 173.
23 "By 1960 as many people lived in the suburbs as in cities." Nigel Whiteley, "Toward a Throw-Away Culture. Consumerism, 'Style Obsolesence' and Cultural Theory in the 1950s and 1960s" (*Oxford Art Journal* 10.2 "The 60s" [1987]: 3–27), p. 7.
24 Richard Rodgers, *Musical Stages: An Autobiography*, updated ed. (New York: Da Capo Press, 2002), p. 293.
25 Philip H. Ennis, *The Seventh Stream: The Emergence of Rocknroll in American Popular Music* (Hanover, NH: Wesleyan University Press, 1992), p. 345.
26 Kenneth Womack and Todd F. Davis, *Reading the Beatles: Cultural Studies, Literary Criticism, and the Fab Four* (Albany: State University of New York Press, 2006), p. 16.
27 Barry Miles, *Paul McCartney: Many Years from Now*, 1st American ed. (New York: Henry Holt, 1997), p. 307.
28 Chris Rojek, *Frank Sinatra* (Cambridge, MA: Polity, 2004), p. 44. For more on Sinatra as one of the innovators of the "concept album," see Elborough, 147.
29 Steven Suskin, ed., *Opening Night on Broadway: A Critical Quotebook of the Golden Era of the Musical Theatre, Oklahoma!*

(1943) to Fiddler on the Roof (1964) (New York: Schirmer Books, 1990), pp. 73–74.
30 Michael Walsh, *Andrew Lloyd Webber: His Life and Works*, updated and enlarged ed. (New York: HarperCollins: 1989), p. 31.
31 Episode Five of *Broadway! A Musical History* with Ron Husmann (Videotape). (Irvine, CA: Chesney Communications, 1988).
32 Lieberson's final cast recording was, serendipitously, the 1976 "Twentieth Anniversary" revival recording of *My Fair Lady*, starring Christine Andreas and Ian Richardson.
33 Quoted in Gary Stevens and Alan George, *The Longest Line: Broadway's Most Singular Sensation, A Chorus Line* (New York: Applause Books, 1995), p. 97.
34 John Lahr, *Toeing the Line: 'A Chorus Line' is back on Broadway* (New Yorker [October 16, 2006], http://www.newyorker.com/archive/2006/10/16/061016crth_theatre, accessed August 19, 2009).
35 Theodore S. Chapin, Kurt Deutsch, Brian Drutman, Thomas Z. Shepard, and Melissa Rose Bernardo, "For The Record: Inside Cast Albums" (American Theatre Wing's Working In the Theatre [April, 2009]), http://americantheatrewing.org/wit/detail/cast_albums_04_09, accessed August 19, 2009.

PART TWO

PERFORMANCE

6

The Institutional Structure of the American Musical Theater

DAVID SANJEK

■ □ ■

IN 1866, NEW YORK PRODUCER William Wheatley found himself in a difficult position. He had contracted a melodrama—*The Black Crook*, by Charles M. Barras—which turned out to be a limp imitation of Weber's *Der Freischütz*. Simultaneously, however, another theater, set to present a ballet troupe newly arrived from Paris, burned down. Wheatley seized the opportunity to hire the stranded dancers, grafting their repertoire onto Barras's borrowed plot in an effort to salvage the situation. As the material evolved in rehearsal, the music director added music by Guiseppe Operti, an immigrant band leader, and interpolated songs by other composers as well, many with little or no connection to the story. To top it off, Wheatley purchased elaborate—and expensive—stage machinery for the show in London.

The first performance of this goulash of ingredients occurred at Niblo's Garden in September 12, 1866 and lasted five and a half hours. One might imagine the public would have felt suffocated by this avalanche of tenuously interconnected elements, but they instead overlooked the emptiness of Barras' imaginings, applauded the opulent production, and ogled the corps de ballet, whose hundred members were, as the *Evening Post* grumbled, "perhaps less concealed than would be deemed proper by those of stout views as to where dresses should begin or end."[1] The three-thousand-seat theater was filled to capacity for the next sixteen months, with Wheatley alluring repeat customers by regularly inserting new production numbers (military drill, "Baby Ballet," ballroom masquerade), even further unhinging *The Black Crook* from its dramatic underpinnings. The show ran for 474 performances, and touring companies kept it playing across the continent for the next fifty years, with eight revivals in New York City alone. As late as 1929, *The Black Crook* played in Hoboken, with a young Agnes de Mille in the role of Queen Stalacta.

It seems appropriate to begin with the cockeyed creation of *The Black Crook*, not only because it has been traditionally dubbed the "first American musical" but also because its evolution from probable bomb to blockbuster incorporates a number of elements that constitute the supporting structure of individuals and agencies through which the American musical has thrived for nearly 150 years. The convulsive manner in which its disparate elements came together recalls the now-clichéd notion of stage production represented in the four Mickey Rooney–Judy Garland musicals released between 1939 (*Babes in Arms*) and 1943 (*Girl Crazy*). These films reinforce the popular belief that concocting a piece of musical theater is mostly a matter of adolescent pizzazz and egoless collegiality, a view promulgated as well by such endearing encomiums to the entertainment profession as Irving Berlin's "There's No Business Like Show Business" (1946). And it's easy to see why these views persist, given the spirit of conviviality instilled by a personal or professional investment in this repertoire. Even if one regards this conviviality as little more than the camaraderie of kitsch, the sense of social adhesion inspired by the American musical has proven hard to resist, especially for those many who are involved in a long-term love affair with the genre.

But such a wide-eyed perspective overlooks the more mundane and possibly mercenary agencies that support and maintain the musical theater as one of the nation's preeminent creative achievements. Even the short narrative of *The Black Crook* illustrates the activity of four of those agencies: producers, publishers, publicists, and property owners. For a piece of musical theater to come into existence, money must be raised; music must be written and protected; audiences must be enlisted to attend; and physical performing spaces must be built and maintained. While this list is not exhaustive, an examination of each of these functions in turn will give some sense of the elaborate superstructure dubbed the "art world" by sociologist Howard S. Becker, at least as it operates in this domain. Becker defines this superstructure as "the network of people whose cooperative activity, organized via their joint knowledge of conventional means of doing things, produce(s) the kind of art works that the art world is known for."[2] In order for someone to put on a show, these networks must marshal their forms of expertise, access to capital, understanding of public opinion, and possession of physical property. Before those individuals whose talents we revere can entertain us, these networks initiate the forces that permit their forms of expertise to have a public forum and enjoy an enduring audience.

THE PRODUCERS

Watergate's "Deep Throat" communicated an abiding truth to Woodward and Bernstein when he advised them to "follow the money." Similarly, it should not be construed as economic determinism to view the checkbook as the principal agent in the creation of a piece of musical theater. Simply put, the producer must collect any necessary number of those checks, by any available means, for a piece of musical theater to be developed, workshopped, previewed, and eventually premiered. Mel Brooks' outlandish exaggeration of the function of these individuals in *The Producers* (1968, 2001) cannot diminish the fact that mounting any piece of theater requires contributions from a pool of investors, even if that pool does not, as in Brooks' fevered imagination, comprise an endless parade of debauched female senior citizens. Professional theater is an innately speculative form of commerce, as much in the financial as the creative sense.

Figures are not available regarding the current average cost of an individual musical or the number of successes versus failures, but the percentages are surely not in the creators' or producers' favor. One might take as a potential benchmark the statistics William Goldman offers in his revelatory analysis, *The Season: A Candid Look at Broadway*, which chronicles the fates of the theatrical premieres mounted during the 1967–68 season. Twenty-two percent of the offerings he discusses made money, a seemingly upbeat calculation until one looks more carefully. Of the twenty-five dramas that opened, only five were hits; of the nineteen comedies, five once again; but of the fourteen musicals, only two succeeded. Goldman concludes,

> Probably no season ever lost more, but I don't know that any of the above should be either surprising or disheartening. The theatre is a high-risk business, and it always has been. And more than that, unlike many businesses, the downside risk in the theatre is greater than almost anywhere else: in most industries you don't stand quite so great a chance of being wiped out completely. But in this decade, if a little over 21% of the productions show a

profit, then a little under 78% show a loss. And most of the shows that do end up being profitable do so only in a small way.[3]

Could it be those seemingly insurmountable odds that have made so many impresarios of the musical theater so idiosyncratic? And "idiosyncratic" is putting it mildly. The most reasonable of them have been downright cockeyed, and some of the most celebrated have been close to pathological. The foremost exemplification of the latter was David Merrick (1911–2000). Acrimony seemed as routine to him as his dour-faced entrepreneur's trademark pinstripe suits. Collaboration in his mind took a back seat to confrontation; the production process was little more than a pretext for transforming allies into adversaries. Merrick seemed to assume that success came only when the participants were routinely made to squirm, fearful that they might be fired without warning; their contributions abandoned without pretext; and their paychecks delayed as long as the most elastic reading of the law would allow. Howard Kissel's 1993 unauthorized biography, *The Abominable Showman*, chronicles the uninterrupted antics of this serial abuser, climaxing with the notorious episode of Merrick's saving the news about the sudden death of director-choreographer Gower Champion until the initial curtain calls of the 1980 production of *42nd Street* in order to milk the maximum publicity out of the tragedy. Merrick reportedly stated, "Most people are weak. I respect no one but myself. . . . There is no such thing as unfair. It is simply a matter of inferiority and superiority. I know more than most people and I use it."[4] Unappetizing as such sentiments might be, the roll call of Merrick's successes indicates that fractiousness can sometimes fuel harmony: *Fanny* (1954), *Gypsy* (1959), *Carnival* (1961), *Hello, Dolly!* (1964), and *Promises, Promises* (1968). At the same time, the sequences of slip-ups that produced such notorious flops as *Breakfast at Tiffany's* (1966) and *Mata Hari* (1967) amply illustrate that aiding and abetting a creative meltdown provides an appetizing spectacle only to those predisposed to schadenfreude.

Florenz Ziegfeld (1869–1932) might have lacked Merrick's most unseemly mannerisms, but he nonetheless possessed his own idiosyncrasies. Impenetrable as an individual, he was selectively consumed by the various elements that made up his lavish productions. Costuming, décor, and casting took precedence over scores, and the verbal element sometimes seemed little more than an afterthought. Repeatedly, he turned to an unregenerate hack, William Anthony McGuire, rather than seek out more sophisticated writers to craft plot and dialogue. Ziegfeld furthermore thought of songwriters as more or less interchangeable employees; Ethan Mordden states, "Historians ask, 'Who wrote the songs!' Ziegfeld asked, 'Who will put them over, and let me see the dress against the backdrop.'"[5] As far back as the operettas featuring his paramour Anna Held through the various permutations of the *Follies* (1907–31), he sought to dazzle audiences with sexual spectacle and stupendous décor rather than leave them with tunes they might whistle as they headed home. One of his most essential employees was designer Joseph Urban, whose elegant and masterful craft can only be appreciated today through the remaining interiors of the producer's eponymous theater, now a single screen film house. Ironically, even his celebrated promotion of comedy had its limits. Though the *Follies* featured some of the major clowns of the age—Bert Williams, Fanny Brice, Eddie Cantor, and W. C. Fields among others—Ziegfeld is said never to have comprehended their appeal until it was recognized by audiences. His on-call talent scout, lyricist, and jack-of-all-trades Gene Buck often protected these talents when Ziegfeld seemed ready to abandon them in rehearsals.

The unique exception to his blinkered notion of production was the landmark 1927 show, Jerome Kern and Oscar

Hammerstein's *Show Boat*, notable as the musical theater's most radical transformation of the genre to that date. But the odyssey of the work's emergence illustrates how both contention and collaboration spurred its completion, reflecting not only the array of these individuals' respective temperaments but also the complex function of the producer as but one of the many agencies engaged in the formation of the American musical theater. Kern was the first of the trio to see musical possibilities in Edna Ferber's novel, published in 1926. He communicated these sentiments to the critic and broadcaster Alexander Woollcott, knowing he was friends with the writer and fellow members of the Algonquin circle. Woollcott introduced novelist to composer at the opening of Kern's *Criss Cross* on October 12, 1926. Ferber expressed doubts about the proposed venture, but Kern felt he could crack the material along with Hammerstein, who had successfully collaborated as both lyricist and libretto writer (along with Otto Harbach) over the past three years with Vincent Youmans (*Wildflower*, 1923), Rudolf Friml (*Rose Marie*, 1925), and Sigmund Romberg (*The Desert Song*, 1926). The two had also worked together once before, on *Sunny* (1925), one of the period's typical grab-bag concoctions with only the most tenuous threads of dramatic logic connecting action and song. Ferber reports in her autobiography that her anxieties evaporated when she heard "Make Believe" and "Why Do I Love You?" and any residual doubts were extinguished altogether when Kern played "Ol' Man River": "The music mounted, mounted, mounted, and I give you my word my hair stood on end, the tears came to my eyes, I breathed like a heroine in a melodrama. This was great music. This was music that would outlast Jerome Kern's day and mine" (Mordden 1976, 103).

Kern and Hammerstein signed a contract with Ferber on November 17, 1926, and nine days later played a portion of the score for Ziegfeld. In a letter written the next day, the producer exclaimed, "This is the best musical comedy I have been fortunate to get hold of. . . . This show is the opportunity of my life."[6] Kern and Hammerstein separately signed contracts with Ziegfeld on December 11, 1926, with the stipulation that the script would be delivered on January 1 of the following year and the work premiere on April 1. These daunting deadlines coincided with the producer's own shift to greater autonomy. For years, the *Follies* had occupied the New Amsterdam Theatre on 42nd Street, which the impresario owned along with theatrical magnates Marc Klaw and Abe Erlanger. With the support of newspaper tycoons William Randolph Hearst and Arthur Brisbane, Ziegfeld financed the building of his eponymous space on 54th Street and 6th Avenue. The cornerstone was laid in an elaborate ceremony, broadcast over the radio and attended by 800 people, on December 9, 1926. On February 2, 1927, the first production, *Rio Rita*, took the stage. Announcements of the immediately forthcoming "*Showboat*" appeared in the program but proved premature. A collision of sensibilities ensued. Ziegfeld was accustomed to libretti being concocted virtually overnight and with little regard to the dramatic or narrative logic of the material. Hammerstein recognized not only the inherent difficulties of accommodating the multigenerational dimension of Ferber's story but also the demands of making the songs and the saga intermingle. For Ziegfeld, the impasse could only be attributed to Hammerstein's refusal to accommodate audience expectations over his own aesthetic standards. He complained to Kern that the work "has not got a chance except with the critics" and worried in particular that the portion that followed Ravenal and Magnolia's wedding proved "too serious, not enough comedy" (Kreuger, 26).

Ziegfeld held off, however, giving Hammerstein enough time to develop the ambitious scenario we know today. *Show Boat* had its world premiere in Washington, D.C., on November 17, 1927, and its New York debut on December 27. The producer, nonetheless, retained his time-honed concern with ostentatious production values virtually up to the last minute, complaining that the dances choreographed by Sammy Lee lacked oomph, whereas they had been intentionally designed to serve the movement of the plot rather than—as in the *Follies* or Ziegfeld's other musicals—stop the production dead in its tracks. Only when audiences and critics alike recognized the coherence and dramatic ambitions of *Show Boat* did Ziegfeld relax and revel in the box-office receipts.

Interestingly, the initial reviews recognized those very qualities of the show that we today revere as a historical precedent. Brooks Atkinson characterized it in the *New York Times* as "one of those epochal works about which garrulous old men gabble for twenty-five years after the scenery has rattled off to the storehouse" and drew attention to the work of the principals: "They blend into the sort of joined, harmonized performance that we extravagantly commend in good dramatic productions" (Kreuger, 53). Even when critics later sometimes objected to what Kern and Hammerstein had accomplished, they underscored the transformation that had taken place, as in George Jean Nathan's lament: "The best musical comedies . . . are those in which sense is reduced to a minimum, the worst, those which aim at rationality. . . . What we want . . . is a return to the old-time absurdity, the old-time refusal to reflect life and reality in any way, the old-time razzle and dazzle and the incredible" (Mordden 1976, 105–6). Ironically, what he describes are precisely those characteristics that typified Ziegfeld's career and that, not altogether with his approval, he helped to eradicate on the occasion of the premiere of *Show Boat*.

PUBLISHERS

If the producer provides the financial and logistic support for the creators of the musical theater, the publisher solicits and merchandises the songs featured in those productions. The relationship between the two groups has always been symbiotic, even if the balance of power may sway according to the relative commercial clout of the creators. For a considerable period of time after the premiere of *The Black Crook*, theatrical songwriters focused mainly on producing their material and left its promotion and legal protection to others. Working out a contractual obligation to a publishing firm allowed them to be single-minded about their craft. These obligations differed from individual to individual, although during the early years of the genre, most negotiations tended to be short and direct. Many would not even pursue a long-term association, selling their songs outright, while others recognized the benefits of a regular paycheck and worked out a system of advances. Whether contract employees or freelancers, most theatrical songwriters have been beholden to publishers in order to maintain their presence in the musical theater and were treated much like workers on an assembly line. Only a few, Irving Berlin most notably, were able to eradicate the middleman and inaugurate their own businesses.

To predict which of the pieces submitted to them might possess commercial viability, publishers needed to act something like social seismologists, attendant to modulations in the public mood and the vagaries of those performers to whom they hawked their wares. Publisher Edward B. Marks' memoir, *They All Sang*, opens with a depiction of the businessman, accompanied by his acolyte Louis the Whistler, ambling from theater to theater in lower Manhattan to convince prominent players to adopt items from his catalog. Hyperbole was the businessman's modus operandi: as Marks states, "We never had anything less than a sensation in those days. Some of them were tremendous, but sensational was moderate praise."[7] John Shepherd stipulates three criteria that needed to be in place for a song to have even a modicum of potential: "It had to be written in a musical style that was in fashion at the time. It had to be about something that was in the public's mind. Or it had to appeal to the public's emotions."[8] In his history of the institution most prominently associated with these practices, Tin Pan Alley, Isaac Goldberg draws attention to how personal emotion played little to no part in this process. Songs were rarely equated with self-expression but rather presumed to serve the requirements of the marketplace. He characterizes the system as "the paradise of Pseudo," for, "In the alley, song became synthetic; one wept, one laughs, at so many per cent."[9]

Publishers realized that they could increase their chances of success by placing their material in the hands of a popular figure on the stage, one who could add it to their act or even interpolate it into a theatrical piece, whether or not it had any bearing upon the plot or the overall tenor of the score. Al Jolson, for example, was famous for stopping a show, coming to the footlights, and letting loose with his best-known repertoire. Early publishers seemed to revel in the competition, thinking of each new composition as something to launch upon its commercial trajectory. Songs were merchandise, not potential masterpieces. Publishers agreed with Ziegfeld and Nathan that the musical theater strayed from its purpose when it failed to emphasize spectacle and sensation. The transition led by *Show Boat* toward the integrated score bemused and befuddled some of them. Some of their shared animosity comes across in Marks' sarcastic denigration of the new narrative format that began to emerge, however raggedly, at the start of the twentieth century: "The new musical comedies, however, marked a distinct retrogression in wit. They were romantic, pretentious; they bequeathed to us the terms 'musical comedy plot' to denote the artificial and saccharine, 'musical comedy heroine' for an insipid girl in tulle and organdie, and 'comic opera kingdom' for a nebulous and absurd locale" (Marks, 114). Over time, publishers accommodated the transformation in form, yet to this day the privileging of hits remains a reflex in the industry. Thus the repeated assertion that Stephen Sondheim does not write with the audience in mind, or the assumed efficacy of wrapping theatrical narratives around commercially proven material, as in jukebox musicals like *Mama Mia!* or *Jersey Boys*. Indeed, while creators of contemporary musical theater may not wish to reside in the "paradise of Pseudo," many would be willing to drum up a set of emotions if it assured the audience's attention and added to ticket sales.

PUBLICITY

Public fascination with American musical theater arguably reached its peak between the 1920s and the 1960s. During this period, the emotional consensus of the nation was that Broadway represented the epitome of glamour and creative ferment. Many yearned to be First-Nighters and thereby to consort with all that was alluring, audacious, and original. Any number of factors fueled these shared feelings, but one of the most influential was the emerging array of journalists, publicists, and others who adopted the entertainment industry as their precinct. They concocted a novel brand of hyperbole, at times nearing hysteria, to embellish the aura that enveloped the stage and the surrounding geography and population of Broadway. The special lexicon of that discourse was a composite of street vernacular, theatrical lingo, and more than a smidgen of Yiddish, laced with striking neologisms that began as part of a minority vocabulary and eventually entered mass culture. For example, the "stix" were the boondocks, "shtick" encompassed an individual's unique behavior, and the "Death Trail" characterized the string of undesirable, cheap hotels that stretched from Chicago across to the West Coast.

No one person originated this phenomenon, but it took root in the pages of the industry publication *Variety* as much as anywhere. Founded by Sime Silverman (1873–1933) in 1905, *Variety* engaged in the dispersal of what he dubbed "slanguage." The boldness and irreverence he brought to the task quickly led to the identification of *Variety*'s pages with not only the activities of the entertainment industry but also a way of life and an emotional disposition. Its reporting remained rooted in the present tense and endeavored to immortalize the immediate, all the while recognizing (if only implicitly) that success was a momentary condition. It acknowledged as well that for most people show business, though nothing more than a circumscribed universe, represented within its narrow precincts limitless energies and ambitions. Both this vocabulary and its accompanying point of view reached an audience unacquainted with *Variety* through the wildly popular short fiction of Damon Runyon (1880–1946). Born in Lawrence, Kansas, Runyon lost his mother before he turned eight, was left on his own by his father, and ditched school before completing the fourth grade; no wonder he retained a lifelong fascination with outlaws and outsiders, while maintaining an aloof exterior and hiding his feelings. Runyon triumphed initially as a reporter, specializing in sports as well as flamboyant murder trials, and soon became one of the best-paid and most widely read contributors to Hearst's *New York American*. Runyon transferred his earlier attraction to cowboys and saloon habitués to the gangsters and chorus girls who flourished in the theatrical district of New York City: the Guys and Dolls of his most famous 1932 short story collection and the source of Frank Loesser's 1950 hit musical.[10] Runyon rarely incorporated the physical attributes of that environment but instead rendered both the mood and motivations of his characters through the voice of interchangeable and typically unnamed narrators. His work became synonymous with both the territory and a sophisticated way of life, but as much as anything, it was Runyon's point of view, hardboiled but ultimately emotionally vulnerable, that others responded to. It allowed them to remain both wide-eyed onlookers and smart-aleck insiders, simultaneously seduced by the Great White Way and cynical about its shabbiness.

The person who most successfully perpetuated this perspective, while epitomizing for many Americans the quintessence of American entertainment, was Walter Winchell (1897–1972). Contemporary audiences may remember him as the gruff-voiced, off-screen narrator of the television series *The Untouchables* (1959–63). In his day, Winchell was ubiquitous, a presence in print and films, and on stage, radio, and television. His sign-on catchphrase, "Good evening Mr. and Mrs. America and all the ships at sea," reached as many as 50 million listeners, and his newspaper column was syndicated in over 2,000 venues. Known as "The Bard of Broadway," Winchell rose from youthful poverty through a hardscrabble stage career to the pinnacle of an environment where his imprimatur made reputations and his dismissal terminated them. Both egocentric and anxious about his professional eminence, Winchell unreflectively kept the machinery of celebrity operating on all cylinders for nearly forty years until age, alterations in social attitudes, and the wreckage strewn by his vindictive temperament unplugged him from the battery of public opinion. Winchell may not have invented gossip, but he crafted and commanded many of its nuances. He introduced the now inescapable practice of piquing the public's fascination with a particular individual or phenomenon, but then just as readily pricking their credulity by revealing just how much of what had bewitched them was as common as dirt. While this process might seem the very opposite of celebratory, it had the undeniable consequence of making the environment Winchell covered continually mesmerizing to his audiences. It is not so much that Winchell enriched the career of any single performer, creator, or production as that he gave a kick-start to the national consensus that entertainment and celebrity were the principal commodities of American society. In the words of his biographer Neal Gabler: "Winchell had helped inaugurate a new mass culture of celebrity—centered in New York and Hollywood and Washington, fixated on personalities, promulgated by the media, predicated on publicity, dedicated to the ephemeral and grounded on the principle that notoriety creates power."[11]

Since Broadway remained one of the touchstones of achievement that Winchell considered fundamental to his beat, he helped thereby to keep the public focused on the achievements of the American musical theater. Who has succeeded him in this function? Parallel with a portion of his long career, Ed Sullivan (1901–74), whom Winchell loathed immoderately, performed a comparable role, particularly when he shifted from print journalism to television with a degree of success that outdid his rival. During the time he ruled the 8 p.m. Sunday night time slot (1948–71), Sullivan was one of the nation's sanctioning authorities; John Leonard persuasively observes, "Never before and never again in the history of the republic would so many gather so loyally, for so long, in thrall to one man's taste."[12] Sullivan revered the theater, and where else did the American public have such easy access to full-dress, uninterrupted segments of hit Broadway shows? *Bye Bye Birdie* (Charles Strouse-Lee Adams, 1960) offers a clever tribute to his influence, when a suburban family sings his praises in mock-ecclesiastical tones. Following Sullivan's departure, there has been only the occasional repetition of this phenomenon, as for example on the Rosie O'Donnell daytime talk show (1996–2002), which served a similar function. The absence of a successor to either Winchell or Sullivan or even O'Donnell fuels the prevailing assumption of Broadway's imminent demise or at least its ongoing desiccation, reminding one as well of how influential such a national discourse can be in promoting forms of commercial entertainment as mass culture.

PROPERTY

In investigating any form of commercial entertainment, one may easily become so enthralled by the final product that one overlooks its mundane causes. For Broadway, one of the most easily bypassed of these is the very space in which it takes place. Obviously, you cannot launch a performance before securing a venue. Creative acts remain flights of the imagination without being anchored in a physical location, which, in the case of the musical theater, requires all the paraphernalia provided by a well-equipped stage. Throughout the history of the genre and its long-term attachment to the real estate of New York City, the principal location of those stages has shifted corresponding to the gravitation of both population centers and centers of public influence from the lower portion of Manhattan to midtown and thence the precinct surrounding Times Square. That migration did not occur without its advance scouts. Although his name and achievements have long since been eclipsed by those of his grandson, Oscar Hammerstein (1847–1919) may well lay claim to being the progenitor and imaginative architect of modern Broadway, as he built five theaters in and around Times Square (before it was so named), beginning with the Olympia in 1895, and thereby founded what Anthony Bianco has described as "the most entertainment-intensive block in the city that is America's once and future cultural capital."[13]

Debates over the commercial fate and physical decay of Broadway have simmered ever since the opening of Hammerstein's venture, accumulating even greater vehemence and ideological baggage when virtually all the live venues transformed into sites for motion picture exhibition after 1930. This led in turn to an influx of what some considered a less desirable clientele, and consternation increased when the sale of drugs and pornography as well as the staging of live sex shows permeated parts of the district. Over time, many in a position of power became convinced that the sophisticated veneer of Broadway had become tacky and tawdry. This interfered as well with marketing the city as a tourist Mecca, and some complained that the advertising motto "Fun City" had become offensively fraudulent. Fervent efforts to oust the interlopers led to the filing of legal briefs and back-room bargaining. Others argued, however, that the theater district provided many citizens with a welcome outlet for letting off steam, and that efforts at censorship and plans for wholesale redesign were informed more by class anxiety than business savvy. The question of who had a right to occupy public space was eventually answered when various parties to the debate conceded the clear-headedness of urban planner and development official Rebecca Robertson, who asserted, in 1990, "Do right by the old theatres and the rest will follow" (Bianco, 6). Those who followed her precept endowed the neighborhood with new or refurbished showcases, as did the management of Playwright Horizons, who engineered the erection of Theatre Row on the western extremity of 42nd Street. More recently, and more controversially, the Disney Corporation renovated the New Amsterdam (1997), the block's 1,800-seat site built by Klaw and Erlanger in 1905. While Theatre Row has been felt to redefine the scene's diversity, many worry that Disney's efforts, and the musical adaptations they have staged, add to both the dumbing-down of the profession and the tackiness of the district as a whole.

    Ownership of physical space does not lead necessarily to the (sometimes controversial) imposition of (usually conservative) taste in theatrical exhibition. The activities of the

Judson Memorial Church in Greenwich Village, and in particular their staging of Marie Irene Fornes's play with music *Promenade* (1965), represents one of several departures from this expectation. The performances at the church were part of the flourishing Off-Off Broadway scene that began in the 1950s following Actors Equity's 1949 ruling that actors could perform in small venues for lower rates. In that first decade, revivals dominated these venues, but the 1960s brought an explosion in experimental pieces staged in small spaces with even smaller casts and few elaborate accoutrements other than could be provided by the imagination. Venues such as Café Cino, La Mama ETC, and St. Mark's Church in the Bowery, in addition to Judson Memorial, opened their doors without charging admission, asking only for donations. Little thought was given to mainstream audiences, as the evolving community conceived itself as separate and self-supporting, even antithetical to the economic and institutional imperatives of mainstream culture. Those in charge of the physical spaces where this community met encouraged their integrity and provided it a refuge. Judson Memorial Church, founded in 1892, stood on the downtown side of Washington Square Park, adjacent to the sprawling campus of New York University and in the midst of a flourishing café, gallery, and club culture. Its director, Howard Moody (appointed in 1956), felt their mission was to serve the immediate neighborhood and initiated an outreach to artists and performers in 1961 by appointing minister-composer Al Carmines as intermediary. They agreed to open the space to any who applied without prior censorship with the only stipulation being that the annual budget for all appearances was $200. Over time, the institution made its setting even more performance-friendly, as the progressive congregation chose to remove all the pews as well as the altar.

The libertory energies unleashed by such decisions are paralleled by the gleefully off-kilter construction of *Promenade*.

Fornes pioneered a form of composition that depended upon the operation of chance and randomness. She created *Promenade* by using three packs of cards: one with scene locations; the second listing character types; and the third containing possible opening lines. Whenever inspiration flagged, she drew from them and continued. Fornes also dispensed with customary forms of character motivation and instead stressed the transformations permitted by sudden revelations and turnabouts of action. Naturalism took a back seat to the free flow of invention. As Stephen J. Bottoms states, "The familiar dynamics of cause-and-effect narrative logic were far less important than the physically limited, but imaginatively limitless potential of the stage event itself."[14] Nothing therefore dictated how an audience ought to respond to her writing, and, ironically, this could be said to have reinaugurated some of the "old time razzle and dazzle and the incredible" that George Jean Nathan felt had fled the stage with the inauguration of the book musical. Furthermore, the songs that Fornes created along with Carmines were equally and eloquently unhinged in their ebullient wrenching from convention. Her lyrics frequently intercut radically disconnected statements—"Chicken is he would does not love me; for there's more to the cake than the icing"—to the tune of Carmines's sprightly melodies.[15] *Promenade* consequently comes across as a one-of-a-kind jeux d'esprit that left downtown denizens delighted. It became one of the exceptions to the rule of appealing only to an insular audience, for it transferred uptown in an elongated version and played for over a year. One cannot imagine such a piece emerging other than in an environment like Greenwich Village and a physical space such as the Judson Memorial Church, a combination that challenged predetermined notions of what a church or a theater or a musical ought to be. Sometimes, real estate can come without any impinging attachments and liberate rather than inhibit its inhabitants.

These four agencies—production, publishing, publicity, and property—have contributed to the repertoire and development of the American musical theater for more than 140 years. But even if one firmly believes they can encourage its continuation, they cannot either guarantee its evolution or outflank its possible extinction. Of course, rumors of the musical's demise are as rife as a cocked hat in a piece of Bob Fosse choreography. Still, there are distressing implications to the rationale behind the recent announcement that the long-standing parody series *Forbidden Broadway*, founded in 1982, shut its doors in March 2009: founder and principal writer Gerard Alessandrini believes that nothing remains to be ridiculed, as Broadway has come to resemble a theme park. An eventual return is not out of the question, but, until then, he waits until Broadway finds a means of renewing itself.[16] In the meantime, might these four agencies, among others, encourage and not disrupt that process.

NOTES

1. Quoted in Ethan Mordden, *Better Foot Forward: The History of American Musical Theatre* (New York: Grossman, 1976), p. 12.
2. Howard S. Becker, *Art Worlds* (Berkeley: University of California Press, 1982), p. x.
3. William Goldman, *The Season. A Candid Look at Broadway* (New York: Limelight Editions, 1984), p. 391.
4. Howard Kissel, *David Merrick: The Abominable Showman* (New York: Applause Books, 1993), p. 190.
5. Ethan Mordden, *Broadway Babies: The People Who Made the American Musical* (New York: Oxford University Press, 1983), p. 36.
6. Miles Kreuger, *Show Boat: The Story of a Classic American Musical* (New York: Oxford University Press, 1977), p. 20.

7 Edward B. Marks, *They All Sang: From Tony Pastor to Rudy Vallee*, as told to A. J. Liebling (New York: Viking, 1935), p. 6.
8 John Shepherd, *Tin Pan Alley* (London: Routledge & Kegan Paul, 1982), p. 2.
9 Isaac Goldberg, *Tin Pan Alley: A Chronicle of American Popular Music*, with a supplement: Edward Jablonski, *From Sweet and Swing to Rock 'n' Roll* (New York: Frederick Ungar, 1961), p. 140.
10 Damon Runyon, *Guys and Dolls and Other Stories* (London: Penguin, 1956).
11 Neal Gabler, *Winchell: Gossip, Power and the Culture of Celebrity* (New York: Alfred A. Knopf, 1994), p. xiii.
12 John Leonard, *Smoke and Mirrors: Violence, Television and Other American Culture* (New York: New Press, 1997), p. 17.
13 Anthony Bianco, *Ghosts of 42nd Street: A History of America's Most Infamous Block* (New York: William Morrow, 2004), p. 7. Modern Broadway is but one of Hammerstein's contributions to New York's cultural map; he also designed, built, and managed nine other venues during the course of his visionary if fiscally erratic career, during which he gained and lost three fortunes, dying penniless but rewarded by his permanent contributions to the metropolitan landscape.
14 Stephen J. Bottoms, *Playing Underground: A Critical History of the 1960s Off-Off-Broadway Movement* (Ann Arbor: University of Michigan Press, 2004), p. 141.
15 Maria Irene Fornes, *Promenade and Other Plays* (New York: PAJ Publications, 1987), p. 16.
16 Julie Bloom, "'Forbidden Broadway' Curtain to Go Down" (*New York Times* [September 13, 2008]: B-9.

7

Orchestration and Arrangement

CREATING THE BROADWAY SOUND

DOMINIC SYMONDS

■ □ ■

> *There are three basic types of orchestration in the Broadway musical. The first comes out of old vaudeville and from military bands; it's what orchestrators call the "Broadway sound" and may be best typified by Hello, Dolly! The second, the "academic school," is based mainly on classical operetta. Candide would be a case in point. Finally, there is the "interpretive style" . . . where the arranger draws from many sources to interpret the lyric in a dramatic sense. Russell Bennett's orchestration of "Lonely Room" in Oklahoma! is a great example of an orchestration that helps set the mood and character, much like a piece of theatre design, like sets and lighting.*[1]

ORCHESTRATION IN MUSICALS IS AN area that has received little attention.[2] In this chapter I consider the orchestrator's role in crafting the distinctive Broadway "sound," from the work of composer Victor Herbert—one of the last to orchestrate his own material—to orchestrators such as Frank Saddler, Robert Russell Bennett, Hans Spialek, and Don Walker, who scored many classic musicals. Finally, I consider several related matters: copyright, union agreements, amplification, the virtual orchestra, and actor-musicianship, all of which have influenced the sound of the Broadway show.

ORCHESTRATION AND ARRANGEMENT

Despite its being a dominant part of musical theater, orchestration is seldom discussed or even defined. Orchestrator Robert Russell Bennett clarifies it as "the rounding out and filling out of the melodic line by means of instrumentation, harmonic color (and all that goes with it) and rhythmic emphases."[3] Don Walker notes that this involves three main stages: arranging—"fitting a song to a dance pattern, the composition of introductions, interludes, modulations, codas and other special material needed for the dance; the decision on the vocal keys and the type of accompaniment for a voice"; orchestration—"the translation of this 'arrangement' into sound . . . by writing notes on pages of score"; and extraction—"the copying of the individual parts for the various instruments of the orchestra from the score."[4] In classical music, orchestration is considered an integral part of composition; certain composers are renowned orchestrators, and Berlioz's *Treatise on Orchestration* has become a seminal text. Broadway composers, however, do not orchestrate their own material. Although some (Jerome Kern) had the ability, others (Irving Berlin) were remarkably illiterate in musical scoring; the composer typically hands over melodies, annotated to varying degrees, and thus much of the "Broadway sound"—and the decision making over how it is created—can be attributed to the orchestrators. Nonetheless, successful collaborations have existed between Jerome Kern with first Frank Saddler (including the Princess Shows) and later Robert Russell Bennett (including *Show Boat, Music in the Air, Roberta*), Rodgers and Hart with Hans Spialek (*On Your Toes, Babes in Arms, Pal Joey*), Rodgers and Hammerstein with Robert Russell Bennett (*Oklahoma!, South Pacific, The King and I, The Sound of Music*), and later Jerry Herman with Philip J. Lang (*Hello, Dolly!, Mack and Mabel, Mame*), Stephen

Sondheim with Jonathan Tunick (*Company, Follies, A Little Night Music, Sweeney Todd, Into the Woods, Passion*), and William Finn with Michael Starobin (*Falsettos, Spelling Bee*).

THE OPERETTA SOUND

A useful starting point is Victor Herbert, the last of the "old-school": a composer who also orchestrated his music. Herbert's experience both as instrumentalist and orchestral conductor made him an "expert at instrumentation"[5] who "conceived everything orchestrally."[6] That Herbert was steeped in the classical tradition is evidenced by his demands for large ensembles: fifty instrumentalists for Broadway and thirty-four when on the road (Gould, 240)—significantly reduced from a symphonic ensemble but enormous by today's standards. These ensembles were modeled on a classical sound:

> the strings massed and predominant; the woodwinds marshalled to speak their humors in choir; the brass discreetly in hand, awaiting a grand tutti; and behind, the simple percussion of tympani and drums, with glockenspiel and triangle for accent, the cymbal for exclamation point.[7]

In scoring for the stage, though, the orchestrator has to consider that a single principal instrument—the voice—demands dominance in the ensemble; Herbert's orchestration was carefully arranged to allow the voice to be heard, using sizable vocal choruses to aid the blend.

Herbert's vocal numbers show typical orchestration of the period: dominant strings supported by wind and brass for color (🔊 Example 7.1). This provides both space and balance for the vocal line: balance from well-blended instruments close in tone and timbre to the voice; space in the layout over several octaves of a chordal structure replicating the harmonic series and using extreme registers (violins at the top of their pitch) to leave room in the vocal register for the voice to carry (🎵 Example 7.2). Herbert's technique stems from traditional musical training—and he was certainly traditional, a musician from the nineteenth century who rebuffed the beginnings of jazz. Herbert's adherence to tradition underscores a persistent cultural tension—"a dual development to suit the tastes of a dual audience"—in the developing landscape of American popular music:

> Those who still dominated society by reason of wealth and prestige still demanded from their entertainment the eccentricities of the European model. . . . The new major players in American society, the new moneyed professionals, demanded a theater more to their own taste: the musical comedy. (Gould, 253)

Musical comedy of the period was typified by vaudevillian George M. Cohan, and the orchestration of his shows was strikingly different from Herbert's. Vaudeville instrumentation, known as "11 and piano," was more focused on brass, woodwind, and percussion, and very distant from the classical European sound (🎵 Example 7.3).

> The basic Broadway pit orchestra of the time consisted of two violins (for the melody), viola, cello (for tender countermelodies), bass, flute (skipping decoratively around the fiddles), clarinet, two cornets (brightly underlining repeats of the violin melody), trombone (swooping up and down), percussion and piano.[8]

It was the classic ragtime band, sometimes decried as "the commonplace rooty-toot of most musical comedy orchestras" with its "blaring brasses, so common in theatrical pits of the time."[9] The next few decades would pit these extremes—and their very different orchestras—in a battle for musical theater dominance.

THE BROADWAY SOUND

Ultimately the Broadway style developed a compromise between the European and vaudeville sounds. "It was the achievement of the [orchestrators] to take the operetta ensemble as Victor Herbert left it and the vaudeville band as George M. Cohan knew it, to weld them together and to make them over in a new image" (Beiswanger, 42). This new "American" music swiftly became "a combination of what was happening in jazz at the time and the basic orchestrational principles anybody who worked in Vienna would know."[10]

For economic reasons, the size of Herbert's orchestra had to be reduced, and orchestrators had to find ways of maintaining both the balance of instruments and the diversity of sounds that gave the score "color." Frank Saddler, "champion of small orchestras" (Bennett, 1999, 279), was the first recognized orchestrator (rather than composer) for Broadway and was Jerome Kern's collaborator for most of his early shows. He "used comparatively few musicians, and his work was contrapuntal and delicate, so that the sound emanating from the orchestra pit was very much in the nature of chamber music."[11] Saddler found ways to reduce the orchestra while still maintaining color, balance, and movement, merging instruments from the vaudeville pit—such as the piano—with a significant but reduced string section.[12] The piano could be used for rhythm, to replace the second violin and viola, or to release them to a lyrical countermelody (⬥ Example 7.4).

Saddler created a number of characteristic techniques, such as his adapted-piano devices, including the "mandolin and banjo attachment" ("a metal tackboard that approximates the sound of a harpsichord")[13] and the "newspaper mute" (a "dull 'thwacking' sound ... accomplished by laying a thick wad of newspaper over the strings"; McGlinn, 5). Saddler and Kern are also credited with the first appearance in the Broadway pit of saxophones—in *Oh, I Say!* (1913)—though Bordman concedes that "any pride Kern took in this progressive innovation was tempered by an eventual distaste for the abuses of jazz orchestras" (90). Saddler's setup became known as "Fifteen and Piano," though this arrangement did not represent just fifteen instruments, since strings usually had several on a part. Typically, he would use six violins (split conventionally in parts), two violas, two cellos, bass, flute, oboe, two clarinets, bassoon, two horns, two trumpets, trombone, and piano, harp, or drums, an orchestra of eighteen to twenty-four players,[14] with eighteen for the tiny 299-seat Princess Theatre (*Zip, Goes a Million!*; 1919), and twenty-six for *Have a Heart* (1917) at the larger Liberty Theatre (Bordman, 138). Bennett explains the arrangement:

> An arrangement of a song was: a loud introduction, a vamp (soft, with oompahs), a soft verse, a soft chorus (refrain) and a loud chorus made by repeating the same arrangement with the brass and drums added and the first violin up an octave. The first violin played the tune throughout, the second violin and the viola played after-beats (the pahs), the violoncello ... had some kind of sustained counter-melody or doubled the bass, who played the ooms. The flute and the two clarinets did "noodles," the oboe played the melody and the bassoon either played in unison with the cello or played ooms and sometimes oom-pahs. The horns were mostly concerned with pahs, but also might reinforce a cello counter-melody; the first trumpet played the melody (on the repeat), the second trumpet found thirds and sixths under the first and the trombone doubled the bass, helped the trumpets to make a triad, or played the tune an octave under the top

trumpet. The drums did oom-pahs and kept the whole thing from dying, just about as they do now.[15]

Saddler's effects "sparkled" (Bennett, 1999, 65), the main vocal melody and its accompaniment ornamented by instrumental "fills" ("noodles"). Take for example Kern's "Till the Clouds Roll By," from *Oh, Boy!* (1917; 🎵 Example 7.5). The short phrases of the vocal line combine long sustained notes ("rain"; "like") with lightly tripping faster motifs ("comes a"; "to be"), a feature of the entire song:

> Oh the rain comes a-pitter patter.
> And I'd like to be safe in bed... (McGlinn, 17)

Saddler exploits this in the chorus, filling in the sustained notes with two closely harmonized flutes playing extensions of the faster motif. Not only does this provide interesting instrumental "noodles," but it also provides a complementary rhythm to the pulse of the double bass "ooms," reminiscent of the pitter-patter of rain. The lower strings and horn provide a more lyrical, sustained counterpoint.

THE CLASSIC ORCHESTRATOR

As operetta waned and the Tin Pan Alley style came to dominate on Broadway, a corps of orchestrators, including Robert Russell Bennett, Hans Spialek, Don Walker, and Ted Royal, introduced important developments. Bennett was the first of these and the most prolific, orchestrating over 300 Broadway shows as well as film scores and TV series. In Banfield's words, "If Saddler was the man who gave Broadway its musical color, it was Bennett who sealed its musical glamour" (2006, 44). Bennett was a traditionalist and a self-confessed snob, traits that colored both the instrumentation and technique of his scores. His sound—featuring classical instrumentation rich in strings and harp—evoked classical Europe even as Broadway was developing its own sound. To him, Broadway was second-rate, and his cherished ambitions to conduct symphony orchestras, his acquaintanceships with Stravinsky and Rachmaninov, and his creditable classical compositions all reveal a serious musician who simply found his metier on Broadway. Bennett's work, however, represents the epitome of one characteristic style of Broadway orchestration (🅰 Example 7.6).

First, the vocal line is doubled by a melody instrument, reflecting a tendency toward softer vocals ("crooning"). Second, a countermelody (or "thumb-line," the middle line often played by composers on the piano with their thumbs) offers a chromatic counterpoint to the diatonic melody. Bennett is the master at this sort of counterpoint, and his work with Richard Rodgers benefits especially from chromatic resonances. Third, carefully spaced families of sounds (strings, winds, brass for effect) produce a rich harmonic balance. Finally, a combination of bass and off-beat "oom-pahs" provides the rhythm, typically from the harp or piano. But while these traits consolidated the conventions of the "classical" orchestration style, many of Bennett's colleagues were embracing the jazz sound, making Bennett's work begin to "sound surprisingly old-fashioned, and he admitted that he was slow in grasping the 'three trumpet sound' that began to revolutionise musicals with the advent of swing around 1930" (Banfield, 2006, 44).

This development reflected the "battle" (Beiswanger, 40) in the 1920s between two prominent aesthetics of the Broadway sound: the classical sound and the dance band sound. The battle was not just over aesthetics but also entailed an ideological contest between cultural discourses of value, race, and class. While the orchestra represented the accepted elegance of European culture, jazz band instrumentation represented a different and denigrated ethnicity, connotations of sexuality, questionable morals and—in an era of prohibition—the taboo of illicit entertainment. Where orchestras had been established as large ensembles with an acoustically balanced blending of instruments, the jazz band operated as a much smaller group of often competing individual sounds—cornet, trombone and clarinet, and a rhythm section of double bass, banjo and drums; sometimes a violin, later (around 1900) a piano, and later still (around 1920) saxophones (Beiswanger, 43).

Many of the songsmiths—often of immigrant stock and Jewish heritage—related to and embraced jazz (as they had ragtime twenty years earlier), not least George Gershwin, a pianist whose rhythms, cadences, and harmonies derived from composing on piano. The piano became even more prominent in the pit for shows such as *Lady Be Good* (1924), *Tip-Toes* (1925), *Oh, Kay!* (1926), and *Funny Face* (1927), which featured two pianos and two regular pianists, Victor Arden and Phil Ohman.

It was around this time—"beginning with such De Sylva, Brown and Henderson shows as *Good News* [1927] and *Hold Everything!* [1928]"—that the now enlarged jazz band "solidly entrenched itself in the pit" (Wind, 65; ◐ Example 7.7). It was well suited to the developing tendencies of songwriters, whose music was becoming increasingly syncopated and chromatically experimental. The principal difference between earlier pit instrumentation and this, "classed as either 'legitimate' or 'non-legitimate'" (Wind, 67), reflected the "choice of woodwind instruments. Operettas used the European light opera complement (flutes, oboe, clarinets, bassoon), whereas dance shows included saxophones, whose assertive tone had become an essential part of the jazz sound."[16] The dominance of three saxophones in the mid-low range and three trumpets on top provided a new punch. And even traditionalists adopted the sound: "It took Bennett a couple of shows to learn how to give the producers the crooning saxophone ensembles and three screaming trumpets, but after doing *Girl Crazy* [1930] he was on easy terms with the lick, rip and break" (Wind, 65; ◉ Example 7.8). By the mid-thirties (Gershwin's later shows, the classic Rodgers and Hart musicals), the sound of the dance band was established and expected, and prominent bands such as Paul Whiteman's were used as pit orchestras, with now-legendary names playing (Benny Goodman) and even co-orchestrating (Glenn Miller).[17]

THE GOLDEN AGE

While—or perhaps because—developments in orchestration largely settled down following these rapid changes, the postwar period is characterized by two predominant orchestrational styles.

The first aligns with the classic integrated musicals of Rodgers and Hammerstein and Bennett's typical orchestrations, using "traditional" orchestral groupings relying heavily on strings. *Carousel* (principally orchestrated by Don Walker) used an enormous thirty-nine-strong orchestra with twenty-two strings, which competes with the orchestras of Victor Herbert or even Berlioz's outline of an opera ensemble (◉ Example 7.9).[18] Given the option, many orchestrators preferred larger numbers, and recordings and concert performances have regularly inflated the number of strings: "When it comes to orchestration, there are never enough strings."[19] However, the predilection for a full orchestral sound is only in part aesthetic: it also assists the ideological claim to high-art status that the musical has always encouraged (alongside the terms "musical play" or "rock opera"). If musicals use classical or "legit" frameworks and terminology, they become increasingly valued artistically and culturally. Tellingly, a classical sound has also formed the basis for more recent megamusicals, from *Evita* (1978, Andrew Lloyd Webber and Hershy Kay) to *Miss Saigon* (1989, William D. Brohn).

The second style is best typified by Robert Ginzler and Sid Ramin's arrangement for *Gypsy* (1959), the "apotheosis of pit band instrumentation," voted by ASCAP the best ever orchestration for a Broadway musical (⏵ Example 7.10).[20] This stems directly from the dance band shows, and along with work by other orchestrators including Walker and Lang captures the quintessence of "Broadway's final era of razzmatazz, through an alchemy of songwriting, orchestration and voices, all of them long on brass."[21] This sound embraces the iconicity of Broadway, incorporating brash performances of stars like Ethel Merman: "that uniquely throat-catching, hair-raising Broadway sound" (Gottfried, 5).

THE MICROPHONE ERA

The introduction of microphone technology (as early as 1937)[22] redefined the acoustic limitations of instruments and voices. Balance had always been a key element of orchestration, and the orchestra had been a brilliant tool for both fortissimo climaxes and sensitive underscoring beneath which dialogue could be heard—"perhaps the most difficult mechanical problem in the business" (Bennett, 1999, 281). But the jazz band's solo instruments threatened to compete with singers in timbre, tone, and volume, and partly in response to this, producers began amplifying both vocals and instruments.

While this offered many benefits, the reconfiguration of sound that the technology introduced disrupted the balance, "the natural color" that reflects "the art of orchestrating" (Pareles, 4): "a solo, muted violin can be made to drown out a full orchestra" (Bennett, 1999, 290). Techniques developed to accommodate this balance had in part defined the Broadway sound: "Stylish singers with small voices like Fred Astaire thrived on Broadway . . . because composers wrote songs suited to his style of delivery and kept orchestrations light."[23] The "noodles" interject *between* vocals specifically so that singers are not drowned out; likewise, orchestrators traditionally doubled the vocal line to support the melody.

Thus, amplification has been blamed for "unbalancing the score": "subtlety is impossible to achieve. The sound is smoothed out, bigger than life, with hardly any dynamics. Everything seems to be at that same mezzo-forte to fortissimo level" (Schonberg, 1); "the louder the orchestra gets, the louder we have to make the singers to ride over the orchestra."[24] Moreover, "inadequate sound design [sometimes] drowned out dialogue and lyrics, leaving audiences confused and frustrated."[25] Since Broadway embraced "rock" orchestration, however, rejecting amplification has not really been practical. Many instruments rely on it, and the mix of acoustic voice against amplified instruments becomes problematic.

ROCK AND THE MEGAMUSICAL

The "rock musical" initiated a trend toward a completely different pit setup, related to the rock band (guitar, bass, drums, keyboard). Surprisingly, shows relying purely on this orchestration or derivations of it have subsequently been relatively rare after the first few (*Hair*, 1967; *Godspell*, 1971; *Grease*, 1972; *The Rocky Horror Show*, 1973). Even classic "rock musicals" have more conventional instrumentation; *The Wiz* (1975) includes harp, woodwind, strings, and brass. On the other hand, the use of rock instruments within a more conventional pit orchestra, as in *Jesus Christ Superstar* (1971), has become common, creating the idiomatic sound of the "megamusical."

The megamusical, then, offers not only more sophisticated sound than its predecessors, but also a more thorough blend of popular music and traditional theatre fare. Whereas rock musicals often feature raw, amplified voices backed by electric instrumentation throughout, rock's direct influence on megamusicals tends to be comparatively tame: an occasional guitar riff, the occasional use of twelve-bar blues form; an electric guitar, keyboard, or bass guitar intermingled with an otherwise standard pit orchestra; the occasional use of vocal techniques that might be heard on FM radio, amid songs otherwise performed by conservatory-trained vocalists. (Wollman, 128)

SYNTHESIZING THE ORCHESTRA

Yet megamusicals have caused no little controversy, largely through scaling down the number of "live" instruments in favor of synthesized sounds. In fact, the use of synthesizers for some shows was part of the original conception: *Phantom of the Opera* (1987) used two synthesizers in David Cullen and Andrew Lloyd Webber's original orchestra of twenty-seven players, partly for the show's crucial pipe organ sound, partly for specialist sound effects such as "glassy lake," and partly to augment other instruments, particularly the strings.[26] In this decision, the economic restraints of even the most lavish shows are revealed, as in the standard Broadway practice of reducing the size of the orchestra after six weeks, once the "full" orchestration of a show is established. While some revivals enjoy the luxury of a return to original orchestrations, such as those of New York's City Center *Encores!* series, many establish new, often reduced orchestrations, using synthesizers. *Sweeney Todd*'s orchestra (1979, Jonathan Tunick) was reduced from twenty-six players to nine for the 1994 Royal National Theatre production (synthesizer, violin, cello, double bass, trumpet, horn, clarinet, bassoon, and percussion).

Although the synthesizer is often used simply to provide a thick string texture otherwise requiring several individual players, it is just one of the "new" instruments that has also developed its own aesthetic:

> The synthesizer is a wonderful tool. Because it can imitate other instruments, the biggest mistake that people make is to use it as an economic means to eliminate instruments. It's fine to use it sparingly to beef up a small orchestra. An ersatz trumpet can be fun. But you have to remember that it has its own personality, and if you write for it as if it's a real trumpet, you're going to get a very tinny, unsatisfying sound. (Winer, 5)

Assassins orchestrator Michael Starobin used the synthesizer as part of the orchestration process: "Starobin, playing the synthesizer, was able with his increasing familiarity with the score to add layers of color (now fixed as an orchestral score on the cast recording)."[27] Banfield suggests that this approach to orchestration may have led to some of *Assassins*' characteristic aesthetic. This is unusual, however, in an idiom that celebrates authenticity. As Maury Yeston puts it, "Musicians have been virtual Luddites at the inception of any electronic simulation of sounds, beginning with electronic pianos" (Yeston, 25).

THE UNIONS

One influence on orchestration has been the Musicians' Union, whose agreements with the League of Broadway Producers stipulate that if live musicians were to be used at all for a theatrical performance, there would be a minimum number set for each theater, proportional to its seating capacity. The precise agreements have changed over the years, but as an example, "twenty-five was the legal minimum for the Shubert in 1973," when Sondheim's *A Little Night Music* was produced. Tunick's orchestrations for the show were therefore destined to be scored for twenty-five players, particularly since the "minimum . . . becomes effectively the maximum" (Banfield 1993, 82). As this highlights, the makeup of the sound is often a compromise between the producer's budget and Musicians' Union regulations, rather than compositional or orchestrational design. As Yeston asserts, "It is sometimes possible, and stylistically appropriate, to accompany Broadway shows with smaller ensembles." Bizarrely, on shows requiring fewer players than the stipulated number, sometimes "nonplaying 'walkers' [are] paid to meet the minimums" (Yeston, 25). More regularly, numbers are reduced when shows play at touring venues with lower minimums, compromising the orchestrator's original work and the "authentic" sound of the show.

One entrenched practice has been to "double" playing responsibilities, particularly among wind players, "a virtuoso speciality not just on the part of the players but for the orchestrator as well" (Banfield, 1993, 85). Doubling arrangements were often written with specific players in mind whose combination of instruments was known; while this expands the possible variety of sounds in the score, particular combinations will inevitably remain impossible if played by the same instrumentalist, since the orchestrator must leave breaks in the score for players to change instruments.

"VIRTUAL ORCHESTRA MACHINES"

More recently still, technology has developed the virtual orchestra, an artificial replacement for live musicians. "Played" from a computer, the machines replicate not just the notes and sound of the instrument(s), but also follow the phrasing, dynamic, and tempo indications of the live conductor. While the Musicians' Union has claimed that this will threaten jobs, manufacturers and producers insist on the reverse: "The show probably wouldn't have toured at all had it been required to maintain the full complement." Indeed, they point out that the software itself is operated "by a live musician."[28]

Perhaps the most compelling argument for the use of such technology is in amateur and school productions of the classic large-ensemble shows, many of which have neither the skill-base nor budget to provide full orchestration. As a supplement to existing musicians, "virtual orchestra machines" at least introduce regional audiences to the true orchestral sound of the Broadway shows. Musicians must trust that the wave of new technology will, in the hands of artists, enhance artistry. There can, and must be, a compromise—one that preserves the large live Broadway ensemble when appropriate (and, essentially, the minimums) but also gives smaller shows the flexibility to make the most of virtual enhancements (Yeston, 25).

NEW AESTHETICS

The notion of the "authentic" in theater orchestration, though, is only a recent phenomenon; historically, the score was updated as shows were revived. Thus, Richard Rodgers assigned Don Walker to reorchestrate both *On Your Toes* and *Pal Joey* for revivals in the 1950s to give the shows a more contemporary feel; when Hans Spialek was called out of retirement to oversee *On Your Toes* in its 1983 revival, the original orchestrations began to be considered integral to the show (🔊 Example 7.11; 🔊 Example 7.12). Subsequently, particularly after the 1987 discovery of hundreds of authentic scores in a Secaucus warehouse,[29] the practice of reviving original, full orchestrations became common: the work of John McGlinn (particularly his 1988 *Show Boat* recording) is especially notable.

Yet the reorchestration of a show need not just be a response to production costs: director John Doyle and musical director Sarah Travis specialize in reconceiving classic shows as actor-musician shows, in which onstage performers provide not only the vocal but also the instrumental performances. Although originally an economic necessity, the reorchestrations required by this have created an aesthetic recognized for "knitting more closely together musical values and narrative shape."[30] Doyle's production of *Sweeney Todd* was particularly effective, and won a Tony award for its orchestration (⬤ Example 7.13; ⬤ Example 7.14).

Tunick's original orchestration of *Sweeney Todd* used twenty-six players in the classical style and has been recognized for its skill in creating "psychological and harmonic complexity." "String harmonics, woodwinds scored in the extreme upper and lower registers, and a whole spectrum of unusual brass sounds are an integral part of the score . . . the instrumentation is as much an identifying factor as the tunes themselves" (Parrent, 35). Yet Sarah Travis's adaptation of the orchestration for just ten versatile instrumentalists gives the show a Grand Guignol, chamber effect whose "sound tilts the production from blockbuster musical towards cabaret."[31] The shift in the audience's experience of this rescoring is palpable, as Sondheim observes:

> The variety of sounds [Travis] has gotten out of the instruments and also the practical way in which they allow [Doyle] to work with the performers onstage is extraordinary. But what got me most about the orchestrations is what they did for the play's atmosphere. These are wonderfully weird textures. The sound of an accordion playing with a violin—it's very creepy. . . . What you gain is a swiftness and intensity that draws the audience into this macabre world, and that is created by a unified ensemble

working in one tone. Here it's as if the audience is drawn into a tunnel. (Quoted in Isherwood, 1)

Actor-musicianship not only works in terms of aurality; it makes visible both the instruments and the physical bodies of the instrumentalists, elements conventionally marginalized from the dramatic space. "What is normally latent, unconsciously symbolic, [becomes] manifest, and a whole new dimension of interaction in music theatre [opens] up" (Banfield, 1993, 85). The music and its orchestration become voiced by characters, part of their expression and integral rather than just an accompaniment to the drama: "Because the performers are the musicians, they possess total control of those watching them in a way seldom afforded actors in musicals. They own the story they tell, and their instruments become narrative tools."[32] Elsewhere this has led to musical theater work wholly conceived for the aesthetic of actor-musicianship.[33]

Of course, there are practicalities involved in the negotiation between score and staging: "If, for instance, the score calls for a tuba (played by [Mrs. Lovett]), to complete a bass harmony, and Mrs. Lovett finds herself embroiled in a dramatic scene, an alternate [sic] musical solution must be found."[34] Similarly, a change of cast may involve changes in orchestration, even if the instrumentation remains consistent. Thus, the Watermill's original Mrs. Lovett, Karen Mann, played trumpet, while Patti LuPone in New York played tuba. As Doyle remarks,

> When the orchestration changes, the physical use of the stage changes as well, because if you're moving a violin around, it's different from moving a flute around, and you have to put it down in different places and use it in different ways, which inevitably means that the whole jigsaw puzzle changes.[35]

COPYRIGHT

Although *Sweeney Todd* is a Sondheim musical, the musical aesthetic of Doyle's production can be attributed to his work with Travis, just as the sound of the original Broadway show can be attributed to Tunick. As is clear, the sort of collaborative and interpretive arrangements that exist between composers and orchestrators complicate the notion of ownership; the orchestration often "creates a sound and feel with which the show will always be associated,"[36] and in this respect, issues of copyright arise.

While certain preemptive contractual arrangements have been made among producers, composers, and orchestrators, Joel Friedman notes a "measure of confusion" regarding this legal arrangement.[37] Some suggest that orchestrators are simply commissioned by composers or producers to fulfill a prescriptive task and that their orchestrations thus constitute "work made for hire," whereby "the employer or other person for whom the work was prepared is considered the author [and] owns all of the rights comprised in the copyright."[38] A second argument explicitly refers to "musical arrangements" in a category alongside translations, dramatizations, and so on, claiming that the work has a degree of originality and is therefore part-copyrightable to the orchestrator but is a "derivative work," one "based upon one or more preexisting works."[39] The counterargument, claiming full recognition for the authorial rights of the orchestrator, labels the whole score a "joint work of authorship":

> Unlike a translation, a movie adaptation of a book, or a musical arrangement of an existing piece of music, an orchestration is not intended to take an already complete underlying work and re-release it under a new form. Rather, the orchestration is meant to be a part of the entirety of the production as intended by the authors. A Broadway musical is not finished or ready

for production until the orchestrations have been completed. (Perkins, 495)

The issue of copyright also affects subsequent arrangements of theater music, traditionally by dance bands—indeed, Jerome Kern prohibited any of the material from his 1924 show *Sitting Pretty* from being "distorted" in this way (Bordman, 249)—but nowadays by electronic sequencing and sampling. In some senses, the increasing use of existing musical material by other creative practitioners has highlighted the issue, and therefore copyright protection for composers is relatively secure. The rights of the orchestrator, however, remain an issue largely unaddressed:

> It is obvious that the official composer of a show produces only a small, though let us say, decisive part of the sounds an audience hears at a musical show. To this man alone go the sometimes fabulous rewards from a smash hit. . . . His associate composers, often protected by unions, collect their adequate fees even if the show fails; but if it clicks, they get nothing more. . . . The music staff's sole extra benefit accruing from helping to make a roaring theatrical success is the honor of being connected with it. [40]

Undoubtedly, the association of any collaborator with a major success will in part recompense the hard work and precise technique that has contributed to it. At last orchestrators are beginning to receive the recognition they deserve for their crucial role in creating the iconicity of the Broadway sound.

NOTES

1. Laurie Winer, "Theater; Orchestrators Are Tired of Playing Second Fiddle" (*New York Times* [July 29, 1990]: 2–5, citing Jonathan Tunick.
2. Recently, however, this topic has received increasing scholarly attention, most notably in "The Sound of Broadway Music: A Symposium on Orchestrators and Orchestrations" (Library of Congress, May 6–7, 2009) and the publication of a comprehensive new book by Steven Suskin, *The Sound of Broadway Music: A Book of Orchestrators and Orchestrations* (New York: Oxford University Press, 2009).
3. Robert Russell Bennett, *"The Broadway Sound": The Autobiography and Selected Essays of Robert Russell Bennett*, ed. George J. Ferencz (Rochester, NY: University of Rochester Press, 1999), p. 293.
4. Don Walker, "Music Goes 'Round: A Gentleman Who Arranges Theatre Tunes Tells How He Works," (*New York Times* [April 12, 1942]: X–1).
5. Joseph Kaye, *Victor Herbert: The Biography of America's Greatest Composer of Romantic Music* (New York: Crown, 2007), p. 7.
6. Neil Gould, *Victor Herbert: A Theatrical Life* (New York: Fordham University Press, 2008), p. 162.
7. George Beiswanger, "After Victor Herbert: The Battle of the Orchestras" (*Theatre Arts* 28.1 [January 1944]: 40–45), p. 40.
8. Barrymore Laurence Scherer, "Benjamin's Ragtime Band Captures the Real Cohan" (*Wall Street Journal* [July 2, 2008]: D-7).
9. Gerald Bordman, *Jerome Kern: His Life and Music* (New York: Oxford University Press, 1980), pp. 211 and 138.
10. John Pareles, "What Is the Sound of Broadway? Hans Spialek Knows" (*New York Times* [April 17, 1983]: 2–4).
11. Richard Rodgers, *Musical Stages: An Autobiography* (New York: Da Capo Press, 2002), p. 20.
12. Stephen Banfield, *Jerome Kern* (New Haven, CT: Yale University Press, 2006), p. 43.
13. See Bordman, 140, and John McGlinn, "Foreword" (Sleeve Notes), *Jerome Kern Treasury*, (Angel D 101,715, 1993), p. 5.

14 Herbert Warren Wind, "Profiles: Another Opening, Another Show" (*New Yorker* [November 17, 1951]: 46–71), p. 67.
15 Robert Russell Bennett, *Instrumentally Speaking* (Melville, NY: Belwin Mills, 1975), pp. 8–9.
16 Jon Alan Conrad, "Let the Drums Roll Out" (Sleeve Notes), *Strike Up the Band* (Elektra Nonesuch 7559-79, 273-2, 1991), p. 44.
17 See Joan Peyser, *The Memory of All That: The Life of George Gershwin* (New York: Billboard Books, 1998), pp. 170–73.
18 Hector Berlioz, *Berlioz's Orchestration Treatise: A Translation and Commentary*, trans. Hugh MacDonald (New York: Cambridge University Press, 2002), p. 321.
19 Maury Yeston, "The Lullaby of Broadway" (*New York Times* [February 28, 2003]: A-25). On recordings, see Amy Parrent, "From 'The Beggar's Opera' to 'Sweeney Todd': The Art of the Broadway Orchestrator" (*Music Educator's Journal* 66:9 [May 1980]: 32–35). On concert performances, see Stephen Holden, "Make It Proud and Loud, with Strings" (*New York Times* [May 22, 2008]: E-7).
20 Martin Gottfried, "Sleeve Notes," *Gypsy: A Musical Fable* (Original Broadway Cast Recording, Sony Classical/Columbia/Legacy SMK 60,848, 1999), p. 6.
21 Frank Rich, "Catching That Fading Sound of Razzmatazz" (*New York Times* [October 10, 1993]: 2–34).
22 According to Harold C. Schonberg, "Stage View: The Surrender of Broadway to Amplified Sound" (*New York Times* [March 15, 1981]: 2–1).
23 Anthony Tomassini, "Pipe Down! We Can Hardly Hear You" (*New York Times* [January 1, 2006]: 2–1).
24 Otts Munderloh, sound engineer for *A Chorus Line*, quoted in Schonberg, 1.
25 Elizabeth Wollman, *The Theater Will Rock* (Ann Arbor: University of Michigan Press, 2006), p. 203.
26 John Snelson, *Andrew Lloyd Webber* (New Haven, CT: Yale University Press, 2004), pp. 103 and 89.
27 Stephen Banfield, *Sondheim's Broadway Musicals* (Ann Arbor: University of Michigan Press, 1993), p. 84.
28 Jesse Green, "Theater's Alive with the Sound of Laptops" (*New York Times* [March 25, 2007]: 2–1).

29 Tim Page, "Broadway Song Trove Tops Original Hopes" (*New York Times* [March 10, 1987]: A-1).
30 Charles Isherwood, "Cutting 'Sweeney Todd' to the Bone" (*New York Times* [October 30, 2005]: 2–1).
31 Stephen Leigh Morris, "John Doyle's *Sweeney Todd*; Who's Your Barber?" (*LA Weekly*, March 17, 2008, http://www.laweekly.com/2008-03-20/stage/major-barber, accessed July 10, 2009).
32 Ben Brantley, "Grand Guignol, Spare and Stark" (*New York Times* [November 4, 2005]: E1–1).
33 See my discussion in "The Corporeality of Musical Expression: 'The Grain of the Voice' and the Actor-Musician" (*Studies in Musical Theatre* 1:2 [2007]: 167–81).
34 Anon, "John Doyle's Production of *Sweeney Todd* to Open A.C.T.'s 41st Season" (American Conservatory Theater, August 5, 2007, http://www.act-sf.org/site/News2?page=NewsArticle&id=5205&news_iv_ctrl=-1, accessed July 23, 2008).
35 In Robert Simonson, "John Doyle's Malicious Musicians: A Chat with the Director" (*New York Sun* [October 31, 2005]: Arts & Letters, 10).
36 Patrick T. Perkins, "'Hey! What's the Score?' Copyright in the Orchestrations of Broadway Musicals" (*Columbia-VLA Journal of Law and the Arts* 16 [1991]: 475–503), p. 494.
37 Joel L. Friedman, "Copyright and the Musical Arrangement: An Analysis of the Law and Problems Pertaining to This Specialized Form of Derivative Work" (*Pepperdine Law Review* 7 [1979]: 125–46), pp. 145–46.
38 17 U.S.C. 101, 201(b) (1988), see Perkins, 481.
39 17 U.S.C. 101 (1988), see Perkins, 493n.
40 Don Walker, "Who Says 'Arranger'?" (*Theatre Arts* 34:11 [November 1950]: 53–54), p. 54.

8

Musical Theater Directors

BARBARA WALLACE GROSSMAN

■ □ ■

In the end, practically and artistically, there can be only one voice to call the shots: the voice of the commander-in-chief. That is the voice of the director.[1]

IT IS NOT UNTIL ALMOST halfway through Michael Kantor's six-part documentary, *Broadway: The American Musical* (2004) that the word "director" appears in the spoken narrative. The first two episodes of the series, covering 1893–1933, present a cavalcade of performers, composers, lyricists, librettists, and producers but do not mention any directors. Even that one-man theatrical conglomerate George M. Cohan (1878–1942) is introduced as a playwright, songwriter, and star who "helped define the Great White Way in a series of shows over forty years," not as someone who also directed many of them. Near the end of Episode Three: "I Got Plenty of Nuttin'" (1929–1942), viewers hear a snippet from John Mason Brown's *New York Evening Post* review of the premiere of *Porgy and Bess* (1935):

> It is a Russian who has directed it, two Southerners who have written its book, two Jewish boys who composed its lyrics and music, and a stage full of Negroes who sing and act it to perfection. The result is one of the far-famed wonders of the melting pot: the most American opera that has yet been seen or heard.

Excepting this oblique reference to director Rouben Mamoulian, however, directors remain tangential until the start of Episode Five: "Tradition" (1957–1979), which states emphatically, "A new generation of creative talent re-imagined what the musical could do. Songwriters like Stephen Sondheim, Jerry Bock and Sheldon Harnick, John Kander and Fred Ebb, along with directors Hal Prince, Bob Fosse, and Michael Bennett created astonishing new work, new sounds, and a bold new tradition for Broadway."[2]

Though perhaps startling in an era when the primacy of directors is indisputable, their invisibility in the first part of Kantor's series accurately reflects their status—but not their actual importance—in the early twentieth century. According to Stephen Citron, directors were simply "hirelings, allowed very little creative input. Their productions were not much more than packages. Even the most successful directors' names are forgotten, and the shows they pied-pipered, if recalled at all, are only remembered for their composers and producers. . . . Directors were not much more than glorified stage managers."[3] That dismissive comment fails to acknowledge the contributions of such prolific talents as Julian Mitchell (1854–1926) and Ned Wayburn (1874–1942), both director-choreographers in these formative decades, although that term was probably not applied to them during their lifetime. Mitchell directed more than eighty musicals including *A Trip to Chinatown* (with Charles H. Hoyt, 1891), *The Fortune Teller* (1898), *The Wizard of Oz* and *Babes in Toyland* (1903), and several editions of the *Ziegfeld Follies* beginning with the first, the *Follies of 1907*, which he choreographed. Wayburn, too, was part of Ziegfeld's stable for several years and directed seven *Follies*—among them the *Ziegfeld Follies of 1916*, which gave Fanny Brice two of her most memorable numbers, "Nijinsky" and "Becky's Back in the Ballet"—as well as other productions including *Star and Garter* (1900), *Mother Goose* (1903), *Tillie's Nightmare* (1910), *The Passing Show of 1912* and

1913, *The Honeymoon Express* (1913), and *Hitchy-Koo* (1920).[4] Nevertheless, it is easy to lose sight of the accomplishments of these early directors because their work, if it received program credit at all, was usually not called directing but was described by a variety of other terms instead: "staged by," "conceived by," "devised by," "supervised by," "musical staging by," "dances and musical numbers staged by," "play staged by," "book staged by," and "dialogue staged by."

The rise of the director as a central artistic figure dates from the nineteenth century, but the emergence of the director as the most powerful member of a musical's creative team, whose vision shapes an entire production and whose authority delivers it, is more recent. This has to do, in large part, with significant changes in the form and content of musicals themselves. It would be a mistake, however, to underestimate the quality of early twentieth-century productions, or to privilege the integrated "book" musical over other forms such as the revue, since, as Bruce Kirle has argued, the collaborative process through which musicals are created precludes the ultimate authority of the text.[5] Nevertheless, an accepted paradigm is that the book was the least important element in musicals before World War II. Whether revue, musical comedy, or operetta, the emphasis was on showcasing stars and offering audiences lively, upbeat, romantic and/or sexually titillating entertainment. With some noteworthy exceptions—including *Show Boat* (1927), *Of Thee I Sing* (1931), *Porgy and Bess* (1935), *Pal Joey* (1940), and *Lady in the Dark* (1941)—books, in Harold Prince's words, "were there to string together really terrific scores."[6] Scripts were considered of far less value than the songs they supported or the talent they featured, so that authentic texts rarely survived from production to production.

The partnership of Richard Rodgers (1902–79) and Oscar Hammerstein II (1895–1960) marked a critical moment in the musical's development. Determined to make musical theater a more serious art form, Rodgers and Hammerstein placed new emphasis on a well-crafted book as the basis for a unified, artistic whole. Beginning with *Oklahoma!* (1943) and continuing through *The Sound of Music* (1959), the story became preeminent in their productions. "From that point on," critic John Lahr asserts, writers provided a show's "creative drive."[7] Writers alone, however, cannot take a work from page to stage, ensuring that it will have maximal audience impact. Telling a story effectively, shaping it into a show with coherent structure, focus, and rhythm, is the director's responsibility. Not surprisingly, given the importance of the book—and hence the director—to Rodgers and Hammerstein, the first person to garner a Tony Award for directing a musical was Joshua Logan (1908–88) for their *South Pacific* (1949), which was named best musical in 1950 and won the Pulitzer Prize for Drama as well.[8] A "writer-director," Logan also shared the Tony award for "Authors (Musical)" with Hammerstein, while Rodgers was recognized as best composer.

The Tony Awards were presented for the first time in 1947 (which is one reason the names of earlier theater artists are so elusive), but a separate category for musical theater direction was not established until 1960. In that year, George Abbott (1887–1995) won it for *Fiorello!*, which he had co-written with Jerome Weidman; he received the prize again for *A Funny Thing Happened on the Way to the Forum* in 1963.[9] After "generations and generations of experience," lyricist Sheldon Harnick explained, this legendary director "was still in his prime" (Rosenberg and Harburg, 243). Known for his disciplined, forthright, pragmatic approach to directing as well as his versatility, "Mr. Abbott" was active as a director, producer, writer, "play doctor," and occasional choreographer for more than seven decades. He specialized in sprightly musical comedies including *The Boys from Syracuse* (1938, writer, director, and producer), *Pal Joey* (1940, director and producer), *On the Town*

(1944), *High Button Shoes* (1947), *Where's Charley?* (1948, writer and director), *A Tree Grows in Brooklyn* (1951, co-writer with Betty Smith, director, and producer), *Wonderful Town* (1953), *The Pajama Game* (1954, co-writer with Richard Pike Bissell, co-director with Jerome Robbins), *Damn Yankees* (1955, co-writer with Douglass Wallop and director), *New Girl in Town* (1957, writer and director), and *How Now, Dow Jones* (1967). Yet his work defies easy categorization. According to director Arthur Masella, Abbott "was in his heyday as great as he was because he was a man who developed. If you look at what he did over his life as a director, you get the sense that he started in this genre, then he moved on to that. He was *constantly changing*" (Rosenberg and Harburg, 104).

Although the eclectic variety of his productions and the longevity of his career make it difficult to describe an Abbott "style," he was a formative influence on subsequent directors, including Harold Prince (b. 1928). In reflecting on his own distinguished career, Prince acknowledged his profound debt to the two men he considered his mentors: Abbott, for whom he began working in 1948 and to whom he remained close for nearly fifty years, and director-choreographer Jerome Robbins (1918–98). As co-producer of *West Side Story* (1957) and producer of *Fiddler on the Roof* (1964), both of which Robbins directed and choreographed, Prince had ample opportunity to watch Robbins work. According to scholar Miranda Lundskaer-Nielsen, "Trained as a ballet dancer, ... Robbins ... introduced Prince to the idea of a unified production vocabulary and to a more fluid use of the stage, ... [as well as to] the effectiveness of improvisation and empathy techniques—elements of 'the method' that he had learned under Lee Strasberg at the Actors Studio."[10]

Dance had always been an essential part of musicals but emerged as a key element in dramatic storytelling with the work of Agnes de Mille (1905–93), who brought ballet to Rodgers and Hammerstein's *Oklahoma!* and *Carousel*

(1945). Notwithstanding the importance of her contributions as choreographer for these shows, however, Rouben Mamoulian (1897–1987) was their director. It was not until Robbins that the director-choreographer became a powerful force in the creation of new work once again. As critic Frank Rich explained, "Jerome Robbins was the prime example of the idea that someone could direct and choreograph a Broadway musical, that they weren't two separate jobs, but the whole thing could move as one.... Other people like Agnes de Mille had done it before him, [but] he took the *Oklahoma!* dream ballet and applied it to the whole piece." According to Arthur Laurents (1917–2011), "When the director of a musical is also the choreographer, his power is absolute; the show is totally in his hands. Or so it would seem if the hands belonged to Jerome Robbins."[11]

In *Bells Are Ringing* (1956, co-choreographed with Bob Fosse), *West Side Story* (which he also is credited with conceiving), *Gypsy* (1959), and *Fiddler on the Roof,* Robbins was integral to shaping and staging all aspects of the production. In Lundskaer-Nielsen's view, he and other director-choreographers in the 1950s, '60s, and '70s—most notably Gower Champion, Bob Fosse, and Michael Bennett—"helped to raise the status of the director in the creative process" and secured the director's preeminent position in the creative team.[12] Each had begun his career as a dancer and had worked his way up through the production hierarchy, graduating from the chorus line to featured dancer, dance captain, assistant or associate choreographer, choreographer, and finally choreographer-director. As Citron notes, "some of them eventually even bypassed the official production system and went directly to record companies for financing of their projects [so that] it became Michael Bennett's *A Chorus* Line or Bob Fosse's *Dancin'* and, assuring his name as part of the logo and title, *Jerome Robbins' Broadway*" (Citron, 86). However idiosyncratic or autocratic their methods may have been, their ability to express a cohesive vision through dance and to make movement of paramount importance in conceptualizing and realizing a production had a transformational impact on musical theater.

The controversial Robbins, known as much for his reputedly tyrannical rehearsal techniques and his testimony as a "friendly" witness before the House Un-American Activities Committee (May 1953) as for his directorial brilliance, made his Broadway debut with *On the Town* (1944), a musical he conceived and choreographed.[13] Inspired in part by his ballet *Fancy Free* (1944), his collaborators were composer Leonard Bernstein, bookwriter-lyricists Betty Comden and Adolph Green, and set designer Oliver Smith. After choreographing *Billion Dollar Baby* (1945)—a show in which the company supposedly disliked him so much that no one stopped him during a rehearsal as he fell backward into the orchestra pit (Lawrence, 101)—Robbins won his first Tony Award three years later for choreographing *High Button Shoes* (1947).

Alternating between the dance and theater worlds for the next two decades, his accomplishments in the 1950s included choreographing dance sequences for *The King and I* (1951), collaborating with George Abbott on *The Pajama Game*, and creating *West Side Story* with Leonard Bernstein (music and uncredited lyrics), Stephen Sondheim (lyrics), and Arthur Laurents (book). Although *West Side Story* lost to Meredith Willson's *The Music Man* in almost every category at the 1959 Tony Awards, Robbins won his second for choreography. Along with Bernstein's brilliant score, Robbins' choreography remains the most memorable part of that production. According to Harold Prince, who co-produced *West Side Story* with Robert Griffith, "Robbins' choreography is authorship in that show. I don't think all choreography is, but certainly Robbins' was in [*West Side Story*]. The marriage of dance movement and storytelling was new to the theater."[14] Beyond that, the show was noteworthy for another reason. In Laurents' words: "Many said *West Side* forever changed the American musical . . . because of its use of dance and music. To me, it used those elements better than they had ever been used before; but what it really changed, what its real contribution to American musical theater was, was that it showed that any subject—murder, attempted rape, bigotry—could be the subject of a popular musical" (Laurents, 145).

Notorious for his dictatorial methods in directing *West Side Story,* which included keeping cast members playing Jets and Sharks apart and mutually distrustful during rehearsals, Robbins deserves recognition for his innovative approach to his dancer-actors. Chita Rivera (Anita in the original stage production) recalled his "genius" in an interview decades later:

> Jerry... really challenged you. If he told me to jump off a building and land on my left foot, I knew it was possible if I did what he told me to do. We used to sit on the steps of the 52nd Street Theatre and talk about my character in colors and textures. Dancers weren't used to this kind of delving. He made us go back into our own histories and make up stories that belonged to us and to the show. Yes, it was tense at times, but it was also amazingly exciting and you felt yourself grow. Suddenly dancers weren't just physical. They were thinking. They were using their own minds. A lot of us came out of that as better actors, better dancers, using ourselves so much more. [15]

Her comments convey a sense of Robbins in rehearsal, with the absolute authority he established and the total control he exerted seen as positive factors in the creative process rather than as inhibiting negatives. Like any director, he understood that he could realize his vision only if he succeeded in embedding his ideas in his actors' bodies. However autocratic he may have been, his reliance on fear as a motivational technique notwithstanding, he empowered many of the performers with whom he worked.

Fiercely protective of his creations, Robbins ensured that his choreography was contractually regarded as part of *Fiddler on the Roof*, for which he won twin Tonys in 1965. (His fifth and last came in 1989 for directing *Jerome Robbins' Broadway*.) For years after his death, his choreographic stranglehold kept directors from reinterpreting the dance sequences, as was the case with David Leveaux's 2004 Broadway revival of *Fiddler*. Denied permission to remove Robbins' choreography, he was forced to recreate it within an otherwise reimagined production. In Leveaux's words, "If he was here, he would be completely ruthlessly redoing and reediting his own work. That's hard for people whose job is to protect his legacy to understand" (Lundskaer-Nielsen, 168). Yet Hofesh Shechter, choreographer for the 2015 Broadway revival directed by Bartlett Sher, seems to have had more latitude. Although he based his work on Robbins' "original conception," he said he felt free "to do something new and . . . did."[16] In 2009, on the other hand, Arthur Laurents' reconceived Broadway production of *West Side Story* featured Robbins' choreography faithfully "reproduced" by Joey McKneely. According to McKneely, "If you remove Jerome Robbins' choreography, you lose significant plot, storytelling moments, and you lose characterization elements that are set in the dance. . . . It's rare that shows have dance as that kind of signature. It's the emotional glue."[17]

As revolutionary a figure as Robbins was, he was not the first person to garner Tony Awards for directing and choreographing the same show. That honor belongs to Gower Champion (1919–80) who won for his work on *Bye Bye Birdie* in 1961. He received that dual recognition twice more, for *Hello, Dolly!* in 1964 and *The Happy Time* in 1968, and was honored posthumously with his eighth Tony as choreographer for *42nd Street* in 1981. Of the major director-choreographers, his particular talent seems the most elusive. Known for bringing a seamless flow to stage musicals, he once said that what he sought in a show was "a constant overall tone . . . We pretty much did it in 'Dolly,'" he noted. "Yes, that kind of precision about time, place, people." His exuberant choreography and skillful direction ably served the shows they enlivened, but did not aggressively scream "Champion."[18]

In that respect his polar opposite is Robert Louis "Bob" Fosse (1927–87) whose now much imitated style is immediately recognizable and remains more distinctive than some of the shows it animated. "When you see his work, you know immediately it's Fosse, like when you see a Picasso," Graciela Daniele explained.[19] Heavily rhythmic music appealed to this award-winning director-choreographer and suited his jazzy idiom, characterized by its intense yet sophisticated sexuality and accentuated by the suggestive use of bowler hats, gloves, and canes. The slinky shuffling of leggy dancers with turned-in toes, thrusting pelvises, and curved, lowered shoulders, sitting seductively astride chairs or locked in erotic couplings is all "Fosse" and infused productions from *The Pajama Game* (1954) to *Chicago* (1975) to *Big Deal* (1986) with a pulsing energy. *The Pajama Game* brought him his first Tony for choreography, followed by five more: *Damn Yankees, Redhead, Sweet Charity, Dancin'*, and *Big Deal*. Rewarded with Tonys for both directing and choreographing *Pippin* (which he also essentially rewrote) in 1973, he became the first person to win Tony, Academy, and Emmy Awards in the same year when he earned an Oscar for directing the film version of *Cabaret* and an Emmy for *Liza with a "Z."*

If Fosse may be credited with forging a style, Michael Bennett (Michael Bennett DiFiglia, 1943–87) was recognized by producer Gerald Schoenfeld for saving the Shubert Organization, revitalizing Broadway, and sparking the renewal of the then-squalid 42nd Street area with *A Chorus*

Line, the 1975 Tony Award–winning musical, which garnered the Pulitzer Prize the following year. The show he originally called "The Dancers' Project" and developed through a series of workshops over eighteen months allegedly "made dancing so popular that leg warmers became a fashion statement"[20] and was for much of the 1980s and '90s the longest-running show in Broadway history. Transforming the traditional chorus kickline into a vehicle for self-revelation, Bennett evoked the pain and the exhilaration professional dancers experience in their challenging, unpredictable careers. Dancers, he seemed to say, have no control over their lives and that may well have been what propelled him from Broadway "gypsy" to choreographer and finally director. Although he often spoke of the joys of collaboration, as a director he sought control over all aspects of a production. He saw his role as that of "a leader who makes everything calm, gives everyone a sense of purpose," engages the audience "from the moment a show starts" and provides "the emotional experience that an audience expects and that is . . . attached to what they consider a great live theatrical experience" (Rosenberg and Harburg, 103).

Bennett's other distinguished work includes *Promises, Promises* (1966, choreography), *Coco* (1969, choreography), *Company* (1970, choreography), and *Follies* (1971, Tony Awards for co-direction with Harold Prince and choreography), *Seesaw* (1973, book, direction, and Tony Award–winning choreography). *Ballroom*, which he produced, directed, and choreographed in 1978, was a disappointment, although Bennett won his sixth Tony Award for choreography (sharing it with Bob Avian). His seventh (with Michael Peters) came three years later for *Dreamgirls* (1981), which he also produced and directed. A critical and popular success, the show ran on Broadway for almost five years. Based on the story of the Motown singing group the Supremes, it, like *A Chorus Line* and *Follies*, evoked the dark underside of American show business and the corrupting power of stardom. While not as groundbreaking as *A Chorus Line*, it was a production in which Bennett found innovative ways to explore stage space. According to critic John Heilpern, he "choreographed the set." Through his manipulation of four large, movable towers designed by Robin Wagner and lit by Tharon Musser, Bennett created "constantly changing perspectives and space, like an automated ballet. . . . Dance and movement were organic to the entire action. But Bennett had made the mechanical set his dancers." As *Wicked* choreographer Wayne Cilento recalled two decades later, whereas Bob Fosse was "meticulous about being very precise about finger turns and hand turns and little wrist movements, . . . Michael Bennett was a genius with choreographing the whole stage, just moving it around and making the whole thing dance."[21]

Some viewed the ascendance of the director-choreographer negatively, claiming that this "hybrid type" exercised undue influence on both script and score and always privileged dance over text. As playwright Peter Stone declared in the early 1990s, "Here was the director or the director-choreographer as 'auteur,' organizing production values (sets, lighting, costume, technology, dance)." With the exception of Jerome Robbins, they were "deadly antagonists to book writers," uncomfortable with text. "They are like abstract painters," he explained, "except their forte is movement." They have no interest in words "that can be directed but can't be *staged*." Unwilling to be part of a creative team, they wanted control of "the whole thing."[22]

Since directorial style is so individual, such generalizations seem unfair to the director-choreographers already discussed as well as to their successors, among them Thomas James "Tommy" Tune, Graciela Daniele, Kathleen Marshall, and Susan Stroman, the first woman to win Tony Awards as director and choreographer for *The Producers* in 2001.[23] Notwithstanding the prominence of director-choreographers in the historical narrative of musical theater, moreover, the two roles are not inseparably fused. There are other kinds of directors of comparable significance, who have exercised artistic control just as stringently. Whether director-producer, director-playwright, director-dramaturg, director-designer, or simply director, they serve as the artistic leader of a production, no matter how collaborative the art form is understood to be. According to Laurents, "In the end, the look of the musical is the director's look. He chooses the designers, he conveys his vision, he guides and edits. He can inspire the best to be even better or he can hamstring them into being less" (Laurents, 11).

The difference in perceived "creative muscle" may stem from the fact that the work of a director-choreographer is so palpable. Even without as distinctive a style as Fosse's, they shape a large part of what the audience sees: the musical numbers as well as the dramatic scenes. When the duties are divided between a director and a choreographer, as Kathleen Marshall explains, "with a lot of directors, if there's music, the choreographer is in charge."[24] Because the musical numbers tend to be the most memorable parts of a production, the contribution of a director, as opposed to a director-choreographer, may be difficult for the average theatergoer to appreciate unless the director is also associated with some other tangible element such as the book (Laurents, *Gypsy* and *West Side Story*), the costumes (Julie Taymor, *The Lion King*), or the set (John Doyle, *Sweeney Todd*, 2005 revival). Doyle, in the last, placed his chilling modern-dress interpretation within what appeared to be a psychiatric ward and put his stylistic imprimatur on the production with his brilliant use of actor-musicians, who served as the show's orchestra, with every cast member responsible for at least one instrument. Whether cello (Joanna) or tuba (Mrs. Lovett), each instrument became an extension of the person playing it, creating great emotional resonance.[25]

As Lundskaer-Nielsen convincingly argues, "It is essential to recognize the vital contribution of a group of American and

British theater directors who have infused the mainstream musical with new ideas, techniques and approaches," beginning with "the work of Broadway producer and director Harold Prince in the 1960s and 70s" and continuing with "Trevor Nunn, John Caird, Nicholas Hytner, James Lapine, George C. Wolfe, Tina Landau, Sam Mendes, Matthew Warchus, and David Leveaux" (Lundskaer-Nielsen, 7–8). That list should expand to include Michael Blakemore, Andy Blankenbuehler, Vinnette Carroll, Stephen Daldry, John Doyle, Richard Eyre, Sam Gold, Michael Greif, Thomas Kail, Arthur Laurents, Joe Mantello, Kathleen Marshall, Casey Nicholaw, Adrian Noble, Jack O'Brien, Diane Paulus, John Rando, Bartlett Sher, Susan Stroman, Julie Taymor, Deborah Warner, Jerry Zaks, and many other theater artists who have made the musical a viable forum for creative expression and imaginative exploration in the twenty-first century.

Lundskaer-Nielsen correctly sees Harold Prince as a seminal figure in the development of the postwar Broadway musical, owing to his "dual identity as the inheritor of Broadway showmanship and as a pioneer in bringing darker themes to the Broadway musical theatre." She credits him with broadening the boundaries of the musical in form and content "through his active participation in the development process, his need for social relevance, and his incorporation of structural formats and staging techniques beyond the traditions of the American musical theatre." Over the course of his multi-faceted, seventy-year career as a producer, producer-director and director, Prince imbued musical drama with a new credibility and, in the words of *The Producers*' irresistible Roger De Bris, proved that musicals could be more than "silly entertainments. Dopey showgirls in gooey gowns. Two-three-kick-turn! Turn-turn-kick-turn!"[26] Determined to engage and challenge his audiences, Prince's work has embraced difficult topics and sobering themes—perhaps none more so than

Parade (1998), which dealt with a shocking episode of anti-Semitism, the 1915 lynching of Atlanta pencil factory manager Leo Frank, as a cautionary tale for a nation still struggling with racism and bigotry.

A collaborative director, Prince has explained, "You must listen to everything, which means to everyone. . . . There's no way of knowing where advice that hits a responsive chord will come from. You've got to be the censor, the editor." He is, however, collaborative only to a point. Although he has sometimes been overshadowed by such creative partners as John Kander and Fred Ebb, Andrew Lloyd Webber and Tim Rice, and Stephen Sondheim, it is clear that he considers his directorial authority sacrosanct: "I must have the final word. People have walked away from that . . . , which is their prerogative. Choreographers can leave or accept the finality of my word. There's no halfway house" (Rosenburg and Harburg, 80, 103). Beginning with the groundbreaking *Cabaret* (1966), for which he earned his first Tony Award for Best Direction of a Musical, his directorial concept has shaped all aspects of a production and determined its style. To date he has won twenty-one Tonys (eight for directing, two as Best Producer of a Musical, eight for producing the year's Best Musical, and three special awards). His career has not been without its critical or commercial failures—among them *Merrily We Roll Along* (1981), which ended his storied partnership with Sondheim, *A Doll's Life* (1982), *Roza* (1987), and *Parade*—but his many more successful productions have validated the musical as an art form worthy of serious consideration and intellectual engagement.[27]

Musical theater now attracts directors who consider it culturally and socially relevant, as credible a creative forum as the other dramatic works they explore. No longer dismissed as frothy, trivial entertainments, musicals have become respectable, while their directors have gained prominence, drawing on a variety of staging traditions to challenge their audiences. In addition to generating new work, moreover, Prince and his successors have sparked an upsurge of interest in musical revivals, which became a separate Tony Award category in 1994. Rather than simply recreating classic texts, they have reinterpreted them from a contemporary perspective and have demonstrated that canonical works must be explored as *living* texts. In Bruce Kirle's words, "Historical context not only influenced the texts of these musicals but also helped shape the way these productions were performed and received by their audiences. New productions. . . will inevitably adapt to new cultural moments and to new audiences. As such, the musical is innately open, subject to a plurality of readings" (Kirle, xix).

Such Tony Award–winning revivals as Nicholas Hytner's *Carousel* (1994), Harold Prince's *Show Boat* (1995), Walter Bobbie's *Chicago* (1997), Rob Marshall and Sam Mendes' *Cabaret* (1998), Michael Blakemore's *Kiss Me, Kate* (2000), Joe Mantello's *Assassins* (2004), Bartlett Sher's *South Pacific* (2008) and *The King and I* (2015), Diane Paulus' *Hair* (2009), *Porgy and Bess* (2012), and *Pippin* (2013), John Doyle's *The Color Purple* (2015), and Jerry Zaks' *Hello, Dolly!* (2017) electrified audiences with their stunning theatricality and proved that mounting revivals is far more than an exercise in nostalgia. As Mendes explains, "*Cabaret* is up there with *The Crucible* or *The Homecoming* or any other great play of the twentieth century that deserves to be reinvented and rediscovered generation to generation. It's a great piece of theatre." For Laurents, "The goal of a revival is to add a fresh take on the material while not losing what made the original worth reviving. The key is to look at the material with fresh eyes rather than merely with the desire to do something different."[28]

Concomitant with these changes and undoubtedly contributing to them is the emergence of American nonprofit theaters as a venue for the development and production of new musicals. Although some shows, such as *Hair* and *A Chorus*

Line, originated Off Broadway and Off-Off Broadway in the 1960s and '70s, the 1980s saw a significant increase in the number of theaters committed to nurturing artists, creating experimental new pieces, and cultivating audiences for them. They attracted intrepid directors seeking an alternative to Broadway, including Des McAnuff (*Big River*), Graciela Daniele (*Once on This Island, Marie Christine*), and Michael Greif (*Rent*). In Lundskaer-Nielsen's view, most influential among them was Tony Award–winning writer-director James Lapine (b. 1949) whose *March of the Falsettos* (1981) helped pioneer nonprofit chamber musicals and whose *Sunday in the Park with George* (1984), which won the 1985 Pulitzer Prize for Drama, introduced the seemingly oxymoronic concept of a noncommercial musical (Lundskaer-Nielsen, 77–78). Lapine has also used his considerable skills as playwright and director to structure, shape, and stage *Into the Woods* (1987), *Falsettos* (1992), and *Passion* (1994), each of which garnered a Tony Award for the Best Book of a Musical.

Whereas Lapine's emphasis has been on story, characters, and songs rather than opulent staging or inventive choreography, George C. Wolfe (b. 1954) is a renowned writer-director and producer who has embraced Broadway staging traditions and whose directorial role models include Jerome Robbins and Michael Bennett. Even more significant, as an African American in a field largely dominated by white men, he has brought the politics of race and the provocative portrayal of African American history and culture to mainstream audiences. From *Jelly's Last Jam* (1991) to *Bring in 'da Noise, Bring in 'da Funk* (1996), for which he earned his second Tony Award for directing, *Caroline, or Change* (2004) and *Shuffle Along, or, the Making of the Musical Sensation of 1921 and All that Followed* (2016), he has succeeded in combining what Lundskaer–Nielsen calls "the traditions of black sociopolitical drama with the storytelling techniques of Broadway choreographer-directors," often in "a new and discomfiting context" (Lundskaer-Nielsen, 89–94, 99). In his words, "the kind of theater I want to craft [is] a theater that's full of delight but also has edge and a sense of responsibility to the world. . . . My theory about musicals is that there is a dark world just waiting offstage and the people are singing and dancing to keep that dark world from coming onstage. The main thing you have to do as a writer or director with this kind of material is to keep things buoyant."[29]

If Wolfe has helped to shatter racial barriers, Julie Taymor (b. 1952)—the first woman to earn a Tony Award for directing, as well as for costume design, for *The Lion King* (1998)—Susan Stroman (b. 1954), Tina Landau (b. 1962), Kathleen Marshall (b. 1962), Diane Paulus (b. 1966), and Rachel Chavkin (b. 1981) among others, have shown that gender equity may finally be within reach for women directors and director-choreographers. Both Stroman and Marshall began as choreographers and moved "up" to directing. As Stroman explains, "It was a natural stepping stone for me. . . . Because I established myself as a credible choreographer, people then believed that I could direct" (Bryer and Davison, 211). Paulus, who became artistic director of the American Repertory Theatre in Cambridge, Massachusetts, in 2008, the year before her acclaimed production of *Hair* won the Tony for Best Revival of a Musical, has demonstrated that it is possible for women as well as men to move between the nonprofit and commercial theater worlds. Whatever the venue or the vehicle, she asserts that her focus as a director is on the audience. In her words: "It's just always been my passion. Whenever I've been asked to direct something, whether it's an opera or it's a musical or a play, I'm always interested in, who is the audience for this? Why are we doing this? Why are we creating this event? And why should I ask people to come and see this? What's the need to do this project now?"[30]

These are questions that any director of musicals should ask and answer. According to Tony Award–winning director Joe Mantello (b. 1962), whose musical theater projects include *Wicked* (2003), *Assassins* (2004), *Pal Joey* (2008), and *9 to 5* (2009):

> The director answers all of the questions, takes all the blame. The director's a combination probably of Dad or Mom, a therapist—hopefully someone who has a little vision and someone who can just lead the troops. You really have to find a way to marshal the troops at all times and say "We're going in this direction, let's go!" And you can't hesitate or they can smell it. [31]

Arthur Laurents, also in martial mode, considers the director the "commander-in-chief." Director, writer, composer, and producer Martin Charnin (b. 1934), best known for his award-winning production of *Annie* (1977), uses similar terms. Calling the director "a visionary who ideally knows everything there is to know... about how to make orchestrations match costumes, dialogue, scenery and performance," he waxes militaristic in likening a show to "an armada, a large fleet, with many ships." The director is the person whose responsibility is to "bring them into port at different times because they arrive at different times. Once that fleet is docked, it's the show." For Prince, taking an aerial view, "the director must see it from a distance, to see the whole arc of the show" (Rosenberg and Harburg, 75, 101, 138).

Given the artistic breadth that characterizes musical theater today, there is no template for directors. Effective directors will have their own individual styles of expression and ways of making a particular production work. In Laurents' view, whether "therapist," "seducer," "psychologist, or lucky," the director is responsible for everything seen, said, or done on the stage. "No musical, no matter how good, can survive a misdirected, misconceived production." A director's work "begins long before the first day of rehearsal—at the moment when he opens the script." At that point, "the first question" should be: "what is it about? The answer tells where to put the focus." Whatever the response, however different each director's approach and techniques may be, the "key always is emotional reality," the ultimate goal to move an audience. For Laurents, "The first five minutes of a musical are crucial; either the audience can be captured, in which case they are the director's, no matter what he or she does, until at least halfway through the first act; or they can be lost, in which case it will take some stage magic to get them back" (Laurents, 3, 7, 29, 31, 76, 132, 154–55).

According to Laurents, who directed into his nineties and who wrote with the authority that only age and experience could bring, "Why? is the most important of questions, certainly the most important a director could ask. Beginning with himself: why is he a director?" He continues thoughtfully, "Why do directors direct? To be in control? To achieve the success they couldn't as actors? To produce theater that gives the audience an experience only theater can—moves them, excites, and entertains, illuminates, and always makes them want to see more theater, that's the desired answer" (Laurents, 175). For every musical theater director, aspiring or seasoned, that edifying answer should be an inspirational first principle as well as a daily mantra.

NOTES

1 Arthur Laurents, *Mainly on Directing: Gypsy, West Side Story, and Other Musicals* (New York: Alfred A. Knopf, 2009), p. 14.
2 *Broadway: The American Musical*, a film by Michael Kantor (Educational Broadcasting Corporation and the Broadway Film

Project, Inc., 2004), Episode Three, track 9, *Porgy and Bess*, and Episode Five, track 1, Introduction.
3 Stephen Citron, *The Musical from the Inside Out* (Chicago: Ivan R. Dee, 1991), p. 85.
4 Other directors and choreographers on whom Ziegfeld relied were George Marion, Joseph W. Herbert, Leon Errol, Edward Royce, William Anthony McGuire, Sammy Lee, and Zeke Colvan. See Ethan Mordden's *Ziegfeld: The Man Who Invented Show Business* (New York: St. Martin's Press, 2008).
5 Bruce Kirle, *Unfinished Show Business: Broadway Musicals as Works-in-Process* (Carbondale: Southern Illinois University Press, 2005), pp. 7 and 23.
6 Kirle, 23; Bernard Rosenberg and Ernest Harburg, *The Broadway Musical: Collaboration in Art and Commerce* (New York: New York University Press, 1993), p. 120.
7 *Broadway*, Episode Four ("Oh, What a Beautiful Mornin'," 1943–1960), track 2, *World War II/Oklahoma!*
8 In 1932, *Of Thee I Sing* (score by George Gershwin, lyrics by Ira Gershwin, book by George S. Kaufman and Morrie Ryskind) became the first musical to win the Pulitzer Prize for Drama. Because the prize only acknowledged literary merit, composer George Gershwin was not recognized. When *South Pacific* became the second Pulitzer Prize-winning musical in 1950, Richard Rodgers was included among the award recipients and thus became the first composer to be honored.
9 *Fiorello!* went on to win both the 1960 Tony Award for best musical and the Pulitzer Prize.
10 Miranda Lundskaer-Nielsen, *Directors and the New Musical Drama: British and American Musical Theatre in the 1980s and 90s* (New York: Palgrave Macmillan, 2008), p. 23.
11 *Broadway*, Episode Five, track 2, *West Side Story*; Laurents, 93.
12 Lundskaer-Nielsen, 7. Others include Joe Layton and Michael Kidd.
13 Greg Lawrence, *Dance with Demons: The Life of Jerome Robbins* (New York: G. P. Putnam's Sons, 2001), 200. Chapter Five, "Betrayals, Triumphs, and Fairy Dust," is particularly informative.
14 *Broadway*, Episode Five, track 2, *West Side Story*.

15 *Broadway*, supplementary material.
16 Ruthie Fierberg, "Hofesh Shechter, *Fiddler on the Roof* and the Choreographic Match Made in Heaven (*Playbill* [June 3, 2016), http://www.playbill.com/article/hofesh-shechter-fiddler-on-the-roof-and-the-choreographic-match-made-in-heaven, accessed November 6, 2017.
17 Julie Bloom, "Rekindling Robbins, a Step at a Time" (*New York Times* [March 4, 2009]), http://www.nytimes.com/2009/03/08/arts/dance/08bloo.html, accessed July 22, 2009.
18 Martin Weil, "Gower Champion Dies as Show Opens" (*Washington Post* [August 26, 1980]), https://www.washingtonpost.com/archive/politics/1980/08/26/gower-champion-dies-as-show-opens/e4463166-f891-41c6-aeac-2b19703327c1/?utm_term=.4a43f9f746d2, accessed November 6, 2017. Ironically, producer David Merrick's dramatic announcement of Champion's death after curtain calls on opening night of *42nd Street*, shocking both audience and cast, is what many people now seem to remember Champion for.
19 *Broadway*, Episode Five, track 9, *Bob Fosse*.
20 *Broadway*, Episode Five, track 8, *A Chorus Line*.
21 John Heilpern, "Bennett's Breakthrough: *Dreamgirls* Remembered" (*New York Observer* [January 7, 2007]), http://wwwobserver.com/node/36503?observer_most_read_tabs_tab=2, accessed July 11, 2009; Broadway supplementary material.
22 Rosenberg and Harburg, 133–34; for a similarly negative evaluation, see "Act Five. Wagging the Musical: How Director-Choreographers Co-opted a Writer's Medium," in Mark N. Grant's *The Rise and Fall of the Broadway Musical* (Boston: Northeastern University Press, 2004).
23 Stroman also won Tonys for choreography in 1992 (*Crazy for You*), 1995 (*Show Boat*), and 2000 (*Contact*). In addition to two Tony Awards for choreography, one for direction, and two for acting, Tune has won twice as a director-choreographer: in 1990 for *Grand Hotel* and 1991 for *The Will Rogers Follies*.
24 Quoted in *The Art of the American Musical: Conversations with the Creators*, ed. Jackson R. Bryer and Richard A. Davison (New Brunswick, NJ: Rutgers University Press, 2005), p. 160.

25 The same technique worked less effectively in Doyle's revival of *Company* (2006), in which some of the musical numbers left the unfortunate impression of a frenetic marching band, its members in dire need of a choreographer. Yet here, too, the device does important dramatic work, enhancing the teeming, oppressive dimension of Bobby's friends, as he experiences them.
26 Lundskaer-Nielsen, 15, 20, 23, 28; Mel Brooks and Tom Meehan, *The Producers: The Book, Lyrics, and Story Behind the Biggest Hit in Broadway History! How We Did It* (New York: Miramax/Hyperion, 2001), p. 130.
27 Lundskaer-Nielsen, 57. Sondheim and Prince did not work together again until *Bounce* (2003), which was not a critical success. When the revised version opened in New York in 2008 as *Road Show*, John Doyle, not Prince, directed it.
28 Quoted in Lundskaer-Nielsen, 117; Laurents, 15.
29 Quoted in Bryer and Davison, 286, 292. Wolfe won his first Tony for directing Tony Kushner's *Angels in America: Millennium Approaches* (a drama, not a musical) in 1993.
30 Interview with Matthew Small (*Talkin' Broadway Regional News* [April 13, 2009]), http://www.talkinbroadway.com/regional/boston/boston128.html, accessed July 9, 2009.
31 *Broadway*, supplementary material.

9

Sets, Costumes, Lights, and Spectacle

VIRGINIA ANDERSON

■ □ ■

Give 'em the old razzle dazzle
Razzle dazzle 'em
Give 'em an act with lots of flash in it
And the reaction will be passionate
Give 'em the old hocus pocus
Bead and feather 'em
How can they see with sequins in their eyes?
　　　　　　　　　　　—BILLY FLYNN, *Chicago*[1]

Color and light.
There's only color and light.
　　　　　—GEORGE, *Sunday in the Park with George*[2]

OVER THE HISTORY OF MUSICAL theater, tendencies in design have swung, pendulum-like, between glittering spectacle and simplicity. This oscillation reflects a symbiotic relationship across the footlights; what the audience has seen on stage has contributed to the success—or failure—of many musicals. Design trends reflect changes in both popular taste and economic investment, even if, ultimately, each theatrical design has been developed to serve the story or mood at the heart of the production as determined through collaboration with writers, composers, and directors. As the economic, social, and political climate in which productions have taken place has in turn determined the definition and feasibility of "spectacle," design trends have moved from the extravagant to the comparatively simple and back again.

As an introduction to the subject of design, this chapter discusses only original productions, not revivals, and focuses on technological and artistic advancements within scenic and lighting design, sometimes incorporating discussion of costumes as they relate to the changing nature of spectacle. A genealogy with a wider scope would also address the work of such costume artists as William Ivey Long and Jane Greenwood, as well as the contributions of hair and makeup artists such as Michael Ward and Candace Carell, and wig makers such as Paul Huntley, each of whom has contributed significantly to characterization and the visual dimension of the stories being told in musicals.[3] In addition, the advancement of design and spectacle would not be possible without the often unsung engineering prowess of individuals such as Edward Kook and George Izenour, lighting technicians who installed the first electronic lighting control system in a professional theater and thereby reduced the amount of time it took to program a lighting cue from hours to seconds.[4]

Real experimentation in musical theater design began in Europe at the turn of the twentieth century with the dance-based work of Adolph Appia and the atmospheric designs of Edward Gordon Craig. Moving productions away from previously established expectations involving lavish sets and lights, these designs brought the notion of spectacle directly to the body. Since then, the presentation of the actor's body has been the central point from which the design pendulum swings. From the silky legs of chorus girls in *The Black Crook* (1866) to the complete baring of the tribe in *Hair* (1967), the revealed body of a performer has captivated musical theater audiences throughout the history of the American musical.

The performer's body as it relates to other scenic elements often illuminates evolving tastes and technological innovation.

COLOR AND LIGHT: EARLY INFLUENCES AND INNOVATIONS

The stagecraft that proved most influential to the American musical developed in Germany in the late nineteenth century. Georg II, Duke of Saxe-Meiningen (1826–1914), was arguably the first modern stage director, with his touring theatrical company laying much of the foundation for modern musical theater. With careful attention to lighting and sound effects, the Duke strove for artistic unity through scenic design, costumes, and intricately choreographed crowd movement.[5] Also in Germany at this time, composer Richard Wagner (1813–83) developed an equally influential approach to design with his theory of the *Gesamtkunstwerk*, or total art work. Wagner called for the complete synthesis of artistic elements, pointing toward opera as the vehicle with the greatest potential for such a totalizing effect. To further his ideas, he opened the *Festpielhaus* (Festival Playhouse) theater in 1876 in Bayreuth, Germany, where he channeled the focus of his audience through several lasting innovations, including a darkened house and surround-sound reverberation. Music, movement, and design further contributed to the total art Wagner desired, and his work profoundly influenced designers who followed. This influential approach to design distinguished itself from the heavily detailed stages of nineteenth-century Realism and Naturalism.

Adolph Appia (1862–1928) drew inspiration from Wagner's *Gesamtkunstwerk*, devoting his designs to the essential mood of a piece as it complemented the embodied actions of performers.[6] He found a muse in Émile Jaques-Dalcroze, a dancer whose art derived from rhythm. Working with Dalcroze, Appia designed sets from pillars, shapes, and objects in a sculptural, nonrepresentational manner (⦿ Example 9.1). He eliminated walls and elaborately painted drop cloths, replacing them with abstract forms to emphasize the actors' movement in space. He simplified costumes to serve the total work and replaced scenic painting with moving projected colored light, always at the service of the actor. Indeed, Appia was one of the first to see the artistic potential of electric light, only recently introduced into theaters.[7] Instead of illustrating a story arc, Appia's approach to design, particularly lighting, intensified the mood and emotion of musical pieces and became the basis for lighting practices that followed.[8]

Like Appia, Edward Gordon Craig (1872–1966) moved theatrical design toward simplified abstraction, paring down his scenic designs to the most essential elements of the stories being told. Also like Appia, Craig found inspiration in dance, but he used light to emphasize scenic design rather than the movement of actors. He ultimately called for the director's complete control over the design of sets, lights, costumes, and choreography, and famously referred to his ideal actor as an "über-marionette," an ego-less performer capable of fulfilling the artistic demands of the director.[9] Over the course of his career, Craig's influential designs were recognized for their simplified scenes, creative use of curtains, emphasis on vertical architecture, and movable screens that allowed space to be redefined from scene to scene.[10]

While Craig and Appia communicated through abstraction in Europe, director/producer/playwright David Belasco signaled the imminent pendulum swing toward the extravagant. Like their European counterparts, Belasco's electrician, Louis Hartmann, with technicians John H. and Anton Kliegl, were devoted to the creation of mood through light, but they strove to create unparalleled realism through lighting. They famously enabled a sunrise to coincide with approximately twenty minutes of action within the saloon setting of Belasco's 1905 play *The Girl of the Golden West*, using tightly controlled lighting cues (⊙ Example 9.2).[11] Hartmann's innovations began in 1879 with the practical lensed spotlight, a device regularly used to separate the stars of musical theater from the chorus. Within an intricate lighting laboratory, Belasco, Hartmann, and the Kliegls developed multiple forms of electronic equipment to advance significantly the lighting technology of the early twentieth century. Belasco wrote, "Lights are to drama what music is to the lyrics of a song. No other factor that enters into the production of a play is so effective in conveying its moods and feeling."[12] Convinced of this principle, Belasco fit lights and their operators into every conceivable place around the stage in order to achieve the desired heavily atmospheric realism. His attention to detail suited well the elaborate artistry of the scenic designs for the musicals of the early twentieth century.

THE SPECTACLE OF THE BODY: THE EARLY CONTRIBUTIONS OF COSTUMING

Before innovations in scenic and lighting design drew their own attention, costumes dazzled audiences. The long-lasting popular success of *The Black Crook*, considered by some to be the first American musical, derived in no small part from the immodest attire of its dancing chorus girls. Advancements in stage machinery also enabled audiences to experience a remarkable and precedent-setting "transformation scene," in which a rocky cavern became a fairyland throne room before their eyes. But it was the daring provocation of nearly-nude dancing girls that brought audiences to this wildly successful show, whose extravagant and often revealing costuming for its leggy chorus members soon become characteristic of the American musical.[13] Direct testimony to the early influence of *The Black Crook* was the wild Broadway success of Lydia Thompson and her English Blondes, who caused a stir with their silky flesh-toned tights in the musical extravaganza, *Ixion* (1868).[14]

Florenz Ziegfeld (1867–1932) capitalized on such lucrative voyeurism in becoming one of the most influential producers of the Broadway musical, famous for sparing no expense while creating spectacular shows with unparalleled production values.[15] Although Ziegfeld's name is well known, those of his chief designers have been widely overlooked. Scenic designer Joseph Urban, along with costume designers Lady Lucile Duff Gordon and John Harkrider, provided significant contributions and innovations to the aesthetic hallmarks of musical theater.

Thirty years before Ziegfeld established the *Follies*, he built a career on the cult of the body, often enshrouded in meticulously designed costumes. With the examples of *The Black Crook* and Lydia Thompson's English Blondes pointing the way, Ziegfeld learned a valuable lesson early in his career: the nearly nude, physically attractive body could serve as a lucrative spectacle in and of itself. His first star, body-builder Eugen Sandow, was famously (barely) dressed in silk trunks or, as some photographs have documented, a strategically placed leaf (⊙ Example 9.3; ⊙ Example 9.4). This approach to costuming proved to be at least as true for feminine beauty, a fact exploited by decades of *Follies* productions, commencing in 1907.

Not all of Ziegfeld's "*Follies* girls" were presented in dishabille. From 1915 to 1921, Lady Lucile Duff Gordon, a high-society women's shop owner in both London and New York, designed elegant gowns for the *Follies*, after her ability to captivate buyers came to the notice of Ziegfeld through his young mistress and star, Anna Held. Lady Duff Gordon introduced the concept of the showgirl whose only responsibility was to look beautiful in spectacular clothing, a mode of presentation quite distinct from that of the singing and dancing chorus girl. As the arbiter of women's fashion in the early years of the twentieth century, she dressed both society ladies and *Follies* girls in extravagant and figure flattering—yet rarely revealing—gowns. Contributing to an enduring trend of emulation, variations of Lady Duff Gordon's stage creations were often on display at society events. Notably, Ziegfeld felt that each gown celebrated individuality, at a time when mass-produced clothing was taking over the fashion industry (◉ Example 9.5; ◉ Example 9.6).

John Harkrider served as Ziegfeld's costume designer throughout the showman's later years, but he owed a great deal to his predecessor. Lady Duff Gordon's gowns for the *Follies* were based on those worn by "living mannequins" who displayed them for the viewing pleasure of New York's elite. These stunning models were cool and detached, providing a prototype for the commanding poise of the *Follies* girls who later, under Harkrider's artistic command, donned the trademark feature of the *Follies*: architecturally extravagant, sculpturesque headdresses. Later parodied in such numbers as "The Money Song" of *Cabaret* and "Springtime for Hitler" in *The Producers*, these headdresses stretched the boundaries of how costumes and the body itself could contribute to spectacle.

Like Lady Duff Gordon, and most likely nurtured by the similarly minded Ziegfeld, Harkrider indulged a passionate affinity for the highest-quality materials, whatever the cost. Wresting control over all aspects of design, the notoriously difficult Harkrider sacrificed professional camaraderie for his own personal achievement in the creation of spectacle. At the age of only twenty-five, Harkrider designed the 1926 *Follies* revue, originally titled *Palm Beach Nights* for its Florida premiere. Feeding Ziegfeld's desire for lavish spectacle, the production's costume costs exceeded $90,000, and scenery expenses reached nearly $50,000 at a time when a loaf of bread cost approximately ten cents. Also in 1926, Harkrider introduced the egret-feather headdresses and costumes that established his place in Broadway history (🅾 Example 9.7; 🅾 Example 9.8; 🅾 Example 9.9).

While Lady Duff Gordon and Harkrider created the look of the world-famous Ziegfeld girls, scenic artist Joseph Urban designed the equally extravagant sets. A noted Viennese architect of pavilions and palaces, Urban had designed operas throughout Europe and was designing for the Boston Opera in 1914 when his work came to Ziegfeld's attention. The designer's opulence and precision in artistry struck the producer immediately as the sort of sophistication he sought for his *Follies*. He immediately wooed Urban for the *Follies* and quickly commenced what proved to be an enduring collaboration, which culminated in Urban's contributions to the architectural and aesthetic design of the Ziegfeld Theatre in New York, an opulent performance space with every available technological extravagance (🅾 Example 9.10).

Often relinquishing credit to his producer, Urban devised scenic innovations crucial to the development of musical theater stagecraft. Like other European designers of his time, Urban experimented with light and scenic painting. Although the lines of his sets were simple, they were frequently complicated by pointillist applications of vibrant color. This technique provided for the appearance and disappearance of shapes and images as well as radical changes of general hue according to the color of light used for illumination. He was among the first to employ platforms and portals in his designs, which allowed him to create an inner proscenium of whatever size best suited the action. Urban championed artistic unity and strove to focus his audience's attention upon a nearly seamless, total production, inspired by Appia and Craig abroad. A key link in an important chain of influence, Urban later inspired Robert Edmond Jones and Norman Bel Geddes, who were trained in scenic construction and painting at the Urban Studio, which he established in 1919 (🅾 Example 9.11; 🅾 Example 9.12).

As collaborators, Urban and Harkrider were often at odds, yet with Ziegfeld's nearly continuous ego-mending assistance, the pair contributed significantly to the watershed musical of their time: *Show Boat* (1927). As the first American musical to present serious themes and highly developed characters, *Show Boat* affected the perceptions and expectations of audiences that had been accustomed to the lighter or more romanticized themes of musical comedy and operetta. With Urban's massive moving set and atmospheric lights, and Harkrider's meticulously period-specific clothing, the designers contributed significantly to a unified generational story of those working on the *Cotton Blossom*, a Mississippi River showboat, between the 1880s and 1920s (◉ Example 9.13).

BACK TO BASICS

With the economic collapse of 1929, the pendulum on Broadway was to swing again, this time away from spectacle and toward a renewed simplicity.[16] While Urban, Harkrider, and Belasco had emphasized beauty through extravagance to mirror popular tastes, visual trends in theater changed, as much of American society was forced to pare down to essentials during the Depression and war years. Seemingly simple and comparatively abstract designs represented a new wave in design, led by Robert Edmond Jones, Norman Bel Geddes, and Lee Simonson, who simultaneously captured the essence of the stories being told and reflected the changing mood of audiences (◉ Example 9.14).

Even prior to this, while spectacle dominated the American musical stage, designers steeped in the work of Appia and Craig introduced the "New Stagecraft," an American design movement defined by the power of simplicity and suggestion, lasting from approximately 1915 through 1930.[17] Chief among these designers, Robert Edmond Jones (1887–1954) was considered "the father of American scenic design." Although he designed relatively few musicals, his influence remains unsurpassed. Turning away from both the ornate designs of Urban and the hyperrealism promoted by Belasco, Jones strove to employ the imagination of his audiences by creating simplified, suggestive settings. He sought to communicate a *feeling* concerning the world of the play rather than construct a concrete reality.[18] Jones was heavily involved in the Little Theatre movement, especially the Provincetown Players and the Theatre Guild (which would produce *Oklahoma!* in 1943). He shared an interest in experimenting with naturalism and expressionism with Donald Oenslager, who contributed a lyrical elegance to even the harshest expressionistic lighting and scenic designs. Norman Bel Geddes (1893–1958) designed both sets and lights, and as with Jones his often "industrial" designs were emblematic rather than realistic. Bel Geddes influenced the focused appearance of later stage productions through his pioneering work with lenses in stage lighting.

Lee Simonson (1888–1967) called for a further simplified realism, eliminating any scenic elements that were not necessary for atmosphere or important information. Perhaps nowhere was Simonson's style felt more keenly than in the original production of the theatrical epitome of American Expressionism, Elmer Rice's 1923 play, *The Adding Machine*, which told the story of Mr. Zero, who murders his employer in a fit of fury when, after twenty-five years of service, he loses his job to new technology. Tried and executed, Mr. Zero awakes in Elysian Fields, where he is forced to work another adding machine before being sent back to Earth. Simonson's designs included a distorted courtroom, an adding machine big enough to walk on, and large numbers that spun across the stage with Mr. Zero's reeling thoughts. Simonson and other designers of the New Stagecraft imparted a less costly but conceptually rich aesthetic to the theater world, which proved invaluable during the troublesome economic period ahead.

Following the stock market crash of 1929 and the ensuing economic depression, most musicals and revues were forced to cut back, if not altogether eliminate expensive scenery and costumes. Instead, a renewed focus on music, choreography, and clever satire created a fertile atmosphere for the creation of a number of shows, including Cole Porter's *Anything Goes* (1934), the Gershwins' operatic *Porgy and Bess* (1935), and Rodgers and Hart's *On Your Toes* (1936). Spectacle was often created not through lights and sets but in other ways, such as with a live elephant in Rodgers and Hart's *Jumbo* (1935). When Marc Blitzstein's *The Cradle Will Rock* (1938), set to open at the Maxine Elliot Theatre with elaborate sets and costumes, was shut down due to budget cuts to the Federal Theater Project (reportedly in reaction to its core communist message), it was performed nearly extemporaneously in the New Century Theatre without the spectacular production values director/designer Orson Welles had created for it. Audiences cheered as Blitzstein told the story from the piano on stage as actors in street clothing sang to one another from across the theater, observing union rules that prohibited them from performing on stage.

While the move away from extravagance conditioned popular taste to a certain degree, musical theater was still associated with leggy showgirls, no matter the setting in which they appeared. Bearing in mind the continued influence exerted by the extravagant sets and costumes of successes stretching from *The Black Crook* to the *Follies*, which continued apace in Hollywood musicals, one may well understand the shock of the audience when the curtain first rose on *Oklahoma!* (1943) to reveal, not a rousing dance number performed by young chorus members, but an older woman in a conservative, floor-length skirt, churning butter in a generally open space. Lemuel Ayers's set and Miles White's costumes, like Urban and Harkrider's designs for *Show Boat*, contributed significantly to the story. Their roots in the Little Theatre movement were evident in sometimes abstract settings and costumes, which, while far from haute-couture, were highly expressive of individual character traits. With the design's emphasis on atmosphere as well as story, the influence of the New Stagecraft was readily apparent.[19]

Jo Mielziner brought the New Stagecraft further into the realm of musical theater, emphasizing a visual metaphor for the essence of each play and musical he designed, creating worlds on stage defined by a sense of poetic realism. He manipulated the styles of painted scenery from the past, adding his own fantastical images, decorations, and softly curved lines. Keeping tight artistic control over sets and lights, Mielziner worked carefully with color, gauze, and scrim to evoke mood, fantasy, dream, and memory. The flow of action from one scene to the next depended not upon the movement of scenery but on the raising and lowering of lights on his often fragmented sets, comprising multileveled playing spaces. This fluidity lent itself to the dream-like quality of the pieces for which he designed. In addition to plays such as *The Glass Menagerie* (1945), *A Streetcar Named Desire* (1947), and *Death of a Salesman* (1949), Mielziner designed such pivotal musicals as *Pal Joey* (1940), *Carousel* (1945), *South Pacific* (1949), and *The King and I* (1951).[20] Mielziner's significant artistic legacy is evident not only in the renderings and production photos he left behind but also through the influential work of his disciples, including Ming Cho Lee, who in turn trained contemporary designer John Lee Beatty and others who have contributed significantly to the way contemporary audiences experience the world of musical theater.

Mielziner's use of lighting to facilitate smooth, cinematic transitions inspired a wave of designers. William and Jean

Eckart matched this fluidity with scenic innovations used to facilitate beautifully choreographed set changes. The designers of such musicals as *The Golden Apple* (1954; the first musical to move from Off Broadway to Broadway), *She Loves Me* (1963), *Anyone Can Whistle* (1964), *Flora the Red Menace* (1965), and *Mame* (1966), the Eckarts remain noteworthy for both their technological advancements and their minimalist aesthetic. Eckart designs were highly stylized, often deriving from symbol-laden modern art. The team introduced a winch-driven device that used hidden tracks to guide set pieces silently into place. They also developed a system for flying in set pieces, or mini-drops, which could drastically change the scenic picture while occupying little space when not in use. Laying the foundation for John Napier's design of *Les Misérables*, the Eckarts developed a system of often overlapping and concentrically revolving turntables. The lengthy breaks in performance required for Joseph Urban's spectacular sets for Ziegfeld were a thing of the past.[21]

The Eckarts and Mielziner contributed to the pendulum swing toward abstraction using color and light to replace the "razzle dazzle" of the earliest musicals, and their work prompted some designers to specialize in lighting for the first time. In the past, even the most intricate use of lights fell under the auspices of the designer of scenery or resident electricians. Lighting pioneers such as Abe Feder (1909–97) and Jean Rosenthal (1912–69) struck out on their own to establish lighting design as an independent craft. Rosenthal is most often credited with the earliest great achievements in lighting design for musical theater. Following an early start working under Orson Welles and John Houseman in the Federal Theatre Project, Rosenthal served as dancer/choreographer Martha Graham's lighting and production supervisor. This early experience illuminating dance prompted Rosenthal to experiment with the communication of mood through light, independent of the space in which it is perceived. Her experiments with light culminated in the 1950s and 1960s with the groundbreaking design collaborations for *West Side Story* (1957), *The Sound of Music* (1959), *Fiddler on the Roof* (1964), and *Cabaret* (1966), traversing the pendulum swing in design trends from spare to decorous once again.[22]

A RETURN TO OPULENCE

The New Stagecraft left a permanent mark on the design aesthetic of the American musical, but as technology advanced, the opportunities and demand for the grandiosity of yesteryear increased accordingly. Following World War II, a renewed artistic interest in spectacle through scenic and costume design emerged. The original production of *My Fair Lady* (1956) embodied this phenomenon, with lighting by Abe Feder, scenery design by Oliver Smith (1918–94), and costumes by Cecil Beaton (1904–80). As with lighting designer Jean Rosenthal, Smith found inspiration for his scenery designs in dance, working throughout his career with the American Ballet Theatre and frequently collaborating with Jerome Robbins. Smith, like the Eckarts, emphasized the graceful choreography of set changes, favoring quick and unobtrusive transitions. His aesthetic combined painting and sculpture, and Smith firmly believed that scenery for musical theater should be bright and entertaining in and of itself. Beaton's costumes for *My Fair Lady* contributed to a pivotal moment in musical theater history. In a brief return to spectacle for spectacle's sake, the scene at Ascot showcased Beaton's neo-romantic designs, placing ladies of the highest fashion on display in a manner unseen since the Ziegfeld *Follies* (🅾 Example 9.15).

While the pendulum remained within the realm of extravagance, the influence of the New Stagecraft continued to be felt in terms of atmosphere, powerful simplicity, and metaphor, all of which were taken to new heights by scenic designer Boris Aronson (1898–1980). Aronson offered strong, clear, and ultimately simple design concepts while making full, expert use of available production values. Born in Kiev and with work experience in Russia and Germany, he designed a number of notable Broadway plays, from Clifford Odets's *Awake and Sing* to Arthur Miller's *The Crucible*. His greatest contributions, however, came in the conceptually driven designs for musical theater throughout the 1960s and 1970s including *Fiddler on the Roof* (1964), *Cabaret* (1966), and four of the Sondheim-Prince collaborations: *Company* (1970), *Follies* (1971), *A Little Night Music* (1975), and *Pacific Overtures* (1976). The early influence of the constructivist aesthetic popular in Eastern Europe during Aronson's youth is apparent throughout his work. Constructivist principles called for strictly functional scenery, often with exposed scaffolding, ladders, and multiple levels that contributed to a kind of celebration of machinery. Aronson employed such techniques to expose cold isolation within the mechanized frenzy of Manhattan society in his design for *Company*, which used steel and Plexiglas to create skeletal apartments complete with a functional elevator timed precisely to match the longest held chord in the musical's opening number.

Aronson's greatest achievements occurred through experimentation with form. One example is the primary drop he designed for the original production of *Pacific Overtures*, which portrays—from the Japanese perspective—the American Commodore Matthew Perry's opening of the island nation. Aronson ran a fine traditional Japanese print through a color-saturated Xerox copier (all the rage in the United States in the late 1970s). Combining the distorted delicacy of the print with tie-dyed fabric, which itself suggested a recent era of change in the United States, Aronson's set communicated, through what his audience saw, the show's central cultural clash. While Aronson also proved himself a master of lavish design, simulating the Ziegfeld era for his Loveland sets in *Follies*, this was not what separated him from other designers of musical theater. Rather, through his clear presentation of an essential concept, Aronson served as a powerful influence on the new generation of scenic artists.[23]

A RENEWED SIMPLICITY

Aronson's work prompted designers to reexamine the contribution of individual visual elements to the story. Designers of the 1970s taking this approach engendered a renewed simplicity that echoed the earliest years of the New Stagecraft. Over his extensive Broadway career, scenic designer Robin Wagner, like Aronson, proved himself capable of both minimalist and lavish designs, contributing the original designs to *Hair* (1977), *42nd Street* (1980), *Dreamgirls* (1987), *City of Angels* (1989), *Crazy for You* (1992), *Side Show* (1997), *The Producers* (2001), and many others. His design for *A Chorus Line* (1975) captures this shift in aesthetic toward powerful simplicity. Collaborating with Michael Bennett, Wagner distilled initial ideas for an expansive and detailed set to the famous black box with a mirror and a line. Aronson had effectively used a mirror in his set for *Cabaret* (1966), and Wagner similarly employed the device to implicate the audience, at the same time serving the practical purpose of evoking a dance studio setting. The famous line, the solitary stage ornament, became the visual focus of the production, with each character's motivation and fate balanced precariously upon it. Powerfully menacing through its simplicity, the line became the spectacle (⏵ Example 9.16).[24]

 A Chorus Line also brought radical innovation in lighting from pioneer Tharon Musser (1925–2009), who introduced an entirely computerized lighting system to Broadway for the first time, marking an important shift away from slower, less consistent, manually operated "piano boards." From her Broadway debut with the mood and atmosphere-driven nonmusical play *A Long Day's Journey into Night* (1956), she meticulously researched the light quality of inspirational sources such as paintings and photographs; indeed, Musser insisted that she "painted with light." Musser collaborated with the Eckarts on *Mame* (1966) and with Boris Aronson on *Follies* (1971), *A Little Night Music* (1973), and *Pacific Overtures* (1976), in addition to her further work with Wagner on *42nd Street* (1980).

CHANDELIERS AND HELICOPTERS: A SPECTACULAR BRITISH INVASION

While audiences grew accustomed to decoding deceivingly simple conceptual designs by the end of the 1970s, the following decade brought another drastic change in design. The "British invasion" of musical theater also brought an epic, and costly, scope in design to Broadway, reflecting the consumerism that dominated the 1980s. John Napier's set designs for *Cats* (1982), *Starlight Express* (1987), *Les Misérables* (1987), *Miss Saigon* (1991), and *Sunset Boulevard* (1994) each centered on a central scenic element and then expanded to fill the rest of the space with a feast for the audience's eyes. A combination of glitz and practicality, Napier's sets employed the latest scenic innovations to dazzle his audiences while suiting the needs of the musical. For *Les Misérables,* Napier began with what he deemed "the centre of the play's biggest moment": the barricade. Comprising objects that could be used as properties by the actors, the barricade was part of a revolving set (echoing the innovations of Eckarts) and was designed to detach into separate levels. Like early scenic designers who also coordinated lights to achieve their artistic visions, a number of set designers for the elaborate musicals of the 1980s and early 1990s also designed costumes. Napier designed sets and costumes for *Starlight Express* and *Cats*, while Maria Björnson designed both costumes and sets for *The Phantom of the Opera* (1988). Björnson, in particular, left a lasting imprint on spectacle through the famous rising— and of course, falling—chandelier, and the visually stunning costumes for the masquerade ball that opens the second act. Her design represented a hybrid less of *practicality* and innovation (like Napier's) than of spectacle and *atmosphere*, recalling the work of Jo Mielziner.[25]

During this period of dazzling spectacle, the scenic environment itself began to change. Often in the hands of Eugene Lee (1939–), who designed musicals well into the twenty-first century, the entire theater was adapted to provide audiences with a carefully conceived experience from the moment they walked through the door. This development also provided ample space and opportunities to sell memorabilia, both providing additional revenue and enhancing mass visibility of Broadway musicals. Even as perceptions of spectacle were to shift again, this total theater experience carried over into the musicals of the twenty-first century.

AN AESTHETIC BACKLASH AND HYBRID DESIGNS: MUSICAL THEATER TODAY

In 1996, Jonathan Larson's *Rent* represented an aesthetic backlash against the illusory extravagance of the Lloyd Webber and Boublil-Schönberg musicals that preceded it on Broadway. *Rent* was not unique in its rejection of massive spectacle— witness the simple, actor-driven unit set of Lynn Ahrens and Stephen Flaherty's Caribbean fable, *Once on This Island*

(1989)—but it represented the greatest critical and commercial success of this new era of design. With echoes of Aronson's constructivist influence, Paul Clay's scenery consisted of multiple levels of pipes and city grates, establishing locales only through introducing props and set pieces. Through this means as well as exposed lighting instruments, Clay visually refused to let audience members retreat fully into the world presented to them—a design well suited to the presentational style of the show (◉ Example 9.17; ◉ Example 9.18). This kind of *verfremdungeffekt* (alienation effect), perhaps modeled on the designs of longtime-Brecht collaborator, Caspar Neher, altered the aesthetic of Broadway musicals after *Rent*. *Urinetown* (2001) and *Spring Awakening* (2006) similarly fight illusion through their alienating set designs and deliberately harsh lighting. Even the production design of the puppet-driven *Avenue Q* (2003) follows this trend of stylization and comparative simplicity.

While production design was pared down to place the emphasis of spectacle on the performers themselves, spectacle through lush design clung tenaciously to the Broadway musicals at the turn of the twenty-first century. As a corporation, Disney Theatricals, like Ziegfeld one hundred years earlier, has invested heavily in an assumption that audiences come to a Broadway musical to be dazzled. Beginning with *Beauty and the Beast* (1994), Disney Theatricals has brought several of its most successful animated film musicals to the stage, recreating effects of animation through stage spectacle. The corporation took a huge but ultimately highly lucrative risk when it hired avant-garde director-designer Julie Taymor for *The Lion King* (1997; ◉ Example 9.19; ◉ Example 9.20). Conveying influences of time she spent in Asia and parts of Africa, Taymor's designs were far from illusory, determinedly resisting "fuzzy animal costumes" and instead showcasing the (human) actor as much as the highly stylized costume and mask he or she wore. Richard Hudson's scenery and Donald Holder's lights complemented this aesthetic approach, creating painterly effects that further distanced the New York audiences from the African Serengeti. Despite the artistic and financial success of *The Lion King*, most of the previously animated Disney stage musicals that followed—*Aida* (2000), *Tarzan* (2006), and *The Little Mermaid* (2008)—returned to the kind of spectacular and semi-illusory effects popular during the 1980s. This trend culminated in the hiring of a "magic/illusion designer," Joe Eddie Fairchild, for *The Little Mermaid*.[26]

Perhaps because audiences today have been conditioned to expect both highly conceptual and elaborately designed productions, only a few individuals have proven themselves as cross-over artists à la Aronson. Eugene Lee mixes core conceptual elements with the grandiosity of design. With a career of theatrical design including the 1974 revival of *Candide*, *Sweeney Todd* (1979), *Merrily We Roll Along* (1981), *Ragtime* (1998), and *Wicked* (2003), Lee's sets are large, include moving parts, and tend to sweep into the area conventionally belonging to the audience. Nodding to the grandiose sets common when he launched his career, Lee's sets range from simple, bare, and abstract to elaborate, detailed, and realistic, sometimes within the same production (as for *Ragtime*).

Designers today often visually acknowledge their predecessors, to the delight of knowledgeable theater audiences. A quarter century after his minimalist design for *A Chorus Line*, Robin Wagner's lavish design for *The Producers* (2001) included notable tributes to both Ziegfeld's designers and Aronson. Thus, "Along Came Bialy" clearly echoes the doily-esque valentine of Aronson's set for Loveland in *Follies*, whereas the costume design for "Springtime for Hitler" offers scantily clad women costumed as if in the *Follies*, complete with massive head pieces in the shape of Bavarian pretzels and sausages that would have pleased (or perhaps insulted) not only

John Harkrider, but also such inspired descendents as Busby Berkeley and Carmen Miranda. Whether such tributes are overt or subconscious, they display the chain of influence in design that forms the backbone of the history of musical theater, a history which, in turn, reflects the changing world in which performances take place. With the pendulum of design trends poised to swing again, one may look to the gravitational pull of popular tastes and the economic climate to predict the designs of the future, yet such predictions cannot encompass the spirit of theatrical innovation that has always propelled the pendulum itself.[27]

NOTES

1 Fred Ebb, Bob Fosse, and John Kander, *Chicago: A Musical Vaudeville* (New York: Samuel French, 1976), p. 75.
2 James Lapine and Stephen Sondheim, *Sunday in the Park with George* (New York: Applause Theatre Book Publishers, 1991), p. 38.
3 The American Theatre Wing offers readily accessible information on these and related topics through online seminars and interviews with contemporary designers, directors, actors, and producers. See http://americantheatrewing.org/wit ("Working in the Theatre") and http://americantheatrewing.org/downstagecenter ("Downstage Center"), accessed September 8, 2009.
4 George C. Izenour, *Theater Technology*, 2nd ed. (New Haven, CT: Yale University Press, 1997).
5 For more on Georg II's use of scenery, costumes, and lighting, see Ann Marie Koller, *The Theater Duke: Georg II of Saxe-Meiningen and the German Stage* (Stanford, CA: Stanford University Press, 1984), pp. 85–113.
6 See George R. Kernodle, "Wagner, Appia, and the Idea of Musical Design" (*Educational Theatre Journal* 6.3 [October, 1954]: 223–30).
7 Here, the innovator was impresario Richard D'Oyly Carte, whose Savoy Theatre in London opened in 1881 with Gilbert and

Sullivan's Patience, becoming the first theater to be lit entirely by electricity. His focus, however, was more on safety and comfort than on enhancing potential for innovative stage design.

8 For an overview of Appia's career, see Richard C. Beacham, *Adolphe Appia: Artist and Visionary of the Modern Theatre* (Philadelphia: Routledge, 1994).

9 See Edward Gordon Craig, *On the Art of the Theatre* (New York: Theatre Arts Books, 1956).

10 For a close examination of Craig's aesthetic and career, see Christopher Innes, *Edward Gordon Craig: A Vision of Theatre* (Amsterdam: Routledge, 1998).

11 For more on this production, see Richard Leppert, "The Civilizing Process: Music and the Aesthetics of Time-Space Relations in The Girl of the Golden West," in *Musical Meaning and Human Values*, ed. Keith Chapin and Lawrence Kramer (New York: Fordham University Press, 2009, 116–49).

12 David Belasco, *The Theatre through Its Stage Door* (Whitefish, MT: Kessinger, 2006), p. 56.

13 For more on this production, see Leigh George Odom, "'The Black Crook' at Niblo's Garden" (*Drama Review*: TDR 26.1 [Spring 1982]: 21–40).

14 For more on Thompson and her English Blondes, see Kristen Pullen, *Actresses and Whores: On Stage and in Society* (Cambridge: Cambridge University Press, 2005), and Faye E. Dudden, *Women in the American Theatre: Actresses and Audiences 1790–1870* (New Haven, CT: Yale University Press, 1994).

15 The myriad resources concerning Ziegfeld and his Follies include Randolph Carter, *The World of Flo Ziegfeld* (New York: Praeger, 1974); Marjorie Farnsworth, *The Ziegfeld Follies* (New York: G. P. Putnam's Sons, 1956); Richard and Paulette Ziegfeld, *The Ziegfeld Touch: The Life and Times of Florenz Ziegfeld, Jr.* (New York: Harry N. Abrams, 1993); and Linda Mizejewski, *Ziegfeld Girl: Image and Icon in Culture and Cinema* (Durham, NC: Duke University Press, 1999).

16 This swing was in sharp contrast to the increasing grandiosity of Hollywood movie musicals during this period, particularly those of Busby Berkeley, which flourished throughout the 1930s.

While Hollywood offered distraction and escape from the economic reality of the Depression era through spectacular sets and elaborately costumed production numbers, Broadway reflected the changing experience of its patrons through comparatively stark designs.

17 For an overview of the New Stagecraft movement, tracing its origins in Appia's work and its legacy, see Orville Kurth Larson, *Scene Design in the American Theatre From 1915 to 1960* (Fayetteville: University of Arkansas Press, 1989).

18 See Jones's manifesto on the theater: Robert Edmond Jones, *The Dramatic Imagination* (New York: Duell, Sloan, and Pearce, 1941).

19 Tim Carter, *Oklahoma! The Making of an American Musical* (New Haven, CT: Yale University Press, 2007).

20 The breadth of Mielziner's work is addressed in Mary Henderson, *Mielziner: Master of Modern Stage Design* (New York: Back Stage Books, 2001).

21 For more on the Eckarts, see Andrew B. Harris, *The Performing Set: The Broadway Designs of William and Jean Eckart* (Denton: University of North Texas Press, 2006).

22 For more on Rosenthal's career and aesthetic, see Jean Rosenthal and Lael Wertenbaker, *The Magic of Light: The Craft and Career of Jean Rosenthal, Pioneer in Lighting for the Modern Stage* (Boston: Little, Brown, 1972).

23 For a comprehensive and lushly illustrated treatment of Aronson's career, see Frank Rich and Lisa Aronson, *The Theatre Art of Boris Aronson* (New York: Alfred A. Knopf, 1987).

24 For more on Wagner's career, as well as other influential scenic designers, see Arnold Aronson, *American Set Design* (New York: Theatre Communications Group, 1985), pp. 153–67 for Wagner; and Ronn Smith, *American Set Design 2* (New York: Theatre Communications Group, 1991).

25 For an overview of design trends within the "British Invasion," see John Goodwin, ed., *British Theatre Design: The Modern Age* (New York: St. Martin's Press, 1989).

26 The use of such a designer is not entirely new, as Roy Benson had served as the "designer and supervisor of magic and illusion"

for Carnival! (1961), which features a love triangle involving a magician.

27 For additional essays on scenography and developments in design, see Arnold Aronson, *Looking in the Abyss: Essays on Scenography* (Ann Arbor: University of Michigan Press, 2005), and Christopher Baugh, *Theatre, Performance, and Technology: The Development of Scenography in the Twentieth Century* (New York: Palgrave Macmillan, 2005).

10

Acting

JOHN M. CLUM

ANDREA MOST HAS WRITTEN THAT "the musical comedy is a celebration of acting, and particularly of American acting."[1] This statement raises a number of questions. How do you define and evaluate acting in musical theater? Lyricist Lynn Ahrens (*Ragtime, Seussical*) wrote of the casting process for *The Glorious Ones*, a musical she co-wrote: "What mattered most to us in casting each role was how well the actor could act, how well he or she embodied the role and whether or not the actor understood the specific world we were trying to create."[2] I am sure that Ahrens assumed that the candidates for her cast had the voices and training to sing the songs she and composer Stephen Flaherty wrote for the musical. Given that, she could be choosy about their acting abilities. Ahrens's criteria may hold for a number of contemporary musicals and major revivals of past classics, such as the 2008 revivals of *Gypsy* (1959: book, Arthur Laurents; music, Jule Styne; lyrics, Stephen Sondheim) and *South Pacific* (1949: book, Oscar Hammerstein II and Joshua Logan; music, Richard Rodgers; lyrics, Oscar Hammerstein II), but the same criteria do not apply to recent rock musicals such as *Spring Awakening* (2006: book and lyrics, Steven Sater; music Duncan Sheik) or *Passing Strange* (2008: book and lyrics,

Stew; music, Stew and Heidi Rodewald) which rethink (in the case of the former) or defy (in the case of the latter) the usual conventions of musical theater regarding continuity of character between dialogue and song and the relevance of realistic acting to a rock musical. Nor were Ahrens's criteria for casting relevant to the producers, directors, and performers of Golden Age musical comedy who put "star turns" before characterization. Notions of acting, then, have to be considered in terms of the history of musical theater and the various subgenres that fall under the name "musical." Furthermore, discussions of theories of acting are inextricably linked with historically inflected concepts of character. In the musical, more than in "straight drama," these discussions also connect to the relationship between character and actor and the contrast between *acting* and *performing*.

Very little has been written directly on the subject of acting in musical theater. The only comprehensive textbook on the subject, Joe Dear and Rocco Dal Vera's *Acting in Musical Theatre: A Comprehensive Course*, underscores the subordinate position acting has had in the training of performers for the musical stage. *Acting in Musical Theatre* begins with basic Stanislavskian concepts of acting, though it is careful to delineate the differences between acting in musicals and "straight plays." The authors discuss key concepts, such as the importance of understanding a character's moment-by-moment objectives and her overall character objective and the obstacles that deter the character from reaching her objective. At the same time, the authors understand that the basic concepts of realistic acting will take the actor in musical theater only so far. They emphasize that "musicals operate on a heightened dramatic scale.... [T]he feelings will be large enough when it feels like life or death for your character" (Dear and Dal Vera, 44). This maxim suggests that acting in musicals needs to be set at a higher emotional pitch than in a play. Even so, there is always a difference in intensity between speech and song. The actor's task is to make both the dialogue and musical numbers real for the audience by finding a balance of scale between dialogue and song. This is a challenge in musical theater because singing requires a different level of physical energy than acting. For there to be a convincing transition between singing and acting of dialogue, the acting must have a different energy than that usually required for spoken theater.

The authors of the textbook also point out that unlike characters in realistic drama, "the characters in musicals... respond to adversity by becoming extraordinarily articulate" (Dear and Dal Vera, 76). Characters in musicals, in other words, tend to sing their subtext. Feelings or motivations may be hidden from other characters onstage but seldom from the audience. The imaginary fourth wall of realistic drama seldom exists in musicals. Characters take the audience into their confidence, which gives them a stronger rapport with those on the other side of the footlights. However, this articulateness is usually in the songs, not the book, for the dialogue of musicals is often far more condensed than that of a play. As actress Joan Copeland, a veteran of many musicals, notes: "In a way, you have to capsulize the characters more in a musical than in a straight play. You have to get to the character more quickly and precisely. You have far less dialogue to establish and develop the character."[3] Most of Dear and Dal Vera's textbook focuses, as it must, on how basic principles of acting are used to sing.

Acting in musical theater has a variety of meanings. It can mean, as we have seen, creating a believable character through speech and song, a criterion that is relevant only if character believability is a goal of the creators of the musical. It can mean the interpretation of the "book scenes" as opposed to "performing" the musical numbers. It can also mean interpreting a song so that it fits character and situation, which is sometimes difficult even in a character-driven musical by someone like

Stephen Sondheim. For instance, do the same criteria of performance apply to *Sweeney Todd*'s (1978: book, Hugh Wheeler; music and lyrics, Stephen Sondheim) "Epiphany," a quasi-operatic mad scene that defines Sweeney Todd's state of mind as he madly resolves to expand his list of victims from Judge Turpin to anyone who sits in his barber chair, and "A Little Priest," the ensuing clever patter song that seems totally "out of character" for the demented man who just roared through "Epiphany"? The challenge for any singing actor who takes seriously playing the role of Sweeney is to find a way of playing his character so that it justifies both songs. But we're talking here about a musical created by artists for whom character was paramount and that demands excellent singing actors. The very term I use, "singing actor," is problematic, for it implies that acting in a musical is more important than singing. Perhaps the term should be "acting singer." In opera nowadays, we expect excellent singers who can also act. The criteria for musicals are actually the same. The singing style may be different, but we expect good singers who are also good actors. Unless one is totally inexperienced at acting, most of the challenge of acting in a musical comes through the singing, not through speaking the lines.

Like most acting texts, Dear and Dal Vera's is most interested in helping performers be *believable* as characters in a musical. However, the issue of believability in a musical raises even more questions. In his book, *The Musical as Drama*, Scott McMillin celebrates the unreality of musical theater performance and suggests that our conventional criteria of "acting" are inappropriate in discussing musicals:

> We do not think of real people while we watch the performance. We think of performance people, people who can sing and dance, numbers people. Chekhov and Shakespeare characters are performance people too, but the song-and-dance performance is

not the same as the Chekhov or Shakespeare performance. If a suspension of disbelief occurs when we watch characters in a Chekhov play, it occurs twice when we watch characters from the book scenes of a musical open themselves into musical performance in the numbers. They are changed by the music. [4]

Are the characters in a musical really "changed by the music"? They are certainly most alive and often most convincing when they are singing. Yet the intensity of those musical moments is stronger when they are contrasted with spoken dialogue. Nonetheless, McMillin is correct in seeing that audiences enjoy the various disparities in a musical. Andrea Most has noted that the musical is more Brechtian (self-consciously performative) than realistic:

> Musical comedy is distinctly *not* realist, and the advent of a musical number—the switch in theatrical modes [from speaking to singing]—does, like Brecht's alienation effect, remind the audience that they are in a theater. But this reminder does not create the alienation effect Brecht describes. Quite the opposite. We might call the result of the separation of elements in a musical an *assimilation effect*. (Most, 9)

Both Andrea Most and Scott McMillin emphasize the paradox of disparity and unity in a musical that makes believability for an actor a challenge. Scott McMillin was also correct in seeing that a discussion of acting in musicals cannot be separated from questions about the very nature of this hybrid art form.

In the history of musical theater, acting was not always a primary concern. In the 1920s and 1930s *musical comedy* meant just that—a genre in which the book was not particularly important, and credible integration of musical number and dramatic situation was not a concern for creators or audience. Stars of musical comedy, as the generic term implies, were either singers (such as Ethel Merman), or comedians who could sing competently (such as Bob Hope, who quickly moved to Hollywood after appearing in a few musical hits in the 1930s) or who couldn't sing at all (such as Victor Moore, who moved back and forth between Broadway and Hollywood in the 1930s). Traditional musical comedy was a hybrid performed by specialists. The chorus was split into singers and dancers. Comics didn't have to be very good singers. Big-voiced singers weren't expected to be great actors. Dancers such as Fred and Adele Astaire did specialty numbers. The baritone who sang the big ballads wasn't expected to have comic timing. Serious actors usually avoided the musical entirely since there was enough serious drama on Broadway to keep them busy. Singers with legitimate voices weren't expected to belt. Operetta, extremely popular in the 1920s, was built on stock characters: the exotic romantic leading soprano and baritone, the comic mezzo and bass, the wistful tenor, and the perky soubrette. These same characters appeared again and again in different settings and costumes. Acting was definitely secondary to quasi-operatic singing. The work we consider the first great "serious" American musical, *Show Boat* (1927: book and lyrics, Oscar Hammerstein II; music, Jerome Kern), combined the conventions of 1920s musical comedy and operetta. The book was by Hammerstein, who had before then been associated with operettas. Magnolia and Gaylord were played by "legit" singers, for the most part performing scenes that could have been out of operetta until Magnolia starts jazzing it up a bit in the middle of the second act. Julie, originally played by Helen Morgan, got the torch numbers, though they are written to be sung with a real, quasi-operatic voice—the belt voice had not yet moved from vaudeville houses and nightclubs into the legitimate theater (which it would do with Ethel Merman in 1930). The older comic characters, Andy and Parthy, don't sing much. In revivals over the years, Captain Andy has become a plum role for an aging comic, the sort of performer who used to be the centerpiece of musical comedy. The song-and-dance team is given specialty numbers. The older black characters, Queenie and Joe, demand more musical versatility, though Queenie, Joe, and mixed-race Julie are doing sophisticated versions of the sort of blackface numbers ("coon songs" as they were called) that had been around since the minstrel show. There are no great acting challenges in *Show Boat*—no one in 1927 assumed that musical comedy performers would be particularly strong actors.

Show Boat is important because it combined musical comedy and operetta to create something more "serious," more character-driven, but for a dozen years after its premiere in 1927, the dominant form of musical would still be the traditional musical comedy driven by star comics (Eddie Cantor, Jimmie Durante, Ed Wynn), who usually had a fixed persona developed in vaudeville, burlesque, and revue. Audiences expected to see that persona, which meant that book writers had to create plots and "characters" built on the pre-packaged characteristics of their stars. Other roles were also types in which performers specialized: the ingénue, the romantic leading man, and so on. A singing star such as Ethel Merman was expected to sing and wisecrack with the comics, which she did in a succession of musicals in the 1930s and early 1940s. Often the book did not provide any consistency of character.

Take for instance, one of the most revived shows of the period (albeit with rewritten dialogue), *Anything Goes* (1934: book, Guy Bolton, P. G. Wodehouse, Howard Lindsay, Russel Crouse; music and lyrics, Cole Porter). The most richly "dramatic" song in the show is the one Reno Sweeney (originally played by Ethel Merman) sings at the opening, "I Get a Kick Out of You," a brilliantly written ballad about unrequited love. Here is a song that cries out for a performer who can act a song as well as sing it, the bored woman of the world who only comes alive at the sight of her beloved's "fabulous face." The lyric specifies the social milieu in which this woman lives and the argot of her world. The problem is that the character the song defines isn't the wisecracking nightclub chanteuse turned evangelist who sings the song. Exactly who owns the "fabulous face" she sings about? Certainly none of the leading men in the original cast had one. When Patti LuPone's leading man is the handsome Howard McGillin (in the 1988 revival) or Elaine Page and Sally Anne Triplett are paired with John Barrowman (in the 1989 and 2005 London revivals) one can think for a moment that Reno pines for her Billy Crocker. However, nothing in the dialogue suggests that is the case. Their duet, "You're the Top," is hardly "You Are Love." Reno ends up with the comic toff—clearly she isn't the romantic lead—and Billy gets the vapid ingénue he has chased throughout the show.

"I Get a Kick Out of You" is thus just a good song inserted into the musical with no character motivation. "Acting" the specifics of this song works against acting the character who sings it. Because *Anything Goes* is constructed as a farce rather than a romantic comedy, feelings and motivation don't matter much. Billy gets the love ballads and no one thought of Ethel Merman as the appropriate object of "Easy to Love." The general problem, then, for thinking about acting in traditional musical comedies of this period is that the songs are self-contained and often have little relationship to the characters who sing them or the overall action of the musical. Indeed, the same could be said of a musical hit like *Phantom of the Opera*. Do the songs of the Phantom, Raoul, or Christine really tell us anything about the specifics of their characters or situation?

No one thought of Ethel Merman, the original singer of "I Get a Kick Out of You," as a great actress. In fact, Merman personifies the problems of discussing acting in musicals. She was famous for facing the audience rather than her partner during dialogue scenes. Fernando Lamas, her leading man in *Happy Hunting* (1956: book, Howard Lindsay and Russel Crouse; music, Harold Karr; lyrics, Matt Dubey), famously asked, "Am I going to read my lines to Miss Merman and Miss Merman read hers to the audience?" The answer, of course, was "Yes." One can even see that trait in some of her film work, which may be one reason she did not become a big Hollywood star. Merman "performed" during both book and musical numbers. Playing a teenaged country girl like Annie Oakley in *Annie Get Your Gun* (1946: book, Herbert and Dorothy Fields; music and lyrics, Irving Berlin) was going to be a stretch for her in the best of circumstances, even more so in the 1966 revival when she was decidedly middle-aged, but Merman knew people went to see *her*, not Annie Oakley, and certainly not anyone else on stage with her. She could belt wisecracks with the same energy and efficiency that she belted her big numbers, but since no one cared about writing a coherent character for her, at least until *Annie Get Your Gun*, there was no need for her to study acting. She was a singer who occasionally said lines. Merman was a great success in *Annie Get Your Gun*, which she played for over 1,000 performances, but part of the frisson of the show was the disjuncture between the performer and the teenage country girl she played.

When Merman triumphed as Madame Rose in *Gypsy* (1959: book, Arthur Laurents; music, Jule Styne; lyrics, Stephen Sondheim), some of her advocates thought she had suddenly become an actress. What really happened was that for the first time she was given a three-dimensional character to play that perfectly fit her personality and hard-driving musical style. Her Rose wasn't as madly driven and unhappy as Tyne Daly's (1989: who acted the role better than she sang it) or as multifaceted as the Roses of Angela Lansbury (London, 1973; Broadway, 1974) or Patti LuPone (2008), who were able to make Rose in turns sexy, funny, manic, and sad. Lansbury and LuPone—and Betty Buckley (Paper Mill Playhouse, 1998) and Bernadette

Peters (2003)—under the leadership of directors who saw the musical as character-driven (the original director, Jerome Robbins, saw it as director- and star-driven) made acting both dialogue and songs the most important aspect of *Gypsy*, which has become the musical version of an operatic vehicle, like *Tosca*—a classic aficionados go to see again and again because they want to see what different great performers will do with its central role.

Hearing Ethel Merman sing "Everything's Coming Up Roses," a perfect belt number for the veteran diva, one was witnessing a singing style that already was passé. Pop music by the late 1950s had moved either to the mellower sound of male and female crooners or the sound of '50s rock. Within a few years, Broadway singers would be wearing wireless microphones. Belters were part of old Broadway, which was to go through a period of experimentation before resolving its split with pop and rock music. Merman could make the moment frightening because the sheer power of her voice, combined with the drive of the Styne-Sondheim song, made the song seem like the utterance of an indomitable will, but was that drive for self-assertion Rose's or Merman's? I don't remember specific details of the original production, but photographs show Rose singing the song as a solo while Herbie and Louise clutch each other in the background. Merman, as usual, did her thing on stage with everyone else in the background. Was this an acting choice or Merman's usual modus operandi? Singers who "act" the song as well as sing it often play more on its irony and its relationship to Louise. Tyne Daly stood apart, as Merman did, but hit herself on "Roses" as if it were "Rose's," thus making the song say something about the driving ego of the character who sang it: everything would come up Rose's way. Patti LuPone's Rose grabs onto Louise as if trying to imbue her with some of Rose's tawdry vision of show business success. The sad thing about Madame Rose is not that she is a stage mother driving her daughters to realize her own ambition but that her dreams are so limited. Vaudeville is dead and burlesque is dying; in response, Rose moves away from Los Angeles, not toward it! In a way, with all her limitations, Merman was perfectly cast to play this character, not because of her acting ability, but because she fit the original conception of the character. She, too, was a representative of a different era of show business. It is no surprise that *Gypsy* was the last musical she originated and one of the last musicals we consider classics.

The star power of Ethel Merman raises other issues about character and actor in musical theater. Audiences went to see Ethel Merman. Did they ever forget that it was Merman, not the character she played, that they were watching and hearing? In her book *Making Americans: Jews and the Broadway Musical*, Andrea Most defines two styles of acting in musicals: what she calls "the performative" and "the psychological." In the former style, "The theatrical characters, comfortable with performance, have control over their self definition. Their singing and dancing styles, their costumes, and their modes of behavior both determine who they are and to which community they belong. They are self-conscious about performance, acknowledging that they are on stage and gleefully making full use of the conventions the stage allows them for self definition" (Most, 31). Ethel Merman would fit into this category, as would most stars of Broadway musicals from the 1920s to 1940 and, in some cases, beyond.

Even in the post–Rodgers and Hammerstein era, many hits were star vehicles that were performer- rather than character-driven. Sometimes these vehicles would show that a star had more versatility than audiences and critics expected. Dancer Gwen Verdon was a passable singer and comedienne who became a star by playing the comic sex-driven females in *Can Can* (1953) and *Damn Yankees* (1955). In her next outing, *New Girl in Town* (1957), a musical adaptation of

Eugene O'Neill's *Anna Christie*, she demonstrated real talent as an actress. Nonetheless, the rest of her Broadway musical vehicles (*Redhead, Sweet Charity, Chicago*) took her back to her "type." Does one "act" Dolly Levi in *Hello, Dolly* (1963: Book by Michael Stewart, music and lyrics by Jerry Herman)? Does Carol Channing, the original Dolly, ever act? Like many musical stars before her, she adapts parts to fit her fixed persona. There is a long list of Dollys who followed Channing during the Broadway run, on tour and in London (Ginger Rogers, Mary Martin, Betty Grable, Phyllis Diller, Pearl Bailey, Yvonne DeCarlo, Ethel Merman, among others, plus a miscast Barbra Streisand in the elephantine film). Most of these replacements for Carol Channing were established stars with identifiable personae rather than actresses. Star turns were popular as long as there were stars.

Nonetheless, different demands were made on performers to act, as specialties and character types combined and broke down when, around 1940, book writers became interested in characters rather than types. Here, what Most calls the psychological mode of performance came into play: "The psychologically defined characters, while more detailed and realistically drawn, have much less control over their identity. These characters have a consistent costume, accent, and gestural style that are fundamentally based on *who they are*. . . . These characters do not redefine themselves every time they sing; rather, the songs form a natural extension of the dialogue" (Most, 31). One could define Most's distinctions as between *performing*, based on the individual style of the performer, and *acting* a coherent character. Joey Evans (*Pal Joey*, 1940: book by John O'Hara, music, Richard Rodgers; lyrics, Lorenz Hart) was not the first lead character who was a dancer as well as a singer (Junior in *On Your Toes* [1936: book, Richard Rodgers, Lorenz Hart, George Abbott; music, Rodgers; lyrics, Hart] made a star out of song and dance man, Ray Bolger), but Joey combined a number of types. He was at once the sexy leading man, like Antipholus in *The Boys from Syracuse* (1938: book, George Abbott; music, Richard Rodgers; lyrics, Lorenz Hart), and the comic con man William Gaxton played so often in musicals of the 1930s. Joey had to sing ballads and comic numbers, and perform jazzy song and dance routines. But Joey also had to be a loser who overreaches. Joey had complexity. Above all, because *Pal Joey* is a musical about sexually driven characters, Joey has to be sexy. It is no wonder the role sent its first incarnation, Gene Kelly, straight to MGM. Joey is a three-dimensional character in an art form where such depth had not appeared before. The same can be said of the complex, psychologically troubled career woman, Liza Elliott, in *Lady in the Dark* (1941: book, Moss Hart; music, Kurt Weill; lyrics, Ira Gershwin). More than most musicals, the experimental *Lady in the Dark* is written for an actress who can sing. The first half of each of the three acts is totally spoken. Legend has it that the original Liza, Gertrude Lawrence, was said to be a variable singer with pitch problems, though her recordings suggest that she was better than that (alas, there is no complete recording of the original production of *Lady in the Dark*). She was considered sui generis, charismatic, and a superb comic actress who moved back and forth between musicals and sophisticated comedies. For its time, *Lady in the Dark* was a hit, and Lawrence stayed through the entire run of a year and a half; producers considered her, like Ethel Merman, irreplaceable, but in a role that really did require a singing actress.

From the beginning of their collaboration in 1943, Rodgers and Hammerstein proudly dubbed their creations "musical plays." This separated their work from the musical comedies they knew well and had mastered separately in the decades before *Oklahoma*. The term "musical play" suggested that the material was to be more character-driven, which meant that more acting would be required of the performers than had been the case before then. Hammerstein had already shown in *Show Boat* that he wanted to create a hybrid of operetta and musical comedy. Now that hybrid would be merged with drama as Rodgers and Hammerstein created adaptations of works that had already appeared as straight plays (*Oklahoma!* was based on Lynn Riggs's folk drama, *Green Grow the Lilacs*, and *Carousel* was based on the Hungarian play *Liliom* by Ferenc Molnar, which appeared successfully on Broadway in 1932 and 1940, and had been adapted for film multiple times), serious films (*The King and I*, based on the book and 1946 film *Anna and the King of Siam*), or fiction (*South Pacific*, based on James Michener's *Tales of the South Pacific*). This involved a modification of previous fixed character types rather than a rejection of them. Laurey in *Oklahoma!* and Julie Jordan in *Carousel* are in some ways typical ingénue roles, sisters of Magnolia in *Show Boat*, but they are also individualized characters whose socioeconomic status is a driving force in their motivation. Ado Annie isn't much different from the man-hungry comic women of previous musical comedies, though she fits more convincingly into the social milieu the musical depicts. Celeste Holm, the first Ado Annie, was more an actress than a singer. Though *Oklahoma!* is mistakenly thought by many to be the first musical in which character complexity is important and songs and narrative are truly integrated, there is only one role in the musical that demands serious acting—that of Jud Fry, played originally by Howard da Silva, a veteran of the Group Theatre. Clearly, the creators felt that this brooding character needed to be played by someone from a different theatrical background than Curly, Laurey, Ado Annie, and Will Parker.

Musicals that require what we conventionally call "acting" are seldom star vehicles. The original casts of the first two Rodgers and Hammerstein musicals contained no established stars. The role was to be more important than the person who played it. It was only in *South Pacific* and *The King and I* that

Rodgers and Hammerstein, who now were producing as well as writing, felt the need to find a balance between character and star, although *South Pacific* ran for years after Mary Martin and Ezio Pinza left the cast and *The King and I*, at first a vehicle for the versatile, charismatic Gertrude Lawrence, has gone through several revivals in which her role has become secondary to the King, which is more an acting role than most musical leads. Both the roles of Nellie Forbush and Anna Leonowens demand more versatility than the usual type, and characterization beyond star persona. Clearly, as musicals became more character-driven than performer-driven, lead performers became more replaceable. Rodgers and Hammerstein's hits of the 1940s and 1950s could survive major cast changes in ways star vehicles could not. Ethel Merman's vehicles closed when she was tired of doing them: *Oklahoma!* and its successors went on for years with a succession of leads. Today, when musicals must last for years just to break even, the star vehicle of old is not economically feasible. Performers are now replaceable parts, asked to give more or less a reproduction of the performances of the original cast. What is being "acted" by a replacement has thus become an imitation of the performance of the original cast member. Star performers in Golden Age musicals were celebrated for their eccentricities, their inimitability. Acting singers in character-driven musicals are not allowed to stand out in the same way. Character comes before performer.

The 2017-18 Broadway season offered a perfect example of the difference between the performative and psychological styles of acting in musicals. At the Shubert Theatre, veteran singer and comedienne Bette Midler returned to Broadway in a revival of *Hello, Dolly!*, a musical that demands above all star presence. To the delight of her fans, Midler played Bette Midler as Dolly. No one in the audience wanted her to be anyone else and the part didn't demand the plumbing of psychological depth. A block away, young Ben Platt offered a powerful example of how a talented acting singer can create a believable character through speech and song in a musical. Platt's performance in *Dear Evan Hansen* (Book, Steven Levenson; Music and lyrics, Benj Pasek and Justin Paul), has made him a star but Platt never breaks character, never acknowledges the audience. Ben Platt convincingly becomes Evan Hansen in both dialogue and song. *Dear Evan Hansen* is a post-Sondheim musical that demands intense acting as well as singing; *Hello, Dolly!* demands personality.

For a brief period in the 1950s and early 1960s, a series of successful musicals were built around leading actors who were at best passable singers (Yul Brynner in *The King and I*, Rex Harrison in *My Fair Lady*, Richard Burton in *Camelot*, Robert Preston in *The Music Man*). In the case of the two Lerner and Loewe musicals (actually, the leading role in their unsuccessful 1951 musical, *Paint Your Wagon*, was also written for an actor who could barely carry a tune), the non-singing male lead supported the notion that these shows were more "serious" than their competition. One could also speculate that the creators thought that the leading men of contemporary musicals weren't good enough actors for the roles they had written. They wanted actors, not singers. Given the attitudes about gender in the 1950s, these older non-singers who became mentors and lovers for younger female characters may have been considered more manly than their singing counterparts. As I write elsewhere, "If you want to be a [male] star in a musical, don't sing the ballads. That's sissy stuff."[5] The long-running 2001 London revival of *My Fair Lady* featured a succession of distinguished actors who could actually sing playing Henry Higgins (Jonathan Pryce, Alex Jennings, Anthony Andrews). As singers are now expected to be good actors, so actors are no longer above singing in musicals.

However honestly and effectively a performer acts the dialogue—in the 2008 revival of *South Pacific*, for instance—we come to hear the songs, and it is in the songs that the characters most come to life for us. After all, both the original creators of *South Pacific* and the director of the 2008 revival cast as their leading man opera singers who had no experience of acting dialogue, particularly dialogue in English. Like all good opera singers, however, Ezio Pinza and Paolo Szot (in the 2008 revival) know how to act a musical number. Daringly, *South Pacific* ends in a silent tableau, as a new family is forged. There is a lot of dialogue in the work, but it is in song or silence that characters reveal who they are and what they feel most deeply. Do we even remember the names of the nonsinging military men who take over the stage for much of act II? Nellie speaks of her racial prejudice but sings of her optimism and her love, which ultimately prevail. The woman behind me at the 2008 revival of *Gypsy* told me that she had come to "hear Patti LuPone sing those songs." She didn't say anything about her expectations of LuPone's acting of the dialogue. As I noted earlier, most of the acting challenge in a musical comes through singing, not speaking the lines. What we expect in a "musical play," then, is someone who can act the songs as well as sing them, someone who can present the songs as utterances of a specific character with specific objectives. Only then are music and spoken dialogue tied together in a meaningful way.

Our criteria for acting in musicals have been changed by the microphone. In the days before body and head mikes, a strong singing voice that could reach the back row of the largest Broadway house was essential. Expertise in naturalistic acting was less important. Many critics have decried what the microphone has done to singing in the musical, but few discuss its effect on dialogue. With the microphone, acting can be less mannered, more naturalistic. This also means that singers are concerned less about volume and more with interpretation. The quasi-operatic legitimate voice and the Merman-like belt voice are no longer necessary to reach the back rows of large

Broadway theaters. As a result, there can be more seamless integration of dialogue and song. The trade-off is that musicals and performers lose some of their spontaneity when the sound is coming from speakers over and around the proscenium rather than from the singing actor's mouth. How "live" is theater without live sound?

Some contemporary rock-inflected musicals emphasize the difference between acting and performing the musical numbers. Michael Greif's original 1996 production of Jonathan Larson's *Rent* had the band on stage, minimal scenery, and a presentational style more like a rock concert than a conventional Broadway musical. In *Spring Awakening* (2006: music, Duncan Sheik; book and lyrics, Steven Sater), directed by Michael Mayer, a character developed in the dialogue pulls a microphone out of his pocket, even though he is wearing a head mike, and performs the song as if he were on *American Idol*. Mayer obviously wants to emphasize the disconnect between the show's source, the period drama written by Frank Wedekind, and the contemporary pop songs the characters sing. (Can't the audience hear this contrast without the visible presence of microphones?) *Spring Awakening* in effect has two styles: the "acting" style required by the book scenes and the rock performance style required by the songs. Mayer and his writing team are fighting the notion of "integration" championed by the advocates of Oscar Hammerstein and Stephen Sondheim (though the latter and his collaborators fought integration in many of their musicals). The performers in *Spring Awakening* need to be both actors and singers, though not simultaneously. Perhaps the kind of performance required by rock music works against a traditional concept of acting. Directors of rock musicals like *Rent* and *Spring Awakening* assume that audiences who are used to rock concerts expect a particular kind of performance associated with rock music.

In her book on rock musicals, Elizabeth Wollman notes that because the rock musical was created out of the desire to capture the sense of immediacy and authenticity, however artificial, of a rock concert, "staged rock musicals have always reflected an interest in finding ways to connect with audiences that are not typical of mainstream theater productions."[6] This may include creating the sense of an improvised performance with the band visible, or a different rapport with the audience than a conventional musical offers. This rapport isn't that different from the relative freedom offered a performer in a musical in the 1920s or 1930s. Rock musicals such as *Spring Awakening* support Scott McMillin's thesis that for all the talk of integration, the inescapable fact of any musical is the "incongruity between book and number" (McMillin, x). Most teachers of acting in musicals will encourage their pupils to reduce that incongruity in their performance.

The relative importance of acting in musicals, then, depends on the style of the show being performed. To a great extent, it depends on the style of the music the actors are required to sing. It is, after all, the songs that define the character and situation more than the dialogue.

NOTES

1 Andrea Most, *Making Americans: Jews and the Broadway Musical* (Cambridge, MA: Harvard University Press, 2004), p. 10.
2 Quoted in Joe Deer and Rocco Dal Vera, *Acting in Musical Theatre: A Comprehensive Course* (London: Routledge, 2008), p. xxii.
3 Dennis McGovern and Deborah Grace Winer, *Sing Out, Louise: 150 Stars of the Musical Theatre Remember 50 Years on Broadway* (New York: Schirmer Books, 1993), p. 51.

4 Scott McMillin, *The Musical as Drama* (Princeton, NJ: Princeton University Press, 2006), p. 59.
5 John Clum, *Something for the Boys: Musical Theater and Gay Culture* (New York: Palgrave, 1999), p. 128.
6 Elizabeth L. Wollman, *The Theatre Will Rock: A History of the Rock Musical from* Hair *to* Hedwig (Ann Arbor: University of Michigan Press, 2006), p. 70.

11

Singing

MITCHELL MORRIS AND RAYMOND KNAPP

THE AMERICAN MUSICAL, AS COMPARED to other theatrical genres that involve singing, such as opera and operetta, is extremely eclectic in its deployment of vocal types and song styles. Musicals not only offer the full range of classic "Broadway" types but may also include "quality" voices and operatic styles, derivatives from popular song, and a variety of comedic, specialty, and character-based vocal types whose entertainment value comes in some measure from vocal inadequacies of one kind or another. While this eclecticism may be understood in part as a legacy of vaudeville and other variety-based genres, it also stems from the musical's responsiveness to emergent popular styles, its penchant for pastiche, and its middlebrow aspirational profile, all of which have conspired to develop a steadily enriching mix of vocal possibilities. To do some justice to this wide range, we will here consider the basis of vocal production in the human body, delineate generally accepted typologies regarding voices and styles, and survey representative examples drawn from two shows especially rich in their deployment of distinctive song and voice types, *Kiss Me, Kate* and *Sweeney Todd*.

BODY TALK

Vocal production has been described in a number of ways, not all of which are commensurate. In the interest of establishing some common points of reference, this section briefly sets out some of the terms that seem most useful in describing singers and singing. This discussion is neither comprehensive nor exhaustive; rather, it establishes a few conceptual markers for the sake of further discussion.

The human vocal apparatus is a complex system involving a number of muscles and organs. The lower part of the system is the less intricate. The (thoracic) diaphragm, for instance, is a large muscle that forms a sheet supporting the chest and abdominal cavities. Above the diaphragm are the lungs and heart, below it the viscera. The diaphragm contracts to expand the lungs, creating inhalation. It expands to push air out of the lungs in exhalation (also assisted by the muscles of the abdominal wall). When vocal instructors speak of "support," they are primarily focused on control of the abdominal wall to better manage the controlled release of air necessary to speaking and singing. Support has a significant effect on singing technique, not only because consistent support helps establish a relatively homogenous sound but also because divergences from this homogeneity then acquire expressive meaning. An "unsupported" sound might strike the ears of listeners as wavering, uncertain, dubious, fragile; and it might be employed by a careful singer for dramatic effects. The lungs, in addition to their necessary functions in ventilation, also act as the reservoir for air that will be used to vocalize. Lung capacity is to some extent a matter of biology: men typically have larger lung capacity than women, taller people tend to have more than short people, those born and living at high altitudes usually have greater capacity than those born and living at sea level, and so on.

Moving from the lungs through the bronchial tubes, air enters the more complex areas of the larynx and the oral cavity. The larynx, composed of cartilage, muscle, and tendon, is an organ that guards the entrance to the trachea and sits just below the hyoid bone, above which lies the pharynx—the place where esophagus and trachea divide. Inside the larynx are the vocal cords, also called the vocal folds, which produce pitch and manage volume. The folds themselves are a pair of mucous membranes that stretch across the interior of the larynx; they produce pitch when air moves across them, causing them to vibrate. The length and thickness of the folds, which determines the pitch produced, is managed by the musculature of the larynx, which shifts the cartilages to control their shape. The size of the vocal folds is the central element in determining vocal range.

The components of the oral cavity take the sound generated in the larynx and shape it in an astonishing variety of ways. The most important features of the oral cavity are the palate or roof of the mouth, the tongue, the teeth, and the lips; the nasal cavity plays a substantial role in managing sound production as well. The soft palate, for instance, can be raised or lowered, not only to make the oral cavity larger or smaller but also to influence the particular overtones that help determine a sound's timbre. The tongue, in addition to its role in articulating consonants, also shapes the oral cavity to produce vowels. (Vowels can be distinguished from one another because each vowel reinforces specific parts of the overtone series.) It is in the oral cavity, in particular, that the concerns of singing merge with those of speaking.

DESCRIBING THE VOICE

The anatomical details just outlined constitute the material grounding of vocal production. Singing, as the term is usually understood, depends upon using the vocal apparatus to create sustained pitches, more or less stable frequencies. ("Middle C," as it is called with respect to the piano keyboard, can also be named as C4 in scientific notation, or c' in the system commonly used by music scholars; middle C is defined as approximately 261.626 cycles per second, or hertz.) In speaking, the voice typically ranges within a general area of frequencies rather than keeping one frequency more or less stable.[1] But musical systems around the world are very often constructed by selecting out a set of frequencies to form some kind of articulated system—often called a scale or a mode, depending on the strategies used in a particular kind of music. Musicals, since they are overwhelmingly based on the systems inherited from Western European music, work mostly within the 12-pitch chromatic scale.[2] Within the usual space occupied by human voices, a number of distinctions have been established that allow us to move beyond the specificity of unique voices and classify them and the ways they work. The terms of greatest use in describing singing are type, register, and production.

Vocal Type

This term refers to the combination of characteristic range and timbre (or vocal "color") of an individual voice. Male singers are named by the vocal types *bass, baritone*, and *tenor*, in order of ascending range; the female equivalents are *alto, mezzo-soprano*, and *soprano*. By convention each voice type centers on a particular segment of the musical system. The bass type spends most of its singing time in the octave-plus-fifth of F2/F-C4/c', though for the sake of special effects some bass parts extend down to C2/C; bass parts also can extend up as high as G4/g' but this is uncommon in the repertory of musicals. The baritone vocal type typically covers the area from F2/F to G4/g', although most singing will occur in the middle of this range.

It is distinguished from the bass voice not as much by the range of possible pitches it can sing, but more by the quality of voice—for most listeners, a baritone voice will sound "lighter," and will tend to be written in the higher parts of its range more often than would be usual in a bass part. The baritone type is considered the most common type of male voice, and this is true for much of the repertory of musicals. Tenor voices are the highest standard male voice type, usually written within the range C3/c-A4/a'. Operatic writing in particular makes some use of the brilliant effects of extensions above A4/a', up to C5/c', the tenor's famous "high C."

The standard complement of female voices parallels that of the male voices. The alto type, occasionally called contralto, is the lowest female voice, with music usually falling between G3/g to F5/f'; in addition, alto voices are often described as "thicker" or "heavier" in timbre. The mezzo-soprano is roughly equivalent to the male baritone and is probably the most common female voice type. Its characteristic range is A3/a-A5/a'. (Note that the range is quite large, and significantly overlaps that of the typical alto range. Once again, the distinction of vocal types is a matter not only of range but also of timbre.) The soprano voice lies within the compass of C4/c' and A5/a', with frequent extensions up to C6/c'; specialists in opera or recent popular music with the necessary skill set can sing even higher.

Especially in the world of opera, subdivisions can be established within each basic voice type. Thus, in the German *Fach* system, which depends on subclassification of voice types and their most suitable operatic roles, it is possible to describe high female voices as lyric coloraturas, dramatic coloraturas, soubrettes, lyrics, young dramatics, dramatics, and Wagnerian dramatics (in order from "highest" and "lightest" to "darkest" and "heaviest").[3] But even the German *Fach* system does not exhaust the roster of possible voice types. In particular, the male vocal type that relies to an especially great extent upon the falsetto register (see below), called *countertenor*, finds wide use in both "classical" and "popular" styles. The highest voice in male quartets is especially likely to be occupied by countertenors. Formerly something of a rare specialty in high- and middlebrow music, associated there primarily with antiquarian or ecclesiastical genres, the countertenor voice type has become much more common, expanding out of the gospel, soul, and rock contexts where it used to flourish most widely.

Register

This word may be used to refer to vocal range, the characteristic feeling of resonance in a specific section of the upper body, a timbre, or a given segment of a singer's range defined by the location of vocal "breaks."[4] Speech pathologists, since they base their classification on physiological distinctions, offer a convenient system through which to offer an overview. There are four registers that differ by the vibratory patterns used to produce them. These registers can be ordered from lowest to highest; if a singer moves from the lowest possible pitch in his or her voice to the highest, the vocal cords will exhibit these vibrational patterns in sequence—though with a degree of overlap between each register and those contiguous to it. The lowest register is called *vocal fry*, and is produced by loose glottal closure, that is, keeping the tension of the vocal folds loose enough to allow air to seep through the apparatus slowly, creating a distinctive buzzing or creaking sound of low frequency. Vocal fry is used in singing to reach low pitches more often than is recognized; it is more common as a technique for bass singers than for the other vocal types.[5] Above the register of vocal fry is the register of *modal* voice, the type of resonance that is used in the majority of singing and speaking. The modal voice typically occurs over the span of an octave and a half or two octaves, depending on the amount of vocal training a singer has had.

The *falsetto* register overlaps the modal voice by as much as an octave. In contrast to the modal register, where the entirety of the vocal folds is energized, in falsetto only the edges of the folds vibrate. Falsetto tends to produce fewer overtones than the modal register, giving a "lighter" or more "transparent" result. The difference between modal and falsetto registers is much more audible in men, thanks to their longer and thicker vocal folds, but the difference in women is significant in the musical (discussed later in the chapter). At the top of the register system is the *whistle* register; at present its means of production is imperfectly understood, but it seems that only the front part of the vocal apparatus is employed. The whistle register is rarely used by men but is often used by women.

It is worth noting that the distinctions offered here do not reflect the most common usages in vocal pedagogy. There, the terms *head* and *chest* voice are more commonly used. Rather than focusing on the specific vibrational patterns occurring in the larynx, these terms draw attention to the subjective experience of the singer. Chest resonance is most commonly experienced when singers are moving through the lower parts of the modal register; head resonance, on the other hand, is typical of the upper part of the modal register. (Some teachers and vocal coaches additionally distinguish further between chest, head, and falsetto voices.)

Production

This is the term used in this chapter to cover the local details of a singer's sound. It is at this point in description that technical vocabulary referring to physiology and bodily sensation tends to recede in favor of a much more figurative language. A whole host of words that may join sound synesthetically to vision (such as "clear," "crystalline," "murky," "dark") or touch ("syrupy," "thin"), or smell and taste, are all just as common and evocative as descriptors that refer one sound to another sound. (It may be that such language tends to proliferate in descriptions of voice because our vocabularies for sound are much less extensive and specific than those for sight, in particular.)

This kind of figurative language is probably the most useful way of describing the singing voice from the point of view of listeners. In addition, however, any quick survey of a selection of musicals will reveal that, quite frequently, performers may employ moments of speech within songs, as well as a huge range of vocal productions that lie somewhere between speech and song as those terms are usually construed. In the history of "classical" music, such liminal styles of production are often collectively referred to as *Sprechgesang*, or "speech-song" (the German name accurately reflects the area of its greatest formal use). Musicals, since they offer a more spacious environment for skilled actors who may not be skilled singers (Rex Harrison comes to mind), tend to feature *Sprechgesang* more than operas do. But even with respect to performers who do have ability as singers, the selective use of speech and semi-speech remains an important dramatic resource.

Another distinctive kind of voice production, one that has been enormously important in musicals, is called "belting," especially important in the careers of performers like Ethel Merman or Judy Garland. Although there are complicated, finicky disagreements about what belting is and how its muscular sound is produced, the most plausible explanation is that belting comes from holding on to the characteristic vibrational pattern of the modal voice, but in a pitch range where the falsetto register would normally be heard. Belting offered one of the most certain ways, before the common use of amplification, of being heard even in the cheap seats of the theater; but more than that, the kind of physical effort that is audible in a belted voice intensifies the energy of the performance, making it viscerally exciting in all senses of the phrase. To the extent that belting is associated with extravagant, outsize female characters, it establishes a very close tie between the timbre of a voice and the kinds of character traits we are likely to read into that voice.

And this leads to the question of "bad" singing in the musical. One way of understanding the particular effects of operatic singing, most especially the powerful tradition known as *bel canto* singing, as well as its relatives, is to observe that the desired characteristics, such as even tone throughout the registers, great agility and flexibility in executing ornaments and passagework, careful control of breath and phrasing, and clear but standardized diction, all have to do with making the voice into something that blends effectively with the instruments of the orchestra (in an era without amplification) while still being able to project over them; furthermore, to the extent that virtuosity of execution is prized in opera, these characteristics make vocal athleticism much easier to manage. The goal of homogeneity within a particular voice is not a special value in most styles of popular music, however. Instead, vocal heterogeneity acquires expressive value: distinctive differences between vocal registers, variations of sound resulting from changes in vocal production, strongly marked accents as well as idiosyncracies of diction—all kinds of "untrained" sound qualities tend to be heard as an index to the individuality of a singer or the character that the singer embodies. Because of this, singing in musicals is often subject to widely, even wildly varying criteria. Rather than attempting to maintain a single standard by which to judge a given performance or set of performances, it is usually more helpful to keep in mind the probability that in any show—sometimes even within a single song—multiple criteria may be operating simultaneously.

THE MATTER OF STYLE

Chapter 3 in this book's companion volume (*Histories*) offers a historically based survey of song styles prevalent in the musical, although a truly comprehensive account could easily fill a separate volume. It seems useful, though, to augment that discussion here by discussing specifically *singing* styles, not only according to the characteristic ways of singing already discussed (belting, speech-song, falsetto, head voice, chest voice, and the like), but also as a representation of time and place. Broadway has always been about creating and enhancing illusions of often exotic temporal and geographic settings, whether through scenery, costume, gesture, and vocal accent, or, most tellingly, through evoking an appropriate "atmosphere" by adopting specific styles of song and of singing. Because of that traditional function of song on Broadway, it seems important to frame our discussion in those terms, even as we underscore that the resulting and potentially endless diversity engendered by the strategy of evoking time and place through song makes cataloging nigh impossible.

Historically, this evocative function of song is a carryover from operetta, where conjuring up a semblance of (often fictional) exotic locales through song, or engaging in nostalgic pastiche (thus with a heavy accent on the first syllable, on the *past*ness of pastiche),[6] have aligned with common operetta themes. Many Broadway practices directly borrow from operetta, which provides access not only to "higher" styles familiar from opera (which on Broadway is also a matter of pastiche), but also provides the basis for easy extensions into other modes of evoking geography and pastness, through variations of what has loosely been termed *ethnic* song and dance, a broad category that may involve not only characteristic singing styles but also, as appropriate, jazz, blues, Latin rhythms, and scales borrowed from Jewish, Eastern European, or Asian traditions (among others), often allied with identifiable (and thus stereotypical) vocal accents and inflections.

Besides this quasi-geographic function of song, it may also evoke place in a more local context, by suggesting venue. A classic case is Kander and Ebb's *Cabaret*, which imitates the style of a Berlin cabaret circa 1930, but examples are legion and extend sometimes to suggest somewhat inappropriate conflations of place, as with the importation of revivalist and gospel styles into secular settings, such as the eleven o'clock numbers "Blow, Gabriel, Blow," "Sit Down, You're Rockin' the Boat," or "The Brotherhood of Man."[7] Venues such as the English music hall, vaudeville, nightclubs, café (or other folk-singing venues), the nineteenth-century parlor, and, more recently, street music (including rap and other contemporary types) are easily evoked through recreations of appropriate singing and musical styles.

The inverse of evoking distant times and places is, of course, creating a semblance of "now" through adopting contemporary styles—which is, again, a matter of pastiche, be it the imitation of rock-and-roll in *Bye Bye Birdie*, of rock in *Hair, Rocky Horror*, and later shows, or of rap in *Hamilton*. For many, the importation of rock to the Broadway stage in the 1960s and '70s was a watershed (see chapter 8 in *Histories*), since it decisively institutionalized amplification as a permanent Broadway reality, complicating the purely biological account of vocal production given above with other modes of vocal "enhancement," ranging from simply allowing singers to be heard over the orchestra, to aiding them in evoking singing styles (such as belting), to helping a falsetto voice carry, to the correction of faulty pitch through auto-tune (which, using current technologies, may efface other aspects of timbre).

KISS ME, KATE AND SWEENEY TODD

This discussion of type, register, production, and style by no means exhausts the ways we may describe and discuss singing, but it offers some useful points of departure when examining specific performances. To open up this consideration to more practical use, the remainder of this chapter turns to two specific case studies. Both *Kiss Me, Kate* (1948) and *Sweeney Todd* (1979) combine a marked aspirational dimension with a deliberate indulgence in cultural "slumming," and their ambitious and deft deployment of a wide range of vocal types and singing styles may be seen to align with both sides of their divided personalities in turn. *Kiss Me, Kate*, being based on Shakespeare in the wake of the Rodgers and Hammerstein revolution, has always worn its gestures toward high(er) culture openly, but it is also based just as squarely on the often petty side of those who perform high culture and gives prominent play to loose living and gangsterism, long-standing affiliates of Broadway. *Sweeney Todd* likewise points in both directions. Its operatic tendencies have been often discussed, along with its political allegories and high tragic tone, whereas Sondheim himself has noted with admiration the blank verse with which Christopher Bond subtly elevated and dignified Sweeney's argot (a feature retained in the musical). But *Sweeney Todd* also panders dreadfully (perhaps campily), trading shamelessly in shocking violence, lurid situations, and crude humor, an outgrowth of Sondheim's originating desire to bring Grand Guignol to the Broadway stage, blood and all. The spread between aspiration and pandering provides each show with a wide field of potential musical styles, and both Porter and Sondheim met their respective challenges well—which is not surprising considering that they rank among the most sophisticated Broadway composers of their respective generations (although both tend to be more celebrated as lyricists than as composers). Thus, both *Kate* and *Sweeney* draw on the full richness of Broadway's voracious capacity to draw on any and all musical styles that suit its purpose, without needing to answer to the standards of aesthetic unity that opera and other "serious" musical genres seem to demand.

Kiss Me, Kate

Kiss Me, Kate employs a pervasive strategy of stylistic layering, first, to establish boundaries between both its strata of characters and its layers of performance, and, second, to overstep those borders repeatedly in order to collapse the difference between performer and character, and between performance on stage and performance in life. In this, it remains true to its origins in the observed intermingling of onstage and backstage drama during a Theatre Guild Production of Shakespeare's *Taming of the Shrew* by the Lunts some years earlier.[8] One of the distinct advantages augured by the decision early on to turn the show into a musical (as well as being able to recruit a reluctant Cole Porter for the project) was the possibilities that a musical could provide for making—and violating—these distinctions in vividly musical terms.

For example, the main couple, Fred Graham and Lilli Vanessi, are alike in aspiring to an artistic level higher than their sensibilities can sustain, and so their theatrical background and musical styles are operetta. Operetta, as a genre within American culture, is firmly ensconced in aspirational middlebrow culture, capable of coupling beautiful, quasi-operatic singing with grand gestures, and unconcerned about (or oblivious to) the yawning gap that separates operetta from actual opera. Thus, early on, Fred and Lilli reconnect through "Wunderbar," a number from an operetta they remember from their past—which is clearly not true operetta but rather an American facsimile of operetta, intermingling German words as an obviously phony marker of old-world authenticity (the song is rumored to have come readymade from Porter's trunk of unused songs). In singing this song together, the two reveal a level of comfort with each other and with themselves that they will not recapture, even in the happy ending that awaits them (🔊 Example 11.2).

Within the musical production of *Taming of the Shrew* that Fred's company is mounting, he (as Petruchio) sings three songs, all deriving from lines in Shakespeare's play. The first, "I've Come to Wive It Wealthily in Padua," adopts an archaic style meant to evoke the Italy of Shakespeare's day, including the "canzona" rhythm that Porter was undoubtedly taught in his music classes at Yale as a hallmark of that style (🔊 Example 11.3). His second song, "Were Thine that Special Face," borrows several operatic tropes, rendered more palatable to Broadway through the modified beguine rhythm that supports the return of the chorus. Porter here creates a kind of da capo structure (ABA) by delaying the recitative-like verse until after the first chorus and letting the verse's more direct text-setting function like a Baroque opera's "B" section, whereas he gives the vocal line an operatic quality through shaping, playing to the rich deeper notes and heroic higher notes of his singer, Alfred Drake, the quintessential "quality" baritone then singing on Broadway (🔊 Example 11.4). Petruchio's third song, "Where Is the Life that Late I Led," is an operatic "list" song, a virtuosic blend of melodramatic and *buffa* elements that ends with an elaborate vocal cadenza across the final three words of the title phrase (🔊 Example 11.5).

In contrast to Petruchio, Kate sings only two songs, near the end of each act, and in each oversteps the role she is supposed to be playing, bringing her (Lilli's) private quarrel with Fred on to the stage, and breaking down Fred's otherwise professional façade (thus, all three of Petruchio's songs remain earnestly in character). "I Hate Men," coming right after Lilli's discovery that the flowers she received from Fred were meant for someone else, gestures toward the "mad" scene by alternating gloomy minor-mode melodrama, set up by an "illogical" chord progression, with a flippant major mode in a more modern idiom (🔊 Example 11.6). Porter withholds the rage aria that he might have opted for in this position, saving that style instead for Kate's interjections during the first act finale, which bring down the curtain in chaos. But her song that opens the second act finale, "I Am Ashamed that Women Are So Simple," derives more directly from the play's dialogue than any other song in the show, holding its simple and direct musical style until the end, where it briefly adopts a militaristic dotted-note (i.e., march-derived) motive ("So wife, hold your temper and meekly put/Your hand 'neath the sole of your husband's foot"), leading to a brief indulgence in the melodramatic scoops of romantic opera ("My hand is ready, ready,/May it do him ease"). It is only in the operatic excesses of the final lines that Kate's song reveals Lilli winking behind the vocal mask of what otherwise seems as earnest a song as any in the show (🔊 Example 11.7).

"So in Love," which Lilli and Fred each sing in turn as a heartfelt soliloquy, she in the first act and he in the second (a reprise that comes across to some commentators as a lapse of dramatic logic),[9] directly links the two original singers, Alfred Drake and Patricia Morison, by playing directly to their mutual strengths: both singers had rich, covered voices, intimate in the lower register and carrying full-bodily into the higher register. Porter shapes the song accordingly, beginning three of the song's four 8-bar phrases at the lowest pitch and ascending an additional step with each phrase, while otherwise following the traditional AABA form common to Tin Pan Alley show tunes. Nevertheless, there is a subtle but telling dramatic difference between the two appearances of the song. Lilli, early on anticipating their reuniting as a couple, soars in her final phrase to the highest notes of the song ("I'm yours till I die"), and then falls away in waves from this vocal climax as if from sexual climax ("So in love, So in love, So in love with you, my love, am I"). Yet, when Fred begins this phrase of the song ("So taunt me and hurt me"), his rich lower register brings reality to the hurt, so that his own heroic ascent ("till I die") comes across as resolve in the face of a bleak future to be endured *without* the consummation Lilli seems to anticipate, brought about in performance by a sotto voce rendering of the final iterations of "so in love" (◉ Example 11.8; ◉ Example 11.9).

The vocal stratum occupied by the secondary couple, while clearly "Broadway," is not so elaborately developed. Harold Lang (the original Bill Calhoun) had to badger Porter to write him a song (owed to him by contractual obligation), and the result, "Bianca," despite its charm, gives credence to the anecdote that Porter deliberately wrote a song so hokey it would have to be cut. This and the second-act song of his counterpart, Lois Lane, "Always True to You in My Fashion," are novelty songs, setting up a dance number for Bill and providing a tour de force Broadway list song for Lois in the best Porter tradition. Lois's earlier song, "Why Can't You Behave?" briefly reprised as a lead-in to "Always True to You," is a conventionally bluesy number, replete with throaty scoops both up and down on the title phrase (◉ Example 11.10). It is in the first-act quartet "Tom, Dick or Harry" that they define both their onstage and offstage relationships, through their mutual occupation of the same level of earthy sophistication, he through dance and she through flirtation and witty wordplay (thus, "Any Tom, Dick or Harry,/Any Harry, Dick or Tom"). As a singer, Bill's Lucentio is comfortably situated between the other two suitors, not only in register and temporally but also because he pretends neither to money (as his lower predecessor Gremio) nor position (as his aristocratic successor Hortensio). As a dancer, he is able to offer the heightened physicality demanded by the (archaizing) rhythms and sexual innuendo of Lois's Bianca. Although occupying the middle (and with only a middling voice), he is thus on an even footing with the more stable bass of Gremio and the aristocratic high operatic tenor of Hortensio—the latter type in any case often marked as effeminate on Broadway (◉ Example 11.11).

As markers for a Broadway (comic) sensibility, Lois and Bill also provide useful points of reference for the lead couple. "Bianca," for example, seems to parody "Were Thine That Special Face" in its overly simplistic recitative-style setting of self-deprecating words (respectively, "So I've written her a love song/Though I'm just an amateur," and "I wrote a poem/In classic style/I wrote it with my tongue in my cheek/And my lips in a smile"; ◉ Example 11.12; ◉ Example 11.13). And "Always True to You" tweaks "Where Is the Life" fairly directly, especially obvious for those who might recognize their mutual origin in Cynara (respectively borrowing the lines "I have been faithful to thee, Cynara! in my fashion," and "gone with the wind"—the latter also the basis for the title of Margaret Mitchell's famous book; ◉ Example 11.14). Thus are the borders both patrolled and violated by musical style, in a trope of parallel construction that dates back at least to eighteenth-century opera.

The lowest musical tier belongs to the gangsters, who perform a vaudeville number, "Brush Up Your Shakespeare," in front of the curtain late in the second act. This is one of the most enduring—and endearing—of eleven o'clock numbers, reinforcing the already established basis for these characters in burlesque caricature, and (depending on casting) often revealing quite skilled performers lurking behind characters who have served mainly as comic relief and a convenient means to force the plot along. The singing style appropriate here has quite a wide range, since a comic effect can be achieved equally from actual singing or from a kind of speech-song (or something in between); as a waltz song, the number is ultimately as much about their surprising turn as comic dancers as about the broad humor of their pun-strewn lyrics (◉ Example 11.15).

Finally, the choral numbers of *Kiss Me, Kate* support and partake of nearly the full range of cross-cultural tweaking already observed between the secondary and lead couples. Fairly obviously, "We Open in Venice" tweaks "Another Op'nin',

Another Show," by revealing, as the flip side of opening-night excitement, the dreary routine of a touring company. More subtle is the send-up of "I Sing of Love" by "Too Darn Hot," displacing the (really, too-) benign pastoral of the first act with the gritty, jazz-based opener to the second. But the chorus's most important function derives from opera, representing the public that underscores the embarrassment of the dysfunctional lead couple in the first-act finale, but also supporting the operatic excess of feeling that invigorates the second-act finale, for which Lilli's Kate substitutes Italian superlatives ("Carissimo!" "Bellissimo!") for the insults she interjected in the first-act finale (🔊 Example 11.16).

Sweeney Todd

Sweeney Todd is a famously class-conscious musical, and differences in songs—both their styles and genres as well as the ways they are performed—are central to the musical's evocation of different social worlds. But the variation of social/musical levels takes place within an overall set of strategies that gives *Sweeney Todd* an operatic flavor: although there is some spoken dialogue, it is relatively sparse, and plot advancement as well as emotional amplification both take place through primarily musical means—a contrast to the Broadway tendency to place action in the book and feeling in the songs; the bitter humor underlying the words and music, however often it may pop up in Sondheim's earlier shows, pervades the entirety of *Sweeney*, darkening the show to a degree much more common in operas than in musicals; although "popular," "lower," or "lighter" musical styles are mixed together with some more overtly modernist ones, they are all rather antiquated—nineteenth-century popular styles, not the jazz-tinted (more recently, rock- or rap-inflected) kind that usually mark Broadway works. Nevertheless, *Sweeney*'s operaticisms take place within a set of assumptions that govern musicals rather than operas. Most crucially, the roles of Sweeney and Mrs. Lovett (and to some extent the role of Judge Turpin) can be quite effectively executed by actors with only moderate musical skills—fabulous voices are not particularly necessary for them, but dramatic skill is paramount.

An overview of singing in *Sweeney Todd* can begin with the assignment of vocal types to characters. To some extent this follows the practices of much nineteenth-century opera: unquestioned romantic leads and younger characters get higher voice types, while more complex, ambivalent, or older characters are written for lower voices. Sweeney and Judge Turpin are cast as bass-baritones or baritones, suggesting that if baritones are cast, those whose voices are a bit heavier and/or darker will match the parts best. Mrs. Lovett is similarly designated as an alto or mezzosoprano, the choice again signaling that a certain vocal heft is desirable. Joanna is a soprano, and by the evidence of her music, one who tends strongly toward the coloratura style or the soubrette type rather than the lyric or the dramatic sopranos—she is an ingénue first and foremost. The Beggarwoman is assigned to the mezzo-soprano type, which is probably meant to match her age and rough life. The tenor roles show the most interesting range of characterizations. Anthony Hope, as a stereotypical handsome young sailor—a Frederic from *Pirates of Penzance*—is either a baritone or a tenor: a young Heldentenor (to simplify brutally, a baritone who has lots of good high notes) would be an effective compromise and would point up the youthful heroics that justify the character's presence in the show. Tobias Ragg is listed as a tenor, which taken together with his rather simple, folkish music, indicates his youth and naiveté. Most interesting of all with respect to vocal type are Adolfo Pirelli, the barber/con man who is cast as the most Italianate of tenors, and Beadle Bamford, whose allotted type of tenor/countertenor reinforces his unctuous foppery.

The most "musical" of *Sweeney*'s numbers is certainly Joanna's "Green Finch and Linnet Bird." To begin with, the song is unproblematically allegorical, commenting on the emotional situation rather than constituting itself as part of the direct action. Joanna is introduced standing on a balcony, in effect giving a little concert. The presence of high style is marked by the song's range of an octave plus fifth, its propensity for wide leaps and somewhat tricky turns of melodic phrase, and above all by the ostentatious trill that leads into the recapitulation of the song's opening material (🔊 Example 11.17). But just as important as all of these musical details is the simple choice of this voice type; for good or ill, the soprano voice type is the stereotypical operatic voice, and the decorum required to make "Green Finch" effective—careful pronunciation, a controlled sound that makes each pitch sound clearly, evenness of tone throughout the voice's range—marks the song as "cultivated." This is of course the character's natural state: as the genteel ward of Judge Turpin, Joanna is a well-brought-up young lady who has been kept "innocent," and the somewhat stock opera-operetta tone of her song signals this to the audience from the moment she opens her mouth.

By contrast, Mrs. Lovett's introductory number, "The Worst Pies in London," uses a bustling lower style with many modernist touches (unpredictable rhythms, some piquant dissonances) to sketch out her broadly comic character—the gruesome facets of her ferocious capitalism come later on. The song requires two kinds of singing. In the fast patter sections of the song, the music aims at rhythmic vivacity. Whether we take the unexpected pauses and sudden accents of the patter sections as syncopations or frequent shifts of meter, the song's bumpy progress comes across as an exemplification of Mrs. Lovett's tendency to chatter interrupted only by the occasional gasping breath or distracted exclamation. What is abundantly clear, as well, is that actual pitches matter less to the song's effectiveness than the accuracy of the rhythms. The more lyrical sections of the songs occur when Mrs. Lovett ruefully describes her wares. Because the deprecation is so broad, her melodic effusions will keep their humor whether the actress cast can sing well or not (🔊 Example 11.18). Mrs. Lovett is an effective part for actresses who can act and count, whether or not they can produce beautiful tones. In fact, it is likely that this song, even more than the rest of Mrs. Lovett's numbers, will gain from being more spoken, less sung. The original cast album of *Sweeney* demonstrates Angela Lansbury managing exactly this kind of vigorous farce in an exemplary matter; specific sonic details might include her management of Cockney-ish vowels and glottal stops to increase the song's rhythmic vitality; her switch between the modal register for patter, and a carefully wobbly falsetto register for her lyrical effusions; and her ways of changing vocal production to increase the song's sense of nonstop breathlessness.

Sweeney's overwhelming mad scene, "Epiphany," is subject to many of the considerations that drive "The Worst Pies." A beautiful sound is not at all the point. "Epiphany" sets up a contrast between more spoken passages, where Sweeney rages at losing his chance with the Judge, and where he imagines slaughtering unwary customers for practice (🔊 Example 11.19), and more lyrical stretches where he alternately pronounces sentence on the whole world and mourns his lost wife and child (🔊 Example 11.20). It's worth noting that the lyrical moments in Sweeney's vocal part are always carefully supported by preparatory instrumental cues and/or helpful doublings. Len Cariou's performance on the original cast album, like Angela Lansbury's, reveals his great success at using vocal production to create many nuances of delivery in the vocal part.

The vocal worlds of Sweeney and Mrs. Lovett represent a demotic level of musical discourse in the musical: they are the equivalent of the show's urban common speech. Joanna and

Anthony operate in a "higher" stylistic world, which is appropriate since of all the characters they are least implicated in the variously sordid and ghoulish happenings on stage. The vocal spaces occupied by both the Beadle and Pirelli, however, are set up to be audibly false instances of high styles. In Pirelli's case, the musical style evoked by his vocal type and his style of singing is distinctively foreign—Italian opera, and a very bad imitation at that. This is not only a matter of his caricatured Italian diction and his gracelessly set up high notes: the minor-mode parodic tone specifically conjures the operas of Rossini, creating an effect not unlike the famous Bugs Bunny/Elmer Fudd travesty "The Rabbit of Seville" (🔊 Example 11.21). Although Sondheim has been criticized for this role, he deserves defending: after all, the whole point of Pirelli is that he is a *fake* Italian; his characterization is meant to be crude and embarrassing, and it makes him contemptible enough as a person that his murder and transformation into meat pies (the first one) does not alienate the audience. (And, since this first one goes down so easily . . .) The Beadle's musical world is different—he belongs to the sentimental, effusive, ultimately mendacious world of parlor song—but its effect is similar (🔊 Example 11.22). Because he is presented vocally as precious, possibly even effeminate in vocal manner, and because of the way his self-importance merges so easily into his occupation as toady and panderer, the Beadle is, like Pirelli, a petty villain, one whose dispatch will not trouble the audience.

The point of all these stylistic juxtapositions, in the end, is their effectiveness at creating an elaborately layered world within which the penny-dreadful action takes place. Certainly, if one were to choose a generic designation for this musical, it would be melodrama. It is to melodrama that *Sweeney Todd* owes its most enduring and spectacular effects; and this is as true of its music as it is of its plot or staging.

NOTES

1 When linguists analyze the pitch systems of tonal language, for instance, they are concerned with relative pitch rather than absolute pitch; even a highly tonal language such as Hmong Der, for instance, defines its tonal levels in general terms such as "high," "middle," and "low" areas of pitch rather than by pitches as they are understood in music.
2 "Octaves" are defined as two notes whose frequencies display a 2:1 ratio. Thus, if A4/a' is the name for the frequency 440 Hz, then A3/a would oscillate at 220 Hz, and A5/a' at 880 Hz. The ear typically recognizes this ratio, hence these frequencies are designated by the letter a. For a more detailed discussion, see ◯ Example 11.1.
3 The *Fach* system is especially important for opera singers, but an acquaintance with it is helpful to those interested in musical theater as well. One account of this can be found in Pearl Yeadon McGinnis, *The Opera Singer's Career Guide: Understanding the European Fach System* (Lanham, MD: Scarecrow Press, 2010).
4 "Breaks" are those segments of a singer's range in which the vocal mechanism shifts between types of resonance. The most important of these breaks is the transition between modal and falsetto registers. The location of breaks is one of the traditional defining characteristics of voice types in vocal pedagogy.
5 Vocal fry is also characteristic of "creaky voice," a device encountered in some tonal languages of Southeast Asia and Mesoamerica.
6 "Pastiche" on Broadway refers to the practice of imitating specific, identifiable styles of song, whether of an era, a song type, or a specific composer, through allusion to or reproduction of key features of the evoked repertory. While the term "pastiche" is often used pejoratively, as part of a claim that a composer relies too much on imitation and not enough on imagination, it is in fact basic equipment for composers on Broadway, who must communicate much in a few deft strokes.
7 The "eleven o'clock number"—so called because it is usually placed strategically late in the show—is designed to elicit extended applause and (usually) encores. For speculation regarding the dramatic import of this theatrical device, see Raymond

Knapp, "Getting Off the Trolley: Musicals *contra* Cinematic Reality" (*From Stage to Screen*, ed. Massimiliano Sala, vol. 18 of *Speculum Musicae* [Turnhout, Belgium: Brepols Publishers], 2012, pp. 157–72).

8 See Charles Schwartz, *Cole Porter: A Biography* (New York: Dial Press, 1977), pp. 230–31. For another discussion of the background, dramatic organization, and songs of the show, see Raymond Knapp, *The American Musical and the Performance of Personal Identity* (Princeton, NJ: Princeton University Press, 2006), pp. 273–84.

9 See, for example, Geoffrey Block, *Enchanted Evenings: The Broadway Musical from* Show Boat *to* Sondheim (New York: Oxford University Press, 1997), pp. 192–93.

12

Dance and Choreography

ZACHARY A. DORSEY

■ □ ■

WARMING UP

My central task in this chapter is to articulate a methodology for analyzing dance in musical theater performance. I begin by discussing definitions of both dance and choreography in this context, assessing the existing body of writings on dance in musical theater, and offering a few observations as to why such scholarship has rarely been pursued. I conclude with an examination of Bob Fosse's 1979 film, *All That Jazz*, to demonstrate the challenges and the joys to be found in looking intensely at dance and choreography in musical theater.

Early in "The Line," Mark Steyn's chapter on dance in *Broadway Babies Say Goodnight!*, he quotes the lyrics to the Irving Berlin song, "Choreography":

Chaps / Who did taps / Aren't tapping anymore
They're doing / Choreography!
Chicks / Who did kicks / Aren't kicking anymore
They're doing / Choreography![1]

Steyn includes Berlin's song to underscore a major shift in the history of dance in musical theater. Steyn relates that in 1936 for *On Your Toes*, George Balanchine became the first member of a production team for a Broadway musical to request that his work be described as "choreography by . . . " rather than "dances by . . . "; Balanchine saw himself as a "choreographer" rather than a "dance director," the title common to the industry at the time. In "The Line," Steyn traces the ascent of the choreographer on Broadway, as well as the relative importance of dance in the Broadway musical from that moment, noting how concert dance choreographers such as Balanchine and Agnes de Mille brought highbrow dance forms like ballet and modern dance to musical theater, paving the way for director/choreographers Jerome Robbins, Michael Bennett, and Bob Fosse, among others.

Berlin's song is just a divertissement for Steyn, but it is instructive, for those of us studying dance and choreography in musical theater, actually to look at the 1954 film *White Christmas*, in which "Choreography" is sung and danced (▶ Example 12.1).[2] As the number begins, a small flock of ponytailed women clad in gray calf-length shifts form a tableau around a single male dancer (Danny Kaye) sporting tight-fitting black clothes and a black beret. Accompanied by music both dissonant and piercing, the women's dancing is asymmetrical, out of unison, and jerky. Their flat-footedness and frequent sinking or falling to the ground suggest a sort of earthbound-ness, and their facial expressions make them seem alternately anguished and vacant. A few moments later, they stomp upstage to form and hold another tableau, even more angular and unnatural, reminiscent of two-dimensional figures frozen on an ancient vase. At the center of the tableau, Kaye wonders aloud, in a "posh" accent, "The theatuh [sic], the theatuh, what's happened to the theatuh, especially where dancing is concerned?" and then breaks into Berlin's song.

As he finishes the lyrics, a woman in a short hot pink skirt and tap shoes (Vera Ellen) descends into the frame from above (presumably lowered in on a trapeze). (▶ Example 12.2) At first, only her legs are revealed, and the women in gray and Danny

Kaye all surround her on the ground, eyes wide and faces nosed curiously toward these tapping pink feet, as if they were some alien object newly fallen to earth, filling them simultaneously with wonder and horror. Shortly, the camera pulls back to reveal this leggy pink and blond confection in her entirety (with hot pink muff on her hand and oversized pink feather in her hair), and she is joined by a male tap dancer in a white suit (John Brascia), who springs up through the stage floor. The two of them hoof it together, and intermittently, dance with Danny Kaye, while the chorus of women swarms around them.

The lyrics and the mise-en-scene make it clear that Kaye's character and his chorines represent the new wave, the "choreography" that is edging out the hoofing and other conventional dance steps of musical theater. Yet by watching the dance, one sees that it's all parody, all over-the-top send-up of both "dance" and "choreography," a fact that might be missed in reading Berlin's lyrics alone. These characters are all larger than life—not just Kaye and his chorus women, but also Ellen and Brascia, each of whom makes a spectacularly ridiculous entrance. And though the song itself might pit dance (or at least the old way of doing things) against choreography, this is not a cage match or a dance-off; Kaye's character reveals himself deft at partnering and well able to share the honor of lifting and twirling Ellen about with Brascia. And importantly, the two groups arrive in a tight tableau at the end of the song, the three leads framed by the chorus, all with arms thrust upward, neither group edging the other out of the spotlight despite their differences in movement styles and appearances.[3] One might imagine, upon listening to and watching this short song and dance, that musical theater would be ever informed by this convergence of dance forms, as well as reassured that the new dance is unlikely to ever replace the old.

I begin with this piece for a few reasons. First, to reiterate Steyn, it is an elaboration of a key moment in musical theater dance history. Even if an audience is lacking the full context—say, that the women in gray are only slightly exaggerated versions of dancers performing modern dance choreographer Martha Graham's technique—one can still see two vastly different dance styles in this number and understand from the spoken text and sung lyrics that change is under way in show dancing. Dance, certainly, can educate, parody, and crystallize a sociocultural moment, and it does all of these things in "Choreography," if only we're willing to look.

Also, I intend this assessment of "Choreography" to demonstrate that studying dance can be a joyful thing, and that this pleasure need not be absented from extensive analysis. "Choreography" might be dismissed as just an elaborate piss-take of pretentious choreographers, but as its staging places bodies on display, it can generate other narratives and hold other significances as well. Further attention to detail and interpretation, for example, might focus on the dancing bodies of the women in gray as juxtaposed to that of Vera Ellen, revealing two dynamically different versions of womanhood. When Ellen first descends, the other women seem mesmerized by her tapping feet, but the camera lens focuses on her bare legs all the way up to her waist. Who or what is being looked at here? And what contexts—gender roles in 1950s America, conceptions of beauty and sex appeal in show dancing, Vera Ellen's anorexia—might enrich our analysis? While dance in musical theater is fun just to watch, the intricacies of moving bodies demand a closer and more measured inspection of the dance itself, as well as considerable thinking about the contexts of the dance and the issues that rise out of it. This work, too, can be tremendous fun.

So what, then, is "choreography"? I examine this number from *White Christmas* not because I want to place choreography and dance as oppositional (as Berlin's song might comically imply), but rather, to show how interconnected they are.

I have delayed the definitional aspect of this chapter purposefully, in part to gesture toward what I believe is the relative unimportance in most cases of parsing out the differences between dance and choreography. First, "choreography" literally means "dance writing" (from the ancient Greek), and as a term, it has become increasingly used since the eighteenth century when the practice of preserving dance steps by writing them down using assorted symbols and systems became popular. More generally, though, choreography refers to the composition of dance—not just putting the dance to the page but rather creating and assembling the dance structures and steps themselves. A choreographer, thus, is the person who creates choreography. I was drawn to using the number from *White Christmas* in part because there is a brief yet memorable moment right before Kaye's character starts singing when he reaches out and adjusts one of the dancer's hands, tugging it upward a few inches, presumably correcting her execution of his character's choreography. As a keyword, choreography is included in this chapter to spotlight the labor of the choreographer, to reiterate that dance steps for musical theater are purposeful creations.[4] Dance is almost never improvised or left to chance in musical theater performance on stage and screen; rather, it is methodically planned, rehearsed, and executed—and we should take for granted that these movements are there for a reason, even if we can't completely fathom what that reason might be.

So what, then, is "dance"? One of the first (and often, most frustrating) tasks in an introduction to dance studies class is the exploration of different definitions of dance. Roger Copeland and Marshall Cohen note that dance "is sometimes defined as any patterned, rhythmic movement in space and time."[5] Such a general definition allows for nonhuman dance, such as the migration of a flock of birds or the falling of leaves and snowflakes. Norman Bryson suggests the utility of looking at any "socially structured human movement," such as parades, weddings, and even bowing, as dance.[6] Joanne Kealiinohomoku, in an effort to define dance cross-culturally, specifies that "dance is a transient mode of expression, performed in a given form and style by the human body moving in space. Dance occurs through purposefully selected and controlled rhythmic movements; the resulting phenomenon is recognized as dance both by the performer and the observing members of a given group."[7] I cite these diverse definitions of dance not with any desire to be pulled into their debates but to suggest the wide range of activities that might be considered dance, depending on one's definition. I suggest not getting bogged down in attempting to define dance within musical theater; if the analysis and understanding of movement is the aim, all that is required from the viewer is the decision (before, during, or after the fact) of where to focus one's gaze.[8]

Thinking and writing about dance in musical theater is difficult, which is evident from the relatively few books and articles on the subject.[9] And yet, for the aspiring student, fan, or practitioner who wants an introduction to the subject of dance in musical theater, there are some fine places to begin. Most generalist books on the musical or its history do include some mention of dance and choreography, if not a complete chapter; beyond Steyn's book, Richard Kislan's *The Musical: A Look at the American Musical Theater* and Gerald Mast's *Can't Help Singin': The American Musical on Stage and Screen* provide balanced discussions of dance as one of the primary elements of the musical form.[10] Two books trace the history of dance in musical theater: Richard Kislan's *Hoofing on Broadway: A History of Show Dancing*, and Robert Emmet Long's *Broadway, the Golden Years: Jerome Robbins and the Great Choreographer-Directors*.[11] Biographies of choreographers are plentiful as well, and most provide not only rich context for the lives and careers of their subjects but also some description of these choreographers' aesthetics, their innovations, and their lasting influence on contemporary musical theater dance practice.[12] More scholarly studies on dance in musical theater are rare, though the last two decades have seen excellent work by scholars such as Andrea Most, Bruce A. McConachie, and Stacy Wolf, who analyze dance as evidence for their individual arguments about musical theater and its contribution to manifold dimensions of American culture, politics, and society writ large.[13]

Truly enterprising musical theater dance scholars will familiarize themselves with all that dance studies scholarship—dance history, world dance, dance ethnography, and so on—has to offer. Though musical theater dance is often marginalized or ignored within these disciplines,[14] one can borrow and adapt methodologies from them for thinking and writing about various movement forms, traditions, and histories. In particular, the work of dance scholars and critics can be helpful in exploring how to write about and make sense of the complexities of dance and choreography in performance. Writings about discourse on dance (whether regarding scholarly research, dance criticism and reviews, or ethnography) by such scholars as Joan Acocella, Janet Adshead, Sally Banes, Roger Copeland, Ann Daly, Jane C. Desmond, Susan Leigh Foster, Deborah Jowitt, and Marcia B. Siegel have been foundational to my own attempts to understand how movement works in musical theater.[15] Beyond academic journals, anthologies about dance, and other scholarly publications, there is great value in reading about dance and movement in newspaper reviews, if only to see how others describe and make sense of live performance.

Why aren't more people writing about dance in musical theater? I sense, first, that nondance specialists may fear they lack either some sort of requisite technical vocabulary or the experience of having danced much themselves. (This phenomenon is curious; fewer shy away from interpreting music, regardless of prior knowledge and familiarity.) All that is required for useful analysis of musical theater dance is careful description of what one sees and a commitment to thinking logically and creatively about it. Choreographers for musical theater, after all, aren't structuring their dances so that only experts can understand them; dances are designed to serve the story that is being told to a general theatergoing audience. In "Imagining Dance," Joan Acocella argues compellingly that the imaginative processes behind choreography have "a strong biological basis,"[16] and that dance is thus a language unto itself that we can all understand without need of having the choreographer explain it to us. She writes,

> So much of life is spent in the difficult task of trying to understand things, to see *through* them to what's on the other side. But the truths of dance are not on the other side. They are in the very bones of the dance, which our bones know how to read, if we let them. (Acocella, 16)

Certainly, the study of many different kinds of dance across cultures and performance styles may provide the viewer with an easier route into a piece of choreography. But movement vocabularies are something that we have all learned and been immersed in since birth—both as spectators of the world around us and as participants moving through it—and this alone should give us much courage as we try to interpret the way that movement, dance, and choreography bear meaning.

A second factor inhibiting musical theater dance scholarship is the ephemerality of dance. Original cast albums make a show's music and lyrics convenient to scholars, and the full scripts for some musicals are published even before the show has closed. Except for a performance presented on the annual Tony awards broadcast, a number excerpted for a variety show (such as the *Ed Sullivan Show* or the *Ellen DeGeneres Show*), or the brief glimpse of a few dance steps recorded illegally in the theater and uploaded to YouTube, dance is not as easily available for close study as the music and book to a show. True, one might write about the choreography in newer shows by attending a performance—or better still, multiple performances, if one can afford it—and scribbling frantic notes during and after. Yet it's frustrating to have the object of inquiry only briefly available, which may render the pursuit of dance scholarship altogether unattractive to even the most diligent of researchers.[17] Of course, in the absence of live or recorded dance performance, it's entirely possible to write about dance from deep archival work. Photographs, prompt books, others' descriptions and recollections of choreography, interviews, and dance notation in scripts, scores, and production notebooks all can reveal much about dance in a particular musical, although they are no substitutes for the movements themselves and require considerable time and energy to assemble, as well as great care and innovation to analyze in any coherent manner.

LEARNING THE STEPS

How then to overcome these challenges to musical theater dance scholarship? The simplest way to understand a live or recorded piece of musical theater choreography is to use what I describe in the next few paragraphs as "dance analysis," a process with which even a novice viewer of dance can address the work's rhetoric: what and how a given piece of choreography means. What follows is my own version of dance analysis, an adaptation of Janet Adshead's ideas laid out in her "An Introduction to Dance Analysis."[18] My methodology is influenced by the writing of dance critics and scholars like Roger Copeland, Ann Daly, and Deborah Jowitt, and is heavily informed by Stacy Wolf's "In Defense of Pleasure: Musical Theatre History in the Liberal Arts [A Manifesto]."[19]

Dance analysis intersects with the work of dance reviewers and critics, though it culminates in the formulation of one or more arguments or interpretations, and ultimately stops short of evaluating a dance. Some reviewers and critics similarly see it as their goal to help make sense of a piece of choreography for their readership, though many just settle for a sort of "thumbs-up/down" mode of criticism, judging a dance "good" or "bad" and making recommendations about whether or not one ought to attend it. Dance analysis is more in line with how Ann Daly delineates criticism: "Criticism... is about sorting out the morass of perception into something orderly and interesting. It's about discerning relationships and making meaning."[20] Dance analysis requires that the meaning we make out of musical theater choreography is not independent from the dance itself—that is, just our own subjective interpretive whims applied to a piece of movement—but rather, firmly grounded in the specifics of the dance and the context of the musical that it comes from. As a scholarly pursuit, dance analysis deepens our understanding of the role of the dancing body within musical theater and can help speak to social ideas and themes prompted by the musical but extending beyond the proscenium arch.

One misconception about musical theater dance is that it is all jazz hands, kicklines, and corny smiles, and that it ultimately can bear little to no structural or thematic weight. Dance analysis forces us to work through this bias and overcome fears that we are reading too much into a dance by revealing its form and structure. Through dance analysis, we can engage with each of a dance's parts separately and then together so as to understand the dance in its entirety and to interpret it. As Janet Adshead states,

> To watch a dance and see and hear its complex interweaving of rhythms and patterns and to perceive the way in which these contribute to the imaginative significance of the whole

construction is, similarly, both the excitement of, and justification for, engaging in analysis. (1998, 165)

Focusing on the minutiae of the dance's construction allows us to appreciate better the art form and to become more active viewers, collaborating with the musical's performers and creators to determine, critically and creatively, what a particular movement means within the musical and beyond.

The first step in dance analysis—and perilously, the most often ignored—is *description*, an extensive series of observations made by the viewer about the dance itself. What steps are taken? What gestures are made? Which parts of the dancing body move? In musical theater, dances are almost always performed by characters whom the audience has met (or will soon meet), and such details become vital to understanding the choreography's relationship to the musical as a whole. Which characters are dancing? Who are they dancing for? Where are they dancing? Because dance analysis doesn't happen in a vacuum, it's also appropriate at this stage to make observations about other elements of the musical during the choreography. What are the characters wearing as they dance? What lyrics are being sung? What does the music sound like? This stage of analysis alone is both exhausting and exhilarating; any eight counts of dance could conceivably result in eight pages of notes.

Description lays the groundwork for the analysis to come. Close observation of diverse elements of dance prevents the viewer from jumping to conclusions without evidence, and it allows for a vocabulary such that viewers can rely on more than just the type of knee-jerk responses consumer society has promoted—"It was good/bad, I loved/hated it." Description is also a way of preserving dance for the viewer, a way of holding on to bits of it despite its fleeting nature. Indeed, such observations, when carefully rendered and artfully assembled, can stand in (imperfectly) for the dance itself to those who haven't seen it. Dance writer Deborah Jowitt is correct in noting that "blow-by-blow accounts of physical actions are useful only in small, skilled doses,"[21] and as a work of criticism, literature, or history, can be deadly to read. But within the lengthy process of dance analysis, such attention to detail is crucial. Later, some notes will be used and interpreted and many others discarded, but as a first step, assembling a wealth of minute descriptions is the best strategy.

The next step in this method of dance analysis is to put these observations into conversation with one another—to begin a *synthesis* of these seemingly disparate descriptions. Here, one might juxtapose the shape of the dance with its speed, or consider together the movement vocabulary allocated to certain characters. One could also look at a repeated gesture or move as it surfaces throughout a musical number over time, with careful attention paid to the similarities and differences between each occurrence. Within this step, additional context can also be productively linked to observations about the dance, such as information about the plot and narrative of the song or the show, details about characters or themes, biographical or stylistic knowledge about the choreographer or performers, the history of a particular dance step, style, or genre, and so on. Though dance analysis doesn't require that one go out and research every aspect of a dance's context, it's clear that richer interpretations of the work might be prompted by the pairing of rigorous descriptions and insightful background material. However, it's important not to clutter an analysis with too much information on authorial intent or anecdotes about the musical's creation; context is meant to aid in the understanding of the dance rather than become the understanding itself. As with the previous step of dance analysis, not every partnering of observations and context will prove illuminating, and yet this methodical and inventive synthesis of observations and contexts is vital to arriving at a nuanced understanding of a dance.

Dance analysis achieves its purpose through *interpretation*, one or more arguments about what a given dance (or section of dance) says, means, or signifies. Interpretations may begin as hunches or suspicions, but when firmly rooted in the synthesis of numerous observations and bits of context, they blossom into compelling arguments that can contribute to better understanding and enjoyment of the work for others. Interpretations can be small or large, obvious or completely original. Again, the complexity of any given eight counts of dance begs for detailed study, and there is great value in being able to voice even the most pedestrian of arguments so long as its logic is made clear. Typically, many interpretations must be combined in analyzing a dance of any length or in understanding how dance functions throughout the entirety of a musical.

What then makes for a strong dance analysis? First, it's imperative to bear in mind that dance analysis is a process. It requires viewing and (if at all possible) reviewing a dance many times, composing and refining interpretations, and discovering which observations and contexts are most relevant and leaving the rest behind. Whether dance analysis is being used in a term paper, a class discussion, or a conversation in line at the bar during intermission, its aim should be a balance of description and ideas—a careful assemblage of observations that elucidate an argument about the dance. Though dance analysis has three distinct steps (description, synthesis, interpretation), these categories need not be relegated sequentially to separate paragraphs or even sentences. As in many forms of oral and written discourse, the argument or interpretation is often best presented up front so as to give those attempting to understand the dance some understanding of what is being discussed and why. And just as the best choreographers are precise and purposeful with every aspect of their dances, so must anyone analyzing dance be precise and purposeful with the language used to analyze these dances; particular attention should be paid to the exacting selection of verbs and adverbs, and to the mindful implementation of figurative language and rhetorical devices.

With a little effort, any "reader" of musical theater choreography can successfully carry out this sort of analysis, no matter how little dance vocabulary or context he or she has mastered. But the complexities of capturing movement in words that are capable of suggesting its significance require that we throw everything we have at the dance, including our own instincts, curiosities, pleasures, and emotional and kinesthetic responses. One might also briefly invoke literary and critical theories—large bodies of ideas, philosophies, and political thought, such as feminism and queer theory—to augment the study of a dance. If used well, these can inspire particular inquiries and might open up the musical's choreography to broader social significances. Not surprisingly, a number of dance scholars have expressed their distaste for analysis or criticism wherein the dancing body is completely eclipsed by the theoretical construct. For example, Susan Leigh Foster says, "These writings seldom address the body I know; instead, they move quickly past arms, legs, torso, and head on their way to a theoretical agenda that requires something unknowable or unknown as an initial premise. The body remains mysterious and ephemeral, a convenient receptacle for their new theoretical positions."[22] In dance analysis, theory should be used sparingly and imaginatively rather than as a replacement for a faithful description and consideration of the musical's choreography on its own terms.

Although there is value in conducting a comprehensive dance analysis for any given number or musical—that is, a description of the entirety of the movements throughout, along with extensive contextualization and the formation of multiple interrelated interpretations—this could easily stretch to hundreds of pages of written work, an undertaking unlikely to appeal to most readers. Whether carried out in a class discussion or put to the page as a term paper, newspaper review, or journal article, dance analysis is often most efficacious as a means of focusing an audience's attention on particular fragments or aspects of the dance through which some significance might be gleaned.

A PERFORMANCE

To provide a brief case study, I conclude by exploring just a few key moments from "Bye-Bye Life,"[23] the nearly ten-minute finale from Bob Fosse's 1979 autobiographical movie musical, *All That Jazz*.[24] First I examine the dominant conventions of dance within the entirety of the film, and then I explore a pivotal piece of choreography from this number—a sequence that also echoes significantly throughout Fosse's career. I end by combining dance analysis with my own kinesthetic and identificatory response. This varied methodology allows me to model each step of dance analysis and to approach from different angles the challenge of figuring out the complicated ways that dance functions in Fosse's film. My choice of *All That Jazz* as a case study may seem obvious—it's all about dance and choreography in musical theater—and yet despite its winning numerous awards and being regarded as the last of Fosse's masterworks, it remains relatively unexamined in dance scholarship.

Joe Gideon, played by Roy Scheider, is Bob Fosse's onscreen stand-in in *All That Jazz*. He starts each day with a well-rehearsed routine of eye-drops, Alka-Seltzer, Dexedrine, and "It's show-time folks," a mantra that he intones to the mirror less and less enthusiastically as the film goes on. *All That*

Jazz documents Gideon casting and choreographing a new Broadway musical, editing a film, and attempting to navigate relationships with his daughter, his ex-wife, his girlfriend, and his assorted one-night-stands. Even while in the hospital recovering from a heart attack, Gideon continues to smoke, to drink, to womanize, and to work himself quite literally to death. A sophisticated and self-involved foretelling of his own death, this biopic chronicles Fosse's own vexed relationship to show-biz, to women, and to his own mortality.

Much as he did in the film version of *Cabaret*, most every number within *All That Jazz* is diegetic, where the characters' singing and dancing fit naturally into the narrative as conscious performance for an audience, such as when Gideon's dancers perform his "Air-otica" number for the show's producers, or when his girlfriend and his daughter perform a practiced dance for him in his apartment. This is vastly different from typical musical theater fare, when characters break out into song and dance as a convention, sometimes with no apparent knowledge that they've done so. Near the end of the film and of his life, Gideon hallucinates bizarre and fantastical song-and-dance routines featuring his loved ones, which he himself watches and directs from behind a camera; his subconscious mind refuses to let someone else choreograph his own life or death. With Gideon at the helm, each of these hospital hallucinations suggests a well-rehearsed number, completely diegetic in its own illogical way—frantic last attempts to capture on film an idea, an aesthetic, an impulse before the ultimate deadline.

Yet "Bye-Bye Life," the final hallucination (if that's truly what it's meant to represent) is different. In it, Gideon emerges from behind the camera and, accompanied by frequent Fosse dancer and collaborator Ben Vereen as a kind of emcee named O'Connor Flood, sings and dances in a finale reminiscent of a surreal rock concert or a glitzy Las Vegas show. Lights of all colors flash and illuminate a multitiered metallic stage, including a pedestal that, with Gideon on it, slowly rises at multiple points in the song. Gideon sings into a microphone and performs in front of costumed band members and backup dancers. True, even in what Flood explains as a "final appearance on the great stage of life," Gideon is a performer who entertains 'til the last; his onscreen audience is made up of characters from throughout his life, all clapping, crying, and witnessing the last act in the spectacle that is Joe Gideon. But "Bye-Bye Life" is less clearly diegetic than every other song and dance in the film. Gideon's performance seems somehow unrehearsed and a bit of a personal journey; he occupies a relatively small kinesphere, and he sometimes dances facing away from the onscreen audience or with his eyes closed. The audience of *All That Jazz* has previously seen Gideon setting his movement vocabulary and style on others—which is easily recognizable as Fosse's own—and these are clearly on display here on the bodies of Gideon, Flood, and the other dancers. Importantly, however, and for the first time, Gideon is no longer shown choreographing anyone or consciously performing his own choreography, but just spontaneously dancing himself, and perhaps even for himself as well. "Bye-Bye Life" is evidence of Gideon finally relinquishing control, embracing the unknown, and just enjoying the ride.

Midway through the number—perhaps its first climax—the two cadaver-esque female backup dancers (who sport skintight white spandex with blue and white lines suggesting veins and arteries) wrap their arms around Gideon's torso, clinging to him, holding him down. As Flood repeatedly sings the lyric "bye-bye your life goodbye," a smiling Gideon thrusts both of his hands outward and upward, almost ecstatically shrugging them off. He then runs and slides feet first across the stage on his side and back, an astonishing way to move, almost transcendent as a departure from normal modes of human locomotion. This slide is expansive and powerful; it takes him far, and with great momentum (▶ Example 12.3). This slide is also exuberant and uninhibited—as opposed to the calmer, more precise, and in-place movements we've seen from him throughout this song (and throughout the film)—and Gideon bursts into this motion with wild and joyful abandon. As he slides, one hand floats skyward triumphant, and the other retains an assured grip on his microphone; contrary to his earlier clumsy attempts to maintain control of his life, here he hurtles toward uncertainty with grace and great style. The onscreen audience goes berserk, of course, applauding Gideon and his apparent acceptance of his own imminent death. Gideon stands and as the rock star of his own hallucination, runs through the audience greeting and glad-handing his adoring fans and all those who have shared in his life.

Fosse's fans may recognize Gideon's athletic slide. Though less iconic than other mainstays of "the Fosse style," feet- and head-first slides turn up in many of his stage shows and films, such as *Damn Yankees* and *Dancin'.* Perhaps most memorable is the slide's appearance in the film version of *Kiss Me Kate* (1953; ▶ Example 12.4).[25] Not content with just performing in a small role, the young Bob Fosse asked choreographer Hermes Pan if he could create a short section of dance for himself and fellow dancer Carol Haney for "From This Moment On." Pan agreed, and Fosse's minute-long choreography—which begins with his own spectacular slide onto stage—was one of the most visually stunning moments of the entire film. An early articulation of an aesthetic that he would return to throughout the rest of his career, this brief section of choreography helped him land his first job as choreographer on Broadway, for *The Pajama Game*. Considered in this context, Gideon's slide toward his exit in "Bye-Bye Life" resonates with Fosse's own entrance during "From This Moment On." As bookends to a career, these slides enunciate both a show-biz maxim and a life philosophy: that entrances and exits truly matter.

All That Jazz is the quintessential musical in which dance is posited as a metaphor for how one lives, and part of the reason that "Bye-Bye Life" is so striking is that it allows its off-screen audience so many ways to relate to it. If death is just a final performance, then those of us watching the film have likely been the audience for many such finales, including Fosse's own—like Gideon, he would later be struck down by a fatal heart attack. Watch *All That Jazz* after Fosse's death in 1987 and it's nigh impossible not to think of the generations of dancers and performers that he's influenced and who have borrowed heavily from his movement style.[26] And if we're willing and able to make these identifications and to reflect on what we've seen and gained from Fosse, then there is a place for us in Gideon's onscreen audience. For me, watching "Bye-Bye Life" also fosters a sort of sympathetic kinesthetic response. In at least three different moments after Gideon's slide, Flood and the two female dancers stand with their elbows near their torsos, their forearms outstretched to the side, and their wrists limp. Then, slowly, and somehow gloriously, their hands begin to rise, still in pronation, and their arms follow in accordance. This repeated ascending motion seems almost a benediction of sorts, and something about the elegance and ease of this particular movement makes me want to stand and join in the celebration, to help the dancers physically and lovingly usher Gideon into the beyond (⏵ Example 12.5). Finally, I would argue that in a surprisingly generous turn, "Bye-Bye Life" opens up a space for us to imagine ourselves in Gideon's position, particularly with the knowledge that we'll all die sometime. Even though Gideon has been a self-indulgent, womanizing, work-obsessed, selfish bastard throughout the film—all fairly well documented personality traits of

Fosse himself—with "Bye-Bye Life" I suddenly identify with Gideon, and find that I want precisely what he wants: to choose how and when I'll leave this life, to be surrounded by those who love and know me best, and to go out singing and dancing to uproarious applause.

NOTES

1 Mark Steyn, *Broadway Babies Say Goodnight: Musicals Then and Now* (New York: Routledge, 2000), p. 179.
2 *White Christmas*, directed by Michael Curtiz and choreographed by Robert Alton (Los Angeles: Paramount Pictures, 1954; DVD release, 2007).
3 Ballet and modern dance have continued to inform musical theater choreography without subsuming it. For instance, although "dream ballets" briefly flourished in the wake of Agnes de Mille's success with "Laurey Makes Up Her Mind" in *Oklahoma!* (1943), they have proved faddish over the years and altogether inappropriate for some shows.
4 It's important to note, though, that particularly when "dance" is defined broadly, other members of the production team such as the director and the actors are also creating choreography, such as setting down entrances and exits (blocking), or even creating a gestural landscape for a character or a show. Choreography, like dramaturgy, is a collaborative act in performance and one that takes place even when there is not someone titled "choreographer" on the production team.
5 Roger Copeland and Marshall Cohen, *What Is Dance?* (Oxford: Oxford University Press, 1983), p. 1.
6 Norman Bryson, "Cultural Studies and Dance History," in *Meaning in Motion: New Cultural Studies of Dance*, ed. Jane C. Desmond (Durham, NC: Duke University Press, 1997, 55–77), p. 58.
7 Joanne Kealiinohomoku, "An Anthropologist Looks at Ballet as a Form of Ethnic Dance," *in Moving History/Dancing Cultures: A*

Dance History Reader, ed. Ann Dils and Ann Cooper Albright (Middletown, CT: Wesleyan University Press, 2001), p. 38.

8 Much of this will be determined by a viewer's particular skill set and investments. Yet these definitions of dance indicate that there is much to be gained in looking beyond conventional dance steps during musical theater dance numbers. Actors' movements across the stage, their individual gestures, the motions of set pieces and lighting elements, and what might be referred to in dialogue and lyrics can all deepen one's understanding, interpretations, and appreciation for dance in musical theater.

9 For instance, *Joseph Swain's The Broadway Musical: A Critical and Musical Survey*, 2nd ed. (Lanham, MD: Scarecrow Press, 2002), is an important resource for learning how the composition of music shapes a musical, with over a dozen chapters, each looking in depth at the music and lyrics of a major musical. No correlate yet exists for musical theater dance studies.

10 Richard Kislan, *The Musical: A Look at the American Musical Theater, revised, expanded* ed. (New York: Applause Books, 1995); *Gerald Mast's Can't Help Singin': The American Musical on Stage and Screen* (Woodstock, NY: Overlook Press, 1987).

11 Richard Kislan, *Hoofing on Broadway: A History of Show Dancing* (New York: Prentice Hall, 1987); Robert Emmet Long, *Broadway, the Golden Years: Jerome Robbins and the Great Choreographer-Directors* (New York: Continuum, 2001).

12 For instance, there is a handful of books exclusively dedicated to the life and legacy of Bob Fosse: *Margery Beddow's Bob Fosse's Broadway* (Portsmouth, NH: Heinemann, 1996), Martin Gottfried's *All His Jazz: The Life and Death of Bob Fosse* (New York: Bantam Books, 1990), Kevin Boyd Grubbs *Razzle Dazzle: The Life and Work of Bob Fosse* (New York: St. Martin's Press, 1991), and Debra McWaters' *The Fosse Style* (Gainesville: University Press of Florida, 2008).

13 See, for example, Andrea Most's "'We Know We Belong to the Land': The Theatricality of Assimilation in Rodgers and Hammerstein's *Oklahoma!*" and "'You've Got to Be Carefully Taught': The Politics of Race in Rodgers and Hammerstein's *South Pacific*," chapters 4 and 6 in her *Making Americans: Jews*

and the *Broadway Musical* (Cambridge, MA: Harvard University Press, 2004), Bruce A. McConachie's "The 'Oriental' Musicals of Rodgers and Hammerstein and the U.S. War in Southeast Asia" (*Theatre Journal* 46 [October 1994]: 385–98), and Stacy Wolf's "'We'll Always be Bosom Buddies': Female Duets and the Queering of Broadway Musical Theatre" (*GLQ: A Journal of Lesbian and Gay Studies* 12.3 [2006]: 351–76) and "'Something Better than This': *Sweet Charity* and the Feminist Utopia of Broadway Musicals" (*Modern Drama* 47.2 [Summer 2004]: 309–32).

14 For example, American musical theater dance is almost entirely exiled to the thirty-second and final chapter of *The Routledge Dance Studies Reader*, ed. Alexandra Carter and Janet O'shea (London: Routledge, 1998), and it is absent altogether from *Moving History/Dancing Cultures: A Dance History Reader*, ed. Ann Dils and Ann Cooper Albright (Middletown, CT: Wesleyan University Press, 2001).

15 In addition to the essays and books that I cite elsewhere in this essay, see Roger Copeland's "Between Description and Deconstruction" (*The Routledge Dance Studies Reader*, pp. 98–107), Jane C. Desmond's "Embodying Difference: Issues in Dance and Cultural Studies" (*The Routledge Dance Studies Reader*, pp. 154–62), Susan Leigh Foster's *Reading Dancing: Bodies and Subjects in Contemporary American Dance* (Berkeley: University of California Press, 1986), Sally Ann Ness's "Dancing in the Field: Notes from Memory" (*Corporealities: Dancing Knowledge, Culture and Power*, ed. Susan Leigh Foster [London: Routledge, 1995], pp. 129–54), and Marcia B. Siegel's "Bridging the Critical Distance" (*The Routledge Dance Studies Reader*, pp. 91–97).

16 Joan Acocella, "Imagining Dance," in *Moving History/Dancing Cultures: A Dance History Reader*, ed. Ann Dils and Ann Cooper Albright (Middletown, CT: Wesleyan University Press, 2001), p. 16.

17 And dance, I would argue, is seldom designed to be catchy, memorable, or easily repeatable for audience members after the performance. Music and lyrics, on the other hand, are often

structured to stick in the audience's minds, to be hummed and sung on the way out of the theater, and to prompt the purchase of sheet music or a cast album for further repetition later.

18 Janet Adshead, "An Introduction to Dance Analysis" (*The Routledge Dance Studies Reader,* pp. 163–70). This essay was, in turn, adapted from her book, *Dance Analysis: Theory and Practice* (London: Dance Books, 1988).

19 Stacy Wolf, "In Defense of Pleasure: Musical Theatre History in the Liberal Arts [A Manifesto]" (*Theatre Topics* 17.1 [March 2007]: 51–60). In her appendix B, titled "Some Elements of Dance Analysis," Wolf presents a series of excellent questions that can further assist one's thinking about dance in musical theater. I see Wolf's questions as specific foci or particular avenues of inquiry that one might use to guide, frame, or organize, Adshead's dance analysis, which is more of a comprehensive methodology that emphasizes, first and foremost, the description of the dance itself.

20 Ann Daly, *Critical Gestures: Writings on Dance and Culture* (Middletown, CT: Wesleyan University Press, 2002), p. xiv.

21 Deborah Jowitt, "Beyond Description: Writing beneath the Surface," in *Moving History/Dancing Cultures: A Dance History Reader,* ed. Ann Dils and Ann Cooper Albright (Middletown, CT: Wesleyan University Press, 2001), p. 9.

22 Susan Leigh Foster, "Dancing Bodies," in *Meaning in Motion: New Cultural Studies of Dance,* ed. Jane C. Desmond (Durham, NC: Duke University Press, 1997, 235–57), p. 235.

23 "Bye-Bye Life" is based on the 1957 song "Bye Bye Love," written by Felice and Boudleaux Bryant and made popular by performances and recordings by the Everly Brothers.

24 *All That Jazz,* directed and choreographed by Bob Fosse (Beverly Hills, CA: Twentieth Century Fox, 1979; DVD release, 2003).

25 *Kiss Me Kate,* directed by George Sidney, choreographed by Hermes Pan and Bob Fosse (Los Angeles: Metro-Goldwyn-Mayer, 1953, DVD release 2003).

26 For instance, Beyoncé recently admitted that the inspiration for her "Single Ladies (Put a Ring on it)" music video was seeing a YouTube video featuring Bob Fosse's choreography for "Mexican Breakfast," a number from a 1969 performance on the *Ed Sullivan Show*. In fact, many versions of this one performance now exist in cyberspace slightly altered; people have taken to trying to synch Fosse's choreography with contemporary music, from rap to pop to death metal.

REFERENCES

Selected References for Volume II, Chapter 1

Altman, Rick. *The American Film Musical*. Bloomington: Indiana University Press, 1987.
Clum, John. *Something for the Boys: Musical Theater and Gay Culture*. New York: Palgrave, 1999.
Kirle, Bruce. *Unfinished Show Business: Broadway Musicals as Works-in-Process* Carbondale: Southern Illinois University Press, 2005.
Knapp, Raymond. *The American Musical and the Formation of National Identity*. Princeton, NJ: Princeton University Press, 2005.
———. "*Assassins, Oklahoma!*, and the 'Shifting Fringe of Dark around the Campfire.'" *Cambridge Opera Journal* 16 (2004): 77–101.
McMillin, Scott. *The Musical as Drama*. Princeton, NJ: Princeton University Press, 2006.
Miller, D.A. *Place for Us (Essay on the Broadway Musical)*. Cambridge: Harvard University Press, 1998.
Miller, Scott. *Deconstructing Harold Hill: An Insider's Guide to Musical Theatre*. Portsmouth, NH: Heinemann, 2000.
Rodgers, Richard. *Musical Stages: An Autobiography*. New York: Random House, 1975; reprinted New York: Da Capo, 1995, 2000.

Wolf, Stacy. "*Wicked* Divas, Musical Theater, and Internet Girl Fans." *Camera Obscura* 65 22.2 (2007): 39–71.

Wollman, Elizabeth L. *The Theater Will Rock: A History of the Rock Musical, from Hair to Hedwig.* Ann Arbor: University of Michigan Press, 2006.

Selected References for Volume II, Chapter 2

Altman, Rick. *The American Film Musical.* Bloomington: Indiana University Press, 1987.

Bazin, André. *What Is Cinema? Essays Selected and Translated by Hugh Gray.* Vol. 1–2. Berkeley: University of California Press, 2005.

Bordwell, David and Kristin Thompson. *Film Art: An Introduction.* 8th ed. Boston: McGraw-Hill, 2008.

Decker, Todd. *Music Makes Me: Fred Astaire and Jazz.* Berkeley: University of California Press, 2011.

Dyer, Richard. *Heavenly Bodies.* New York: St. Martin's Press and Basingstoke: Macmillan, 1986.

Feuer, Jane. *The Hollywood Musical.* 2nd ed. Bloomington: Indiana University Press, 1992.

Knapp, Raymond. "Getting Off the Trolley: Musicals *contra* Cinematic Reality." *From Stage to Screen:Musical Films in Europe and United States (1927–1961).* Ed. Massimiliano Sala. Vol. 18 of *Speculum Musicae.* Turnhout, Belgium: Brepols Publishers, 2012, pp. 157–172.

———. *Making Light: Haydn, Musical Camp, and the Long Shadow of German Idealism.* Durham: Duke University Press, 2018.

McMillin, Scott. *The Musical as Drama: A Study of the Principles and Conventions behind Musical Shows from Kern to Sondheim.* Princeton, NJ: Princeton University Press, 2006.

Pysnik, Steven. "Musical Camp: Conrad Salinger and the Performance of Gayness in *The Pirate.*" *Music and Camp.* Ed. Christopher Moore and Philip Purvis. Wesleyan Unviversity Press, forthcoming.

Selected References for Volume II, Chapter 3

Altman, Rick. "Toward a Theory of the History of Representational Technologies." *Iris*, 2 (1984):111–125.
Block, Geoffrey. *Richard Rodgers*. Yale Broadway Masters Series. New Haven, CT: Yale University Press, 2003.
Kemp, Peter. "How Do You Solve a 'Problem' Like Maria von Poppins?" *Musicals: Hollywood and Beyond*. Edited by Bill Marshall and Robynn Stilwell. Portland: Intellect, 2000, pp. 55–61.
Wolf, Stacy Ellen. *A Problem like Maria: Gender and Sexuality in the American Musical*. Ann Arbor: University of Michigan Press, 2002.

Selected References for Volume II, Chapter 4

Bell, Elizabeth, Haas, Lynda, and Sells, Laura, eds. *From Mouse to Mermaid: The Politics of Film, Gender, and Culture*. Bloomington: Indiana University Press, 1995.
Dyer, Richard. "Entertainment and Utopia." *Genre: The Musical*. Ed. Rick Altman. London: Routledge & Kegan Paul, 1981, p. 177. Originally published in *Movie* 2, Spring 1977, pp. 2–13.
Eisenstein, Sergei. *Eisenstein on Disney*. London: Methuen, 1988.
Feuer, Jane. *The Hollywood Musical*. 2nd ed. Bloomington: Indiana University Press, 1992.
Pinsky, Mark I. *The Gospel According to Disney: Faith, Trust and Pixie Dust*. Louisville, KY: Westminster John Knox Press, 2004.
Thomas, Frank and Johnston, Ollie. *Disney Animation: The Illusion of Life*. New York: Abbeville Press, 1981.
Wells, Paul. *Understanding Animation*. London: Routledge, 1998.
Zipes, Jack. "Breaking the Disney Spell." *From Mouse to Mermaid: The Politics of Film, Gender and Culture*. Ed. Elizabeth Bell, Lynda Haas, and Laura Sells. Bloomington: Indiana University Press, 1995, pp. 21–40.
———. *Happily Ever After: Fairy Tales, Children and the Culture Industry*. New York: Routledge, 1997.

Selected References for Volume II, Chapter 5

Anderson, Tim. "'Buried under the Fecundity of His Own Creations': Reconsidering the Recording Bans of the American Federation of Musicians, 1942–1944 and 1948." *American Music* 22.2 (Summer 2004): 231–69.

Brooks, Tim. "Early Recordings of Songs from *Florodora*: Tell Me, Pretty Maiden . . . Who Are You?—A Discographical Mystery." *Association for Recorded Sound Collections Journal* 31 (2000): 51–64.

Chapin, Theodore S., Kurt Deutsch, Brian Drutman, Thomas Z. Shepard, and Melissa Rose Bernardo. "For The Record: Inside Cast Albums." *American Theatre Wing's Working In the Theatre*, April, 2009). http://americantheatrewing.org/wit/detail/cast_albums_04_09

Drowne, Kathleen and Patrick Huber. *American Popular Culture through History: The 1920s*. Westport, CT: Greenwood Press, 2004.

Eisenberg, Evan. *The Recording Angel: Music, Records and Culture from Aristotle to Zappa*. 2nd ed. New Haven, CT: Yale University Press, 2005.

Grant, Mark N. *The Rise and Fall of the Broadway Musical*. Boston: Northeastern University Press, 2004.

Katz, Mark. "Making America More Musical through the Phonograph, 1900–1930." *American Music* 16.4 (Winter 1998): 448–75.

Marmorstein, Gary. *The Label: The Story of Columbia Records*. New York: Thunder's Mouth Press, 2007.

Miletich, Leo N. *Broadway's Prize-Winning Musicals: An Annotated Guide for Libraries and Audio Collectors*. New York: Haworth Press, 1993.

Mordden, Ethan. *Beautiful Mornin': The Broadway Musical in the 1940s*. New York: Oxford University Press, 1999.

Selected References for Volume II, Chapter 6

Becker, Howard S. *Art Worlds*. Berkeley: University of California Press, 1982.

Bianco, Anthony. *Ghosts of 42nd Street: A History of America's Most Infamous Block*. New York: William Morrow, 2004.

Bottoms, Stephen J. *Playing Underground: A Critical History of the 1960s Off-Off-Broadway Movement*. Ann Arbor: University of Michigan Press, 2004.

Bloom, Julie. "'Forbidden Broadway' Curtain to Go Down." *New York Times* (September 13, 2008): B-9.
Fornes, Maria Irene. *Promenade and Other Plays*. New York: PAJ Publications, 1987.
Gabler, Neal. *Winchell: Gossip, Power and the Culture of Celebrity*. New York: Alfred A. Knopf, 1994.
Goldberg, Isaac. *Tin Pan Alley: A Chronicle of American Popular Music*. Including Edward Jablonski's *From Sweet and Swing to Rock 'n' Roll*. New York: Frederick Ungar, 1961.
Goldman, William. *The Season. A Candid Look at Broadway*. New York: Limelight Editions, 1984.
Kissel, Howard. *David Merrick: The Abominable Showman*. New York: Applause Books, 1993.
Kreuger, Miles. *Show Boat: The Story of a Classic American Musical*. New York: Oxford University Press, 1977.
Leonard, John. *Smoke and Mirrors: Violence, Television and Other American Culture*. New York: New Press, 1997.
Marks, Edward B. *They All Sang: From Tony Pastor to Rudy Vallee, as told to A. J. Liebling*. New York: Viking, 1935.
Mordden, Ethan. *Better Foot Forward: The History of American Musical Theatre*. New York: Grossman, 1976.
———. *Broadway Babies: The People Who Made the American Musical*. New York: Oxford University Press, 1983.
Runyon, Damon. *Guys and Dolls and Other Stories*. London: Penguin, 1956.
Shepherd, John. *Tin Pan Alley*. London: Routledge & Kegan Paul, 1982.

Selected References for Volume II, Chapter 7

Bennett, Robert Russell. *Instrumentally Speaking* (Melville, NY: Belwin Mills, inc., 1975).
———. *"The Broadway Sound": The Autobiography and Selected Essays of Robert Russell Bennett*, ed. George J. Ferencz (Rochester: University of Rochester Press, 1999).
Harrison, Jeremy. *Actor-Musicianship* (London & New York: Bloomsbury, 2016).
Kaye, Joseph. *Victor Herbert: The Biography of America's Greatest Composer of Romantic Music* (New York: Crown Publishers, 2007).

Parrent, Amy. "From 'The Beggar's Opera' to 'Sweeney Todd': The Art of the Broadway Orchestrator" (*Music Educator's Journal* 66:9 [May 1980]: 32–35).
Perkins, Patrick T. "'Hey! What's the Score?' Copyright in the Orchestrations of Broadway Musicals" (*Columbia-VLA Journal of Law and the Arts* 16 [1991]: 475–503).
Suskin, Steven. *The Sound of Broadway Music: A Book of Orchestrators and Orchestrations* (New York: Oxford University Press, 2009).

Selected References for Volume II, Chapter 8

Broadway: The American Musical. A Film by Michael Kantor. Educational Broadcasting Corporation and the Broadway Film Project, 2004.
Brooks, Mel and Tom Meehan. *The Producers: The Book, Lyrics, and Story Behind the Biggest Hit in Broadway History! How We Did It.* New York: Miramax/Hyperion, 2001.
Bryer, Jackson R., and Richard A. Davison, eds. *The Art of the American Musical: Conversations with the Creators.* New Brunswick, NJ: Rutgers University Press, 2005.
Grant, Mark N. *The Rise and Fall of the Broadway Musical.* Boston, MA: Northeastern University Press, 2004.
Citron, Stephen. *The Musical from the Inside Out.* Chicago: Ivan R. Dee, 1991.
Ilson, Carol. *Harold Prince: From* Pajama Game *to* Phantom of the Opera. Ann Arbor: UMI Research Press, 1989.
Kirle, Bruce. *Unfinished Show Business: Broadway Musicals as Works-in-Process.* Carbondale: Southern Illinois University Press, 2005.
Laurents, Arthur. *Mainly on Directing: Gypsy, West Side Story, and Other Musicals.* New York: Alfred A. Knopf, 2009.
Lawrence, Greg. *Dance with Demons: The Life of Jerome Robbins.* New York: G.P. Putnam's Sons, 2001.
Lundskaer-Nielsen, Miranda. *Directors and the New Musical Drama: British and American Musical Theatre in the 1980s and 90s.* New York: Palgrave Macmillan, 2008.
Mordden, Ethan. *Ziegfeld: The Man Who Invented Show Business.* New York: St. Martin's Press, 2008.
Prince, Harold. *Sense of Occasion.* Milwaukee, WI: Applause Theatre & Cinema Books, an Imprint of Hal Leonard LLC, 2017.

Rosenberg, Bernard, and Ernest Harburg. *The Broadway Musical: Collaboration in Commerce and Art*. New York: New York University Press, 1993.
Vaill, Amanda. *Somewhere: The Life of Jerome Robbins*. New York: Broadway Books, 2006.
Viertel, Jack. *The Secret Life of the American Musical: How Broadway Shows are Built*. New York: Sarah Crichton Books/Farrar, Straus and Giroux, 2016.

Selected References for Volume II, Chapter 9

Aronson, Arnold. *American Set Design*. New York: Theatre Communications Group, 1985.
———. *Looking in the Abyss: Essays on Scenography*. Ann Arbor: University of Michigan Press, 2005.
Baugh, Christopher. *Theatre, Performance, and Technology: The Development of Scenography in the Twentieth Century*. New York: Palgrave Macmillan, 2005.
Belasco, David. *The Theatre through Its Stage Door*. Whitefish, MT: Kessinger, 2006.
Craig, Edward Gordon. *On the Art of the Theatre*. New York: Theatre Arts Books, 1956.
Goodwin, John, ed., *British Theatre Design: The Modern Age*. New York: St. Martin's Press, 1989.
Izenour, George C. *Theater Technology*. 2nd ed. New Haven, CT: Yale University Press, 1997.
Jones, Robert Edmond. *The Dramatic Imagination*. New York: Duell, Sloan, and Pearce, 1941.
Larson, Orville Kurth, *Scene Design in the American Theatre From 1915 to 1960*. Fayetteville: University of Arkansas Press, 1989.
Smith, Ronn. *American Set Design 2*. New York: Theatre Communications Group, 1991.

Selected References for Volume II, Chapter 10

Clum, John M. *Something for the Boys: Musical Theatre and Gay Culture*. New York: Palgrave, 1999.
Deer, Joe, and Rocco Dal Verra. *Acting in Musical Theatre: A Comprehensive Course*. London: Routledge, 2008.

McGovern, Dennis, and Deborah Grace Winer. *Sing Out, Louise: 150 Stars of Musical Theatre Remember 50 Years on Broadway.* New York: Schirmer Books, 1993.

McMillin, Scott. *The Musical As Drama.* Princeton, NJ: Princeton University Press, 2006.

Most, Andrea. *Making Americans: Jews and the Broadway Musical.* Cambridge, MA: Harvard University Press, 2004.

Wollman, Elizabeth L. *The Theatre Will Rock: A History of the Rock Musical from* Hair *to* Hedwig. Ann Arbor, MI: University of Michigan Press, 2006.

Selected References for Volume II, Chapter 11

Block, Geoffrey. *Enchanted Evenings: The Broadway Musical from Show Boat to Sondheim.* New York: Oxford University Press, 1997.

Knapp, Raymond. *The American Musical and the Performance of Personal Identity.* Princeton, NJ: Princeton University Press, 2006.

McGinnis, Pearl Yeadon. *The Opera Singer's Career Guide: Understanding the European Fach System.* Lanham, MD: Scarecrow Press, 2010.

Selected References for Volume II, Chapter 12

Adshead, Janet. *Dance Analysis: Theory and Practice.* London: Dance Books, 1988.

Bryson, Norman. "Cultural Studies and Dance History." *Meaning in Motion: New Cultural Studies of Dance.* Ed. Jane C. Desmond. Durham, NC: Duke University Press, 1997, pp. 55–77.

Copeland, Roger and Marshall Cohen. *What Is Dance?* Oxford: Oxford University Press, 1983.

Daly, Ann. *Critical Gestures: Writings on Dance and Culture.* Middletown, CT: Wesleyan University Press, 2002.

Dils, Ann and Ann Cooper Albright, eds. *Moving History/Dancing Cultures: A Dance History Reader.* Middletown, CT: Wesleyan University Press, 2001.

Foster, Susan Leigh. "Dancing Bodies." *Meaning in Motion: New Cultural Studies of Dance.* Ed. Jane C. Desmond. Durham, NC: Duke University Press, 1997, pp. 235–57.

———. *Reading Dancing: Bodies and Subjects in Contemporary American Dance*. Berkeley: University of California Press, 1986.

Kislan, Richard. *Hoofing on Broadway: A History of Show Dancing*. New York: Prentice Hall, 1987.

Long, Robert Emmet. *Broadway, the Golden Years: Jerome Robbins and the Great Choreographer-Directors*. New York: Continuum, 2001.

Wolf, Stacy. "In Defense of Pleasure: Musical Theatre History in the Liberal Arts [A Manifesto]." *Theatre Topics* 17.1 (March 2007): 51–60.

INDEX

Note: Page numbers in *italics* indicate photographs.

Abbott, George, 176–77, 179
The Abominable Showman (Kissel), 131
abstraction: and cast recording, 110; and theatrical design, 184, 200, 208–9, 216
Academy Awards, 182
Acocella, Joan, 271–72
Acting in Musical Theatre (Dear and Dal Vera), 222
actors and acting, 165–66, 185, 221–39; and animation, 83–85; and casting, 221–22; performance vs., 222–23, 232, 238
Actors Equity, 144
Actors Studio, 177
Adams, Edie, 58
adaptations, 34–38
The Adding Machine, 206
Adshead, Janet, 271, 273–75
AFM (American Federation of Musicians), 103–4

African Americans. *See* race issues and racism
Ahrens, Lynn, 214, 221–22
Aida, 216
Alessandrini, Gerard, 146
Alexander, Jason, 62, 69
All That Jazz, 265, 279–84
"Along Came Bialy," 216
Altman, Rick, 24n1, 27, 77n2
alto voices, 244–45
"Always Look on the Bright Side of Life," 41
"Always True to You in My Fashion," 256–57
American Ballet Theatre, 210
American Expressionism, 206
American Federation of Musicians (AFM), 103–4
American Idol, 238
American Playhouse, 36
American Repertory Theatre, 190
American Theatre Wing, 117

Amos and Andy, 94
amplification, 159–60, 237–38, 251
Andrews, Anthony, 236
Andrews, Julie: and cast recordings, 111–12; and *Cinderella,* 58, 66–74, 67, 111–12
angels, 129–35
Anger, Kenneth, 49
animation, 5, 79–98; and *Bambi,* 80–82; and *Dumbo,* 79–81; Eisenstein on, 85–93, 97; etymology of, 98n2; and ideological issues, 94–97; as performance, 80–84
animism, 85–86
Anna and the King of Siam, 234
Anna Christie (O'Neill), 232
Annie, 191
Annie Get Your Gun, 229
"Another National Anthem", 16
"Another Op'nin', Another Show," 257–58
anthropomorphism, 91, 93
anti-Semitism, 186–87
Anyone Can Whistle, 209
Anything Goes, 207, 227–28
Appia, Adolph, 198–200, 204–5
Arden, Victor, 157
Aronson, Boris, 211–13, 215–16
arrangement of music. *See* orchestration and arrangement of music
Assassins, 16, 162; and direction, 188, 191
Astaire, Adele, 226
Astaire, Fred: and orchestration/arrangement of music, 160; and race/ethnicity issues, 31–32; and rhythm songs, 51n5; and romantic pairings, 33–34; and singing, 226

Atkinson, Brooks, 135
audiences: and expectations for actors, 226; interaction with, 11–24, 38; and rock musicals, 238–39
audio recordings. *See* cast recordings
authenticity, 163–64
authorship (attribution) issues: and authorial intent, 75–76; and copyright issues, 167–68, 181
Avenue Q, 215
Awake and Sing, 211
Ayers, Lemuel, 207–8

Babes in Arms, 128
Babes in Toyland, 174
"Baby Mine," 79–81, 89, 91
backstage musicals, 32–34, 37
Baensch, Otto, 101
Bagdad Cafe, 41–42
Balanchine, George, 265–66
Ballard, Kaye, 58, 60, 69
Ballroom, 183
Bambi, 80–82
The Band's Visit, 4
Banes, Sally, 271
Banfield, Stephen, 162
"Bare Necessities," 96
baritone voices, 244–45
Barras, Charles M., 127
Barrowman, John, 228
bass voices, 244–45
Bat Boy: The Musical, 22
Bazin, André, 38–39
Beardsley, Aubrey, 44
The Beatles, 112–14, 116
Beaton, Cecil, 210
Beatty, John Lee, 208
Beauty and the Beast, 58, 215
Becker, Howard S., 129

INDEX | 301

"Becky's Back in the Ballet," 174
Beg, Borrow or Steal, 113
Belasco, David, 200–201, 205–6
bel canto singing, 249
Bel Geddes, Norman, 204–6
Bells Are Ringing, 178
"belting," 248–49
Bennett, Michael: choreography style of, 182–84; and director/choreographers, 178, 189, 266
Bennett, Robert Russell, 149–50, 154–55, 158
Berkeley, Busby, 40, 217, 218–19n16
Berlin, Irving, 128, 265–68; and cast recordings, 106; and orchestration, 150; and song publishing, 136
Berliner, Emile, 105
Berlioz, Hector, 150, 158
Bernstein, Leonard: and cast recordings, 109; and direction, 179; and *West Side Story,* 179
"Bianca," 256–57
Bianco, Anthony, 143
Big Deal, 182
Billion Dollar Baby, 179
Björnson, Maria, 214
The Black Crook, 127–29, 136, 198, 201–2, 207
blackface minstrelsy, 30–32
Blakemore, Michael, 186, 188
Blankenbuehler, Andy, 186
Blitzstein, Marc, 105–6, 207
Block, Geoffrey, 77–78n8, 121n11
Bloomer Girl, 107
"Blow, Gabriel, Blow," 251
Bobbie, Walter, 188
Bogart, Anne, 18
"Bojangles of Harlem," 31–32, 51n5
Bond, Christopher, 252

Bottoms, Stephen J., 145
Boublil, Alain, 214
"The Boy Next Door," 33
The Boys from Syracuse, 233; and direction, 176
Brando, Marlon, 35
Brascia, John, 267
Bread and Tulips, 41–42
Breakfast at Tiffany's, 131
Brett, Jeremy, 30
Brice, Fanny, 132, 174
Brigadoon, 107
Bring in 'da Noise, Bring in 'da Funk, 189
Brisbane, Arthur, 134
British Invasion, 213–14
Broadway: and cast recordings, 102; and publicity for musicals, 140–41; and theater properties, 142–46
Broadway, the Golden Years (Long), 270
Broadway Babies Say Goodnight!, 265
"Broadway Melody" films, 37
"Broadway Sound." *See* orchestration and arrangement of music
Broadway: The American Musical (Kantor), 173
Brooks, Mel, 130
"The Brotherhood of Man," 251
Brown, John Mason, 173
Brown, Lew, 157
"Brush Up Your Shakespeare," 257
Brynner, Yul, 236
Bryson, Norman, 269
Buck, Gene, 132
Buckley, Betty, 229
burlesque, 227, 231
Burton, Richard, 236

"Bushel and a Peck," 35
Bye Bye Birdie, 141, 181, 251
"Bye-Bye Life," 279–84

Cabaret, 280; and costuming, 203; and dance/choreography, 182; and direction, 188; and film adaptations, 37–38; and theatrical design, 210–12; Tony Award for, 187
Caird, John, 186
Callaway, Cab, 32
Camelot, 236
camera technology, 70–75, *73*
camp, 44–50, 53n13
Can Can, 231
Candide: and orchestration/arrangement of music, 149; and theatrical design, 216
Can't Help Singin' (Mast), 270
Cantor, Eddie, 132, 227
capitalism, 88
Capitol Records, 107
Carell, Candace, 198
Carmines, Al, 144–45
Carnival, 131
Caroline, or Change, 189
Carousel, 64, 158, 177, 234; and direction, 188; revival of, 4; and theatrical design, 208
Carroll, Pat, 58, 60
Carroll, Vinnette, 186
casting: acting and, 221–22; of African Americans, 122n21; for *Cinderella,* 59, 62, 65–70, *67*, 76, 77–78n8; and Ziegfeld, 132
cast recordings, 101–19; and concept albums, 112–17; contrasted with live performance, 101–2; and development of the LP record, 107–12; and early recording technology, 102–7; future of, 117–19; and LP records, 107–17; popularity of, 102
Cats, 213–14
censorship, 50
CFM (Chicago Federation of Musicians), 104
Champion, Gower, 131, 178, 181, 194n18
Channing, Carol, 232
Chapin, Ted, 118
Chaplin, Charlie, 86
Chavkin, Rachel, 190
chest voice, 247
Chicago, 72; and direction, 182, 188; film adaptation, 37; and theatrical design, 197
Chicago Federation of Musicians (CFM), 104
choreography. *See* dance and choreography
"Choreography" (song), 265–68
A Chorus Line: and cast recordings, 115–16; and communal focus of musicals, 16, 18; and direction, 178, 182–84; and nonprofit theaters, 188–89; and theatrical design, 212–13, 216
Cilento, Wayne, 184
Cinderella: and casting choices, 59, 62, 65–70, *67*, 76, 77–78n8; and cast recordings, 111–12; and television musicals, 57–76
cinematography, 29
Citron, Stephen, 174, 178
City of Angels, 212
Clara, 113
classical orchestration, 155–58
Clay, Paul, 215

A Clockwork Orange (film), 76
Clum, John, 21
Coco, 183
Cohan, George M., 152–53, 173
Cohen, Marshall, 269
"Colonel Hathi's March," 96
The Color Purple, 188
Columbia Pictures, 37
Columbia Records, 107–9, 115
Comden, Betty, 179
comedy and comics: and concept albums, 113; and orchestration/arrangement of music, 152
Come from Away, 4
commercialism, 1
compact discs (CDs), 116
Company, 183, 211
conservatism, 89, 93
constructivism, 211, 215
contralto voices, 244–45
Copeland, Joan, 223
Copeland, Roger, 269, 271, 273
copyright issues, 167–68
costuming, 132, 185, 198, 201–5, 207–8, 214–16
countertenor, 246
Cox, Veanne, 60
The Cradle Will Rock, 105–6, 121n11, 207
Craig, Edward Gordon, 198, 200, 204–5
Crazy Ex-Girlfriend, 5, 77n1
Crazy for You, 212
Criss Cross, 133
Crosby, Bing, 106
The Crucible: and direction, 188; and theater design, 211
Cullen, David, 161
Culshaw, John, 108
Cypher, Jon, 58, 64, 70, 73–74

Daldry, Stephen, 186
Dal Vera, Rocco, 222–24
Daly, Ann, 271, 273–74
Daly, Tyne, 229–30
Damn Yankees, 177, 182, 231, 282
Damon, Stuart, 58, 61, 68, 70, 74–76
dance and choreography, 265–84; and animated musicals, 91; ascent of the choreographer, 265–66; and audience response, 263n7; and copyright issues, 181; dance analysis, 273–79, 285n8; definitions of, 268–70, 284n4; Fosse's influence on, 279–84; interpretation and, 277; scholarship on, 269–73; and *Show Boat,* 135; and television musicals, 72–74
dance band sound, 156–58
Dancin', 178, 182, 282
Daniele, Graciela, 182, 184, 189
Darrell, R. D., 104
da Silva, Howard, 234
Davis, Todd F., 112, 114
Dear, Joe, 222–24
Dear Evan Hansen, 235–36
Death of a Salesman, 208
Decca Records, 105–8, 117
Decker, Todd, 31, 51n5
de Mille, Agnes: and *The Black Crook,* 128; and direction, 177–78; and highbrow dance forms, 266
Der Ring des Nibelungen (Wagner), 108
design. *See* theatrical design
Desmond, Jane C., 271
Desselle, Natalie, 60
De Sylva, Buddy, 157
Deutsch, Kurt, 117

digital downloads, 116
directors, 173–92. *See also specific individuals; specific titles*
Disney: and animated musicals, 61, 68, 85–98; and television musicals, 58–59; and theater properties, 143; and theatrical design, 215–16
"Do I Love You," 74
A Doll's Life, 187
Donen, Stanley, 32
Don Juan in Hell, 109
"Do-Re-Mi," 19
Doyle, John, 165–66, 186, 188
Drake, Alfred, 254–55
Dreamgirls, 183, 212
Dr. Horrible's Sing-Along Blog, 20
Drutman, Brian, 117
dubbing, 51n4
Duff Gordon, Lucile, 202–4
Dumbo, 79–81, 89–94
Durante, Jimmie, 76, 227
Dyer, Richard, 1, 87

Eastman School of Music, 109
Ebb, Fred, 187
Eckart, Jean, 208–10, 213
Eckart, William, 208–10, 213
economics of musical productions, 153, 165, 207. *See also* producers
Eddy, Nelson, 70
editing, 29
Edwards, Cliff, 76
Eisenberg, Evan, 101
Eisenstein, Sergei, 85–93, 97
"eleven o'clock numbers," 263n7
Ellen, Vera, 266–68
EMI, 114
Emmy Awards, 182
Engel, Lehman, 111
ensembles, 11–12, 151
"Epiphany," 224, 261

Erlanger, Abe, 134, 143
ethnicity, 47, 157, 186–87, 250. *See also* race issues and racism
European influences, 156–57, 213–14
Evans, Joey (character). *See Pal Joey*
"Everything's Coming Up Roses," 230–31
Evita, 69, 115, 159
extraction, 150
Eyre, Richard, 186

Fach vocal system, 245–46, 263n3
Fairchild, Joe Eddie, 216
"Falling In Love with Love," 69
falsetto, 246–47
Fame, 37
Fancy Free, 179
Fanny, 131
fans and fan practice. *See* audiences
Feder, Abe, 209–10
Federal Theater Project, 207, 209
femininity and feminism. *See* gender and sexuality
Ferber, Edna, 133–34
Ferrer, José, 122n21
Festpielhaus (Festival Playhouse) theater, 199
Feuer, Jane, 88
Fiddler on the Roof: and choreography, 181; and direction, 177–78; and theatrical design, 210–11
Fields, Dorothy, 33
Fields, W. C., 132
The Film Musical (Altman), 27–28
films and filmed musicals, 27–50; and adaptations, 34–38; and camp, 44–50; elements of, 28–30; live performance compared to, 13–14; and race/ethnicity issues, 30–32; and

realism, 38–42; and sung intimacy, 42–44; technical capabilities of, 4; and television musicals, 56
Finn, William, 151
Fiorello!, 176
Flaherty, Stephen, 214, 221
Flora the Red Menace, 209
Florodora, 105
Floyd Collins, 19
Flynn, Errol, 53n13
Foley effects, 40, 43
Follies (1971 play), 183, 211, 213, 216
Follies (Ziegfeld). *See* Ziegfeld Follies
Forbidden Broadway (parody series), 146
Fornes, Marie Irene, 144–45
The Fortune Teller, 174
42nd Street: and Champion's death, 131, 194n18; and cinematic realism, 40; and direction, 181; and theatrical design, 212–13
Fosse, Robert Louis "Bob": and *All That Jazz*, 265, 279–84; choreography style of, 146, 282; death of, 283; and direction, 178, 182, 185; and film musicals, 38; influences on, 266
Foster, Susan Leigh, 271, 278
Frank, Leo, 187
Freed, Arthur, 48
Freedman, Robert L., 60
Der Freischütz, 127
Friedman, Joel, 167
Friml, Rudolf, 133
"From This Moment On," 282
Fun Home, 4
Funny Face, 157
A Funny Thing Happened on the Way to the Forum, 176

Gabler, Neal, 141
Galavant, 5, 77n1
Garber, Victor, 60, 69
Garland, Judy, 70, 76; and camp, 48; and film musicals, 33, 44; musicals with Rooney, 128; vocal production of, 248
Garrett, Betty, 113
Gaxton, William, 233
gays and gay characters, 47–50
gender and sexuality: and acting criteria, 234; and animated musicals, 96; and camp, 47–50; and choreography, 268; and directors, 190; and singing, 247, 249
Gennaro, Liza, 265
Gentlemen Prefer Blondes, 38
Georg II, Duke of Saxe-Meiningen, 199
Gershwin, George, 193n8; and orchestration/arrangement of music, 157–58; and theatrical design, 207
Gershwin, Ira: and cast recordings, 120n9; and theatrical design, 207
Gesamtkunstwerk, 199
Ghostley, Alice, 58, 60, 69
Ginzler, Robert, 159
Girl Crazy, 128, 158
The Girl of the Golden West, 201
The Glass Menagerie, 208
The Glorious Ones (Ahrens), 221
Godspell, 160
Goffman, Erving, 47
Gold, Sam, 186
Goldberg, Isaac, 137
Goldberg, Whoopi, 60, 69

Golden Age of the Broadway Musicals: and acting criteria, 235; and casting, 222; and film musicals, 27; and orchestration, 158–59
The Golden Apple, 209
Goldman, William, 130–31
Goodman, Benny, 158
Good News, 157
"Goodnight My Someone", 17
Graham, Martha, 75, 209, 268
Grant, Mark N., 117
Grease!, 22, 160
Green, Adolph, 179
"Green Finch and Linnet Bird," 260
Green Grow the Lilacs (Riggs), 17, 234
Greenwich Village, 144–45
Greenwood, Jane, 198
Greif, Michael, 186, 189, 238
Griffith, Robert, 179
Grimm's Fairy Tales, 58
Group Theater, 234
Guys and Dolls: and communal focus of musicals, 22; and film adaptations, 35; and publicity, 139–40
Gypsy: and acting criteria, 229–31, 237; and casting, 221; and cast recordings, 116; and direction, 178; and Merrick, 131; and musical montage, 51n3; and orchestration/arrangement of music, 159

Hagen, Uta, 122n21
Hair: and amplification, 160; and direction, 188, 190; and musical styles, 251; and nonprofit theaters, 188–89; and theatrical design, 198, 212

Hairspray, 22
Hall Johnson choir, 94
Hamilton, 4
Hammerstein, Oscar, 142, 147n13
Hammerstein, Oscar, II. *See also* Rodgers and Hammerstein productions: and acting criteria, 238; and cast recordings, 106, 107; and direction, 175–78; and orchestration, 150, 158; and production, 134; and *Show Boat,* 132–35; and television musicals, 57, 59–62
Haney, Carol, 282
Happy Hunting, 229
The Happy Time, 181
Harbach, Otto, 133
Harkrider, John, 202–5, 208, 217
Harrick, Sheldon, 176
Harrison, Rex, 236
Hart, Lorenz, 150, 158; and television musicals, 69; and theatrical design, 207
Hartmann, Louis, 200–201
Have a Heart, 154
head voice, 247
Hearst, William Randolph, 134, 139
Heilpern, John, 184
Held, Anna, 132, 202
Hello, Dolly!: and acting criteria, 232, 235–36; and direction, 181–82, 188; and Merrick, 131; and orchestration/arrangement of music, 149
Henderson, Ray, 157
Hepburn, Audrey, 30, 66, *67*
Herbert, Victor, 149, 151–53, 158
Herman, Jerry, 150
High Button Shoes, 177, 179
Hitchcock, Alfred, 71

Hitchy-Koo, 175
Holder, Donald, 216
Hold Everything!, 157
Hollywood, 218–19n16, 226, 229. *See also* films and filmed musicals
Holm, Celeste, 58, 234
The Homecoming, 188
The Honeymoon Express, 175
Hoofing on Broadway (Kislan), 270
Hope, Bob, 226
Horne, Lena, 32
"Hot Patootie-Bless My Soul," 49
Houseman, John, 209
House Un-American Activities Committee, 179
Houston, Whitney, 59, 62, 69, 73
How Now, Dow Jones, 177
Hudson, Richard, 216
humor in musicals. *See* comedy and comics
Huntley, Paul, 198
Hytner, Nicholas, 186, 188

"I Am Ashamed that Women Are So Simple," 255
"If I Were King of the Forest," 41
"I Get a Kick Out of You," 227–28
"I Hate Men," 254
"Imagining Dance" (Acocella), 272
"I'm Gonna Wash that Man Right Outa My Hair," 18, 63
imitation, 20, 241, 250–51, 263n6
"Impossible," 63, 65, 73
improvisation: and animation, 84, 88; and dance/choreography, 269; and jazz, 108; and Method Acting, 177; and rock musicals, 239
"In Defense of Pleasure" (Wolf), 273

ingénue roles, 234
in-jokes, 46
"In My Own Little Corner," 62–64
institutional structure of musical theater, 127–46; and *The Black Crook,* 127–29; and producers, 129–35; and publicity, 138–42; and publishers, 135–38; and theater properties, 142–46
integration of musicals: and acting styles, 238; and *Oklahoma!,* 234; and song publishing, 137–38
interpretation, 277
intimacy, sung, 42–44
Into the Woods, 4, 189
"An Introduction to Dance Analysis" (Adshead), 273
investors, 129–35
iPods, 116
"I Sing of Love," 258
"It's Possible," 72
"I've Come to Wive It Wealthily in Padua," 254
"I Wanna Be Like You," 95–96
"I wish" songs, 61–62
Ixion, 202
Izenouer, George, 198

Jack and the Beanstalk, 56
Jaques-Dalcroze, Émile, 199–200
jazz dance, 182
jazz music: and concept albums, 113; and orchestration/arrangement, 152–54, 159; and race/ethnicity issues, 94–97; and recording formats, 108
The Jazz Singer, 30, 32, 34
Jelly's Last Jam, 189
Jennings, Alex, 236

Jepson, Helen, 105
Jerome Robbins' Broadway, 178, 181
Jersey Boys, 22, 138
Jesus Christ Superstar: and amplification, 160; and cast recordings, 114–15
Jews and Jewish Americans. *See* ethnicity; race issues and racism
"Jim Crow" (animated character), 94
"John 19:41, " 114
Johnson, Van, 56
Johnston, Ollie, 83–84
Jolson, Al, 32, 137
Jones, Robert Edmond, 204–6
Joseph and the Amazing Technicolor Dreamcoat, 114
Jowitt, Deborah, 271, 273, 276
Judson Memorial Church, 144–45
Jumbo, 207
"Jumpin' Jive," 32
The Jungle Book, 95–97

Kail, Thomas, 186
Kander, John, 187
"Kansas City," 63
Kantor, Michael, 173–74
Kantor, Tadeusz, 11
Kapp, Jack, 106
Katz, Mark, 103–4
Kaye, Danny, 266–67
Kealiinohomoku, Joanne, 270
Kelly, Gene: and animation, 82; and camp, 48, 53n13; and film productions, 76; and race/ethnicity issues, 32; star status of, 233; and television musicals, 56, 70, 72

Kern, Jerome: and cast recordings, 105; and copyright issues, 168; and orchestration/arrangement of music, 150, 153–55; and rhythm songs, 51n5; and *Show Boat,* 132–35; and star teams, 33
The King and I: and acting criteria, 234–36; and direction, 179, 188; and theatrical design, 208
Kirle, Bruce, 175, 188
Kislan, Richard, 270
Kissel, Howard, 131
Kiss Me, Kate, 188, 241, 252–58, 282
Klaw, Marc, 134, 143
Kliegl, Anton, 200–201
Kliegl, John H., 200–201
Knapp, Raymond, 16, 24n1
Komack, James, 113
Kook, Edward, 198

La Bohème, 22
Lady Be Good, 157
Lady in the Dark, 105, 120n9, 175, 233
Lahr, John, 116, 176
Lamas, Fernando, 228–29
Landau, Tina, 186, 190
Lang, Harold, 256
Lang, Philip J., 150, 159
Lansbury, Angela, 229, 261
Lapine, James, 186, 189
Larson, Jonathan, 214, 238
Laughton, Charles, 109
Laurents, Arthur: and direction, 178–81, 185–86, 191–92; and *West Side Story,* 180–81
Lawrence, Gertrude, 105, 120n9, 233, 235
League of Broadway Producers, 162

Lee, Eugene, 214, 216
Lee, Sammy, 135
Legally Blonde, 117
Leonard, John, 141
Le Prevost, Nicholas, 18
Lerner, Alan Jay, 107, 236
Les Misérables: and filmed musicals, 4; and theatrical design, 209, 213; and "visual spectacle," 4
"Let Me Entertain You," 51n3
Leveaux, David, 181, 186
Liberty Theatre, 154
Lieberson, Goddard, 102, 107–11, 115–16, 118, 122n21
The Life of Brian, 41
lighting, 199–201, 204, 207–10, 214
Liliom, 234
Lindsay, Howard, 58, 60, 69
The Lion King, 190, 215–16
"Little April Shower," 80–82
The Little Mermaid, 216
A Little Night Music, 163, 211, 213
"A Little Priest," 224
Little Theater Movement, 206, 208
Liza with a "Z," 182
Lloyd Webber, Andrew: and cast recordings, 114–15; and orchestration/arrangement of music, 161; and Hal Prince, 187; and theater design, 214
Lockwood, Don, 42
Loesser, Frank, 139
Loewe, Frederick, 107, 236
Logan, Joshua, 37, 176
"The Loneliness of Evening," 61
"Lonely Room," 149
Long, Robert Emmet, 270
Long, William Ivey, 198

A Long Day's Journey into Night, 213
longevity of musicals, 20
long-playing records (LPs), 102, 107–12
Louis the Whistler, 136
"Loveland," 216
"Lovely Night," 64–65, 69, 74
Lundskaer-Nielsen, Miranda, 177–78, 185–86, 189–90
LuPone, Patti, 166, 228–30, 237
Luske, Hamilton, 83
Lydia Thompson and her English Blondes, 202

MacDonald, Jeanette, 70
"Make Believe," 133
Making Americans (Most), 231
Mame, 209, 213
Mamma Mia!, 22, 138
"Mammy," 32
Mamoulian, Rouben, 174, 178
Mann, Michael, 71, 166
Mantello, Joe, 186, 188, 191
March of the Falsettos, 189
marketing musicals, 23
Marks, Edward B., 136–37
marriage trope, 24n1
"Marry the Man Today," 35
Marshall, Kathleen, 184–86, 190
Marshall, Rob, 72, 188
Martin, Mary, 235
Masella, Arthur, 177
Mast, Gerald, 270
Mata Hari, 131
Maxine Elliot Theatre, 207
Mayer, Louis B., 50
Mayer, Michael, 238
McAnuff, Des, 189
McCartney, Paul, 112–13
McClaren, Norman, 98n2

McConachie, Bruce A., 271
McGillin, Howard, 228
McGlinn, John, 165
McGuire, William Anthony, 132
McKneely, Joey, 181
McMillin, Scott, 2, 12, 14, 224–25
media and the press, 140–41
Meet Me in St. Louis, 33, 41, 43
megamusicals: and amplification, 160–61; and orchestration/arrangement of music, 159
Mendes, Sam, 186, 188
MERM (Musically Enhanced Reality Mode), 38–42
Merman, Ethel: and acting criteria, 226–32, 235; and camp, 45; and cast recordings, 105, 116; and film musicals, 30; and orchestration/arrangement of music, 159; vocal production of, 248
Merrick, David, 131–32, 194n18
Merrily We Roll Along, 187, 216
Method Acting, 177
mezzo-soprano voices, 244–45
Michener, James, 234
microphones, 159–60, 237–38, 251
Midler, Bette, 235
Mielziner, Jo, 208–9, 214
Miller, Arthur, 211
Miller, D. A., 21
Miller, Glen, 158
Miller, Susan, 95
Ming Cho Lee, 208
Minnelli, Vincente, 48
minstrelsy. *See* blackface minstrelsy
Miranda, Carmen, 217
Miranda, Lin-Manuel, 6
miscegenation, 31–32
mise-en-scène, 28–29, 36, 39–40, 48–49

Miss Saigon: and orchestration/arrangement of music, 159; and theatrical design, 213
Mitchell, Julien, 174
Mitchell, Margaret, 257
Moana, 5
modal voice, 246–48
Moesha, 67
Molnar, Ferenc, 234
"The Money Song," 203
montage, 51n3
Montalban, Paolo, 59, 68–70, 73
Moody, Howard, 144
Moore, Victor, 226
Mordden, Ethan, 111, 132
Morgan, Helen, 226
Morrison, Patricia, 255
Most, Andrea, 221, 225, 231–32, 271
Mother Goose, 174
motion pictures. *See* films and filmed musicals
Moulin Rouge, 43
movies. *See* films and filmed musicals
MP3s, 116
multiculturalism, 77–78n8
music. *See* cast recordings; orchestration and arrangement of music; singing; *specific music styles*
The Musical (Kislan), 270
The Musical as Drama (McMillin), 2, 12, 224
Musically Enhanced Reality Mode (MERM), 38–42
Musical Stages (Rodgers), 15
Musicians' Union, 162–64
The Music Man: and acting criteria, 236; and communal focus of musicals, 16–17; and film adaptations, 35; and Tony Awards, 179

Musser, Tharon, 184, 212–13
My Fair Lady: and acting criteria, 236; and audience interaction, 20; and casting choices, 66; and cast recordings, 102, 109, 112; and communal focus of musicals, 18; film, 30; original cast recording, 66; revival of, 4; and theatrical design, 210
"My Own Little Corner," 69
Mystery Science Theater 3000, 20

Napier, John, 209, 213–14
Nathan, George Jean, 135, 137, 145
naturalism, 199
Nederlander Theater, 23
Neher, Caspar, 215
New Amsterdam Theater, 134, 143
New Century Theatre, 207
New Girl in Town, 177, 231–32
New Stagecraft, 205–6, 208, 210, 212
New York American, 139
New York City theater district, 142–46
New York Evening Post, 128, 173
New York Theater Workshop, 23
New York Times, 135
Nicholas Brothers, 32, 34
Nicholaw, Casey, 186
The Nightmare before Christmas, 88
"Nijinsky," 174
9 to 5, 191
Nixon, Marni, 30
Noble, Adrian, 186
Noguchi, Isamu, 75
nonprofit theater, 188–89
Norwood, Brandy, 59, 67–70, 73, 77n7
nostalgia, 22
No Strings, 62–63

"Notes on Camp" (Sontag), 47, 52n11
Noyes, Betty, 79
Nunn, Trevor, 186

O'Brien, Jack, 186
O'Connor, Donald, 32
Odets, Clifford, 211
O'Donnell, Rosie, 141
Oenslager, Donald, 206
Off and Off-Off Broadway shows, 144
Of Thee I Sing, 175, 193n8
Oh, Boy!, 155
Oh, I Say!, 154
Oh, Kay!, 157
"Oh, What a Beautiful Mornin'," 106
Ohman, Phil, 157
O'Horgan, Tom, 115
Oklahoma!: and acting criteria, 233–35; and audience interaction, 15; and cast recordings, 105–11; and communal focus of musicals, 15, 17; and direction, 176, 178; emphasis on community, 12; and nostalgia, 22; and orchestration/arrangement of music, 149; and show-based albums, 34; and theatrical design, 207–8
"Ol' Man River," 133
Once on This Island, 214–15
"One," 16, 18
O'Neill, Eugene, 232
One Touch of Venus, 107
On the Town, 107, 176–77, 179
On Your Toes: and acting criteria, 232; and dance/choreography, 265; and orchestration/arrangement of music, 164; and theatrical design, 207

operetta: and acting criteria, 226, 234; cultural context of, 253; and orchestration/arrangement of music, 149, 151–53, 157–58; and singing, 250
Operti, Guiseppe, 127
orchestration and arrangement of music, 149–68; classic orchestration, 155–58; and copyright issues, 167–68; described, 150–51; and the Golden Age of musicals, 158–59; and labor issues, 162–64; and megamusicals, 160–61; and microphones, 159–60; new aesthetics of, 164–66; and operetta sound, 149, 151–53, 157–58; and sung intimacy, 42–43; and synthesizers, 161–62; and television musicals, 65; types of, 149; and virtual orchestra machines, 163–64
organicism, 184
original cast recordings. *See* cast recordings
Othello (Shakespeare), 122n21
Our Town, 69
"Over the Bannister," 43–44

Pacific Overtures, 211, 213
Page, Elaine, 228
Paint Your Wagon, 236
The Pajama Game, 177, 179, 182, 282
Pal Joey, 111, 164; and character, 232–33; and direction, 175–76, 191; and theatrical design, 208
Palm Beach Nights, 203
Panama Hattie, 105

Parade, 16, 186–87
Partridge, Pauline, 103
The Passing Show, 174–75
Passing Strange, 221
Passion, 36, 37, 189
pastiche, 241, 250–51, 263n6
Paulus, Diane, 186, 188, 190
"People Will Say We're in Love," 106
Perrault, Charles, 58
Peter Pan Live!, 4
Peters, Bernadette, 62, 69, 229–30
Petrillo, James Caesar, 104, 106–7
The Phantom of the Opera: and acting criteria, 228; and orchestration/arrangement of music, 161; popularity of, 2; and theatrical design, 214
phonograph, 104–5. *See also* cast recordings; long-playing (LPs), 102, 107–12
Phonograph Monthly Review (journal), 103
Pidgeon, Walter, 58, 60, 69
Pied Piper of Hamelin, 56
"Pink Elephants on Parade," 89–94
Pinza, Ezio, 235, 237
Pippin, 20–21, 182, 188
Pippin, Donald, 115
The Pirate, 48, 50
Pirates of Penzance, 259
Place for Us (Miller), 21
plasmaticness, 86, 90, 93, 97
Platt, Ben, 235–36
"playback," 40
Playwright Horizons, 143
politics, 4
popular music, 230, 246, 249
Porgy and Bess: and cast recordings, 105, 111; and direction, 173,

175, 188; and theatrical
design, 207
Porter, Cole: and camp, 48; and
Kiss Me, Kate, 252–56; and
theatrical design, 207
post-production manipulation, 40,
51n4, 72
Presley, Elvis, 116
Preston, Robert, 236
Prima, Louis, 97
Prince, Harold "Hal," 179, 183,
186–88; and Abbott, 177; and
concept musicals, 115; and
direction, 175, 177, 191; and
theatrical design, 211
"The Prince Is Giving a Ball," 71
Princess Theatre, 154
print media, 140–41
producers, 129–35
The Producers: actual production
contrasted with, 130; and
costuming, 203; and direction,
184, 186; and theatrical design,
212, 216
Promenade, 144–45
Promises, Promises, 131, 183
Provincetown Players, 206
Pryce, Jonathan, 236
psychological mode of
performance, 231–33
publicity, 138–42
publishers, 135–38
Puccini, Giacomo, 21
Pulitzer Prizes, 176, 183, 189

"The Rabbit of Seville," 262
race issues and racism. *See
also* ethnicity: and anti-
Semitism, 186–87; and
blackface minstrelsy, 30–32;
and *Dumbo*, 94–95; and
filmed musicals, 30–32; and

multicultural casting,
77–78n8; and *Othello*,
122n21; and segregation,
31–32; and stereotypes,
94–97; and Wolfe,
189–90
Rachmaninoff, Sergei, 156
Ragtime, 216
Ramin, Sid, 159
Rando, John, 186
Reading the Beatles (Womack and
Davis), 112
realism, 37–42, 45–48, 93,
199, 224–25
The Recording Angel
(Eisenberg), 101
recording ban, 104–6, 122n21
recording industry. *See* cast
recordings; phonograph
Redhead, 182
Rent: and communal focus of
musicals, 22–24; and stage
design, 238; and theatrical
design, 215
revisals, 38. *See also* revivals
revisionism, 18–19
revivals. *See also* revisals:
and *The Black Crook*, 128;
and changing perspectives,
4; and direction, 188–89;
and orchestration/
arrangement of music, 161–62,
164–65; and television
musicals, 76
revues, 227
Rhode, Greg, 95
Rice, Elmer, 206
Rice, Tim, 114–15, 187
Rich, Frank, 178
Riggs, Lynn, 17, 234
Rio Rita, 134
Rivera, Chita, 180

Robbins, Jerome: and Abbott, 177; and direction, 177–81; as director-choreographer, 184; influences on, 266; and theatrical design, 210; and Wolfe, 189
Robertson, Rebecca, 143
Robeson, Paul, 122n21
Robinson, Bill "Bojangles," 31–32
rock-and-roll: acting criteria in rock musicals, 238–39; and concept albums, 112–17; and LP records, 109, 112; and megamusicans, 160–61; and *Rent*, 22–24
"Rock Island," 35
The Rocky Horror Picture Show: and amplification, 160; and audience interaction, 20, 38; and camp, 49–50; and musical styles, 251
Rodgers, Richard, 193n8; and aesthetic choices, 15; and direction, 175–78; and orchestration/arrangement of music, 150, 156, 158, 164; and television musicals, 57, 62–64, 69; and theatrical design, 207
Rodgers and Hammerstein Organization, 118
Rodgers and Hammerstein productions. *See also* Hammerstein, Oscar, II; Rodgers, Richard: and acting criteria, 233–34; and audience interaction, 15; and authorial intent, 75–76; and cast recordings, 111–12; and communal focus, 18; emphasis on community, 12; influence of, 252

Rodgers and Hart productions. *See* Hart, Lorenz; Rodgers, Richard
Rogers, Ginger: and *Cinderella*, 58, 60, 69; and film musicals, 31–32; and romantic pairings, 33–34
Rojek, Chris, 113
Romberg, Sigmund, 133
Rooney, Mickey, 33, 128
Rosenthal, Jean, 209–10
Royal, Ted, 155
Roza, 187
Ruick, Barbara, 58, 60
Runyon, Damon, 139–40

Saddler, Frank, 149–50, 153–55
Sandow, Eugen, 202
satire, 22
Schneider, Roy, 279
Schoenfeld, Gerald, 182
Schönberg, Claude-Michel, 214
Schrank, Joseph, 60–61
scores and scoring, 42–44, 167. *See also* cast recordings; orchestration and arrangement of music; songs and songwriting; *specific title*
The Season (Goldman), 130–31
Seesaw, 183
segregation, 31–32
Selden, Kathy, 42
sets and set design. *See* theatrical design
"Seventy-Six Trombones", 17
Sgt. Pepper's Lonely Hearts Club Band (Beatles), 112–14
Shakespeare, William, 122n21, 252–54
"Shall We Dance," 63
Sharman, Jim, 115

Shechter, Hofesh, 181
sheet music, 102
She Loves Me, 209
Shepherd, John, 136–37
Sher, Bartlett, 181, 186, 188
Shirley, Bill, 30
Sh-K-Boom/Ghostlight Records, 117
Show Boat: and acting criteria, 226–27, 234; and cast recordings, 105, 107; and choreography, 135; and direction, 175, 188; and film versions, 76; ingénue roles, 234; production of, 132–35; and song publishing, 137; and theatrical design, 205, 208
"Show Girls" concept, 202–4
Shubert Theatre, 235
Shuffle Along, 189
Side Show, 212
Siegel, Marcia B., 271
"Silly Symphonies," 88
Silverman, Sime, 139
Simonson, Lee, 205–6
Sinatra, Frank, 35, 106, 113, 116
The Sing-Along Sound of Music, 20
Sing Along with Mitch, 20
singing, 241–62. *See also* songs and songwriting; and acting criteria, 222–23, 235–38; amplification of, 251; "bad," 249; case studies, 251–62; and intimacy, 42–44; and register, 246–47; "singing actors," 224; styles of, 250–51; and vocal anatomy, 242–43; and vocal production, 247–49; and vocal type, 244–46
Singin' in the Rain, 32, 42
"Singin' in the Rain" (song), 76, 82

"Sit Down, You're Rockin' the Boat," 251
Sitting Pretty, 168
Skeleton Dance, 88
Smith, Jack, 49
Smith, Oliver, 179, 210
"So in Love," 255
Something for the Boys (Clum), 21
"Something's Coming," 61
"Somewhere Over the Rainbow," 43
Sondheim, Stephen, 6; and acting criteria, 224, 238; and cast recordings, 109; and film adaptations, 36; and orchestration/arrangement of music, 150–51, 163, 165; and Hal Prince, 187; and song publishing, 138; and *Sweeney Todd,* 252, 259; and theatrical design, 211; and *West Side Story,* 179
Song of Norway, 107
songs and songwriting. *See also* orchestration and arrangement of music; singing: and communal focus of musicals, 19; "I wish" songs, 61–62; and Louis the Whistler, 136; and publishers, 135–38; *Sprechgesang* (speech-song), 248; and Ziegfeld, 132
Sontag, Susan, 47, 49, 52n11
soprano voices, 244–45
sound design, 29–30
The Sound of Music, 62, 77n1; and communal focus of musicals, 19; and direction, 176; film adaptations, 36–37; popularity of, 2; and sing-alongs, 20; and theatrical design, 210

South Pacific, 193n8; and acting criteria, 234–37; and casting, 221; and cast recordings, 108–9; and communal focus of musicals, 18; and direction, 176, 188; and film adaptations, 37–38; and theatrical design, 208
Soviet filmmakers, 51n3
special effects, 71–72
spectacle: and audience interaction, 12–13; and British Invasion, 213–14; and design trends, 197–98; and New Stagecraft, 205, 207, 210; and sung intimacy, 42; and theatrical design, 197–98, 205, 207, 210, 212–15
"The Spectre of the Gun" (*Star Trek* episode), 75
Spialek, Hans, 149–50, 155, 164
Sprechgesang (speech-song), 248
Spring Awakening: and acting criteria, 238–39; and book/music incongruity, 238–39; and casting, 221; and theatrical design, 215
"Springtime for Hitler," 203, 216
stage and set design. *See* theatrical design
staging, 76
Star and Garter, 174
Starlight Express, 213–14
Starobin, Michael, 151, 162
Star Trek, 75
State Fair, 76
Steamboat Willie (animation), 82
"Stepsisters' Lament," 71
stereotypes. *See* race issues and racism

Steyn, Mark, 265–67, 270
Stickney, Dorothy, 58, 60, 69
St. Louis Woman, 107
Stone, Peter, 184
Stonewall Rebellion, 49
stop-motion animation, 88
Stormy Weather, 32, 34
Stothart, Herbert, 43
Strasberg, Lee, 177
Stravinsky, Igor, 156
A Streetcar Named Desire, 208
Street Scene, 107
strikes, 104–6
Stroman, Susan, 186, 190
subcultural references, 46
subtext, 223
Sullivan, Ed, 141
Sunday in the Park with George, 189, 197
Sunny, 133
Sunset (journal), 103
Sunset Boulevard, 213
"Superstar," 114
surrealism, 90–92
"The Surrey with the Fringe on Top," 63
Swanson, Gloria, 109
Sweeney Todd, 241; and acting criteria, 224; and copyright issues, 167; and direction, 185; music of, 252, 258–62; and orchestration/arrangement of music, 161–62, 165–67; and theatrical design, 216
Sweet Charity, 182
"The Sweetest Sound," 62–64
swing music, 157
Swing Time, 31, 33
symphonies, 108–9
synthesizers, 161–62
Szot, Paolo, 237

INDEX | **317**

Tales of the South Pacific (Michener), 234
The Taming of the Shrew, 253–54
tap dance, 31–32
Tarzan, 216
Taymor, Julie, 185–86, 190, 215–16
Technicolor, 37–38, 48
technological advances: and amplification, 159–60, 237–38, 251; and animation, 82–83; development of the LP record, 102–7; technological frames, 70–75, 73; and television musicals, 56, 77n2; and theatrical design, 209–10; virtual orchestration machines, 163–64
television musicals, 55–76; audience response to, 75–76; book for, 59–62; casting and performance, 65–70; *Cinderella*, 57–76, 111–12; as episodes/series, 4–5, 56–57, 77n1; live broadcasts of, 5, 57–58, 77n1; music for, 62–65; and orchestration, 155; and Sullivan, 141; and technology issues, 70–75, 73
"Ten Minutes Ago," 64, 68, 73, 73–75
tenor voices, 244–45
TER/Jay Records, 118
theaters, 142–46. *See also specific theater names*
Theatre Guild, 206
Theatre Row, 143
theatrical design, 197–217; and British influences, 213–14; costuming, 132, 185, 201–8, 214–16; and hybrid designs, 215–16; lighting, 199–201, 205–10, 214; sets and set design, 70–75, 185, 203–4, 207–9, 213–16; and simpler designs, 205–10, 212–13; and spectacle, 201–5, 210–12
"There's No Business Like Show Business," 128
They All Sang, 136
This Is the Army, 106
Thomas, Frank, 83–84
Thompson, Lydia, 202
3 for Bedroom C (Lieberson), 109
Tibbett, Lawrence, 105
Tillie's Nightmare, 174
"Til There Was You", 17
Times Square, 142
Tin Pan Alley: and orchestration/arrangement of music, 155; and Porter, 255; and song publishing, 137
Tip-Toes, 157
"Tom, Dick or Harry," 256
Tommy (The Who), 113
Tony Awards, 165, 176, 179–90, 193n9, 194n23, 195n29, 272
"Too Darn Hot," 258
Tosca, 230
totemism, 86, 88–93, 97
touring companies, 128, 163
Travis, Sarah, 165, 167
Treatise on Orchestration (Berlioz), 150
A Tree Grows in Brooklyn: and direction, 176
Triplett, Sally Anne, 228
A Trip to Chinatown, 174
Tune, Thomas James "Tommy," 184
Tunick, Jonathan, 151, 163, 165

unions, 162–64
The Untouchables (television), 140
Urban, Joseph, 132, 202, 204–6, 208–9
Urinetown, 22, 215
utopianism, 87–88, 92–94, 97

Van Vleet, Jo, 58
Variety, 139
vaudeville: and acting criteria, 227; and *Gypsy*, 231; and orchestration/arrangement of music, 149, 152–53
venues for musicals. *See* theaters; *specific venue names*
Verdon, Gwen, 231–32
Vereen, Ben, 280
Victor Light Opera Company, 105
videotape, 72
vinyl records, 107–12
virtual orchestration machines, 163–64
vocal fry, 246, 263n5
The Voice (Sinatra), 113
voice and vocal style, 243–49
"Voodoo," 50

Wagner, Richard, 108, 199
Wagner, Robin, 184, 216
Waiting for Godot, 109–10
Walker, Don, 149–50, 155, 158–59, 164
waltzes, 64
Warchus, Matthew, 186
Ward, Michael, 198
Warhol, Andy, 49
Warner, Deborah, 186
Warren, Lesley Ann, 58, 66–68, 67, 70, 74, 76
Waverly Theater, 38

Wayburn, Ned, 174
"The Way You Look Tonight," 31
WCharley?, 177
Weber, Carl Maria von, 127
Wedekind, Frank, 238
Weidman, Jerome, 176
Weill, Kurt, 120n9
Welles, Orson, 207, 209
Wells, Paul, 98n2
"We Open in Venice," 257
"Were Thine that Special Face," 254, 257
West Side Story, 61; and communal focus of musicals, 15; and dance/choreography, 179–81; and direction, 177–78; and theatrical design, 210
Wheatley, William, 127–28
Whedon, Joss, 20
"When I See an Elephant Fly," 92, 95
"Where Is the Life that Late I Led," 254, 257
"Whistle a Happy Tune," 62–63
Whistler, James Abbott MacNeill, 44
whistle register, 247
White, Miles, 208
White Christmas, 266–69
Whiteman, Paul, 158
The Who, 113
"Why Can't You Behave?," 256
"Why Do I Love You?," 133
Wicked: and direction, 184, 191; and theatrical design, 216
Wilde, Oscar, 44–45
Wilder, Thornton, 69
Williams, Bert, 132
Willson, Meredith, 179
Winchell, Walter, 140–41

The Wiz, 160
The Wizard of Oz: and cinematic realism, 41; and direction, 174; and film musicals, 33; and special effects, 72; and sung intimacy, 43
The Wiz Live!, 4
Wolf, Stacy, 271, 273
Wolfe, George C., 186, 189–90
Wollman, Elizabeth, 23, 239
Womack, Kenneth, 112, 114
women. *See* gender and sexuality
Wonderful Town, 176
Woollcott, Alexander, 133
"Working in the Theatre," 117
World War II, 106–7
"The Worst Pies in London," 260–61
"Wunderbar," 253
Wynn, Ed, 227

Yap, John, 118
Yeston, Maury, 162–63
"You Are Love," 228
Youmans, Vincent, 133
"You're the Top," 228
"Your Song," 43
"You Were Meant for Me," 42

Zaks, Jerry, 186
Ziegfeld, Florenz: and costuming, 202–5; and music publishing, 137; and production, 132–35; and theatrical design, 215, 216
Ziegfeld Follies: and direction, 174; and production, 132–35; and theatrical design, 202–5, 207, 210, 216
Ziegfeld Theater, 204
Zipes, Jack, 93–94

www.ingramcontent.com/pod-product-compliance
Ingram Content Group UK Ltd.
Pitfield, Milton Keynes, MK11 3LW, UK
UKHW041414180426
11947UKWH00007B/125